GENOCIDE AND HUMAN RIGHTS

A Global Anthology

Edited with an Introduction by
Jack Nusan Porter

UNIVERSITY
PRESS OF
AMERICA

LANHAM • NEW YORK • LONDON

Copyright © 1982 by

University Press of America,™ Inc.

4720 Boston Way
Lanham, MD 20706

3 Henrietta Street
London WC2E 8LU England

Library of Congress Cataloging in Publication Data
Main entry under title:

Genocide and human rights.

Bibliography: p.
1. Genocide–Addresses, essays, lectures. 2.
Holocaust, Jewish (1939-1945)–Addresses, essays,
lectures. 3. Civil rights–Addresses, essays, lectures. I.
Porter, Jack Nusan.
HM281.G43   305.8   81–40580
ISBN 0–8191–2289–0   AACR2
ISBN 0–8191–2290–4 (pbk.)

All University Press of America books are produced on acid-free
paper which exceeds the minimum standards set by the National
Historical Publications and Records Commission.

ACKNOWLEDGEMENTS

I would like to thank the following authors and publishers for permission to reprint their articles and documents: Humanity and Society (Vol. 5, No. 1, March 1981) and the Association for Humanist Sociology for "What is Genocide? Notes Toward a Definition;" Midstream, the Theodor Herzl Foundation, and the authors for "America's Shame: The Unratified Genocide Treaty" by William Korey (Vol. 27, No. 3, March 1981) and "Whose Genocide?" by Yehuda Bauer (Vol. 26, No. 9, November 1980); European Judaism (Vol. 13, No. 1, Autumn 1979) and author Alan Rosenberg for "The Genocidal Universe: A Framework for Understanding the Holocaust;" the American Jewish Historical Society, American Jewish History (Vol. 48, No. 3, March 1979) and Henry L. Feingold for "Who Shall Bear Guilt for the Holocaust: The Human Dilemma;" Byron Sherwin of Spertus College and the Wein Foundation for Jack Nusan Porter's "Why Didn't the Jews Fight Back?" from Byron Sherwin and Susan Ament (eds.), Encountering the Holocaust: An Interdisciplinary Survey, (Chicago: Impact Press, 1979, pp. 189-195); Marjorie Housepian and Commentary (Vol. 42, December 1966) for "The Unremembered Genocide;" Leon Chorbajian and The Armenian Review (Vol. 32, Nos. 2-126, June 1979) for "Massacre or Genocide: An Essay in Personal Biography and Objective Experience;" James H. Tashjian for Genocide, the United Nations, and the Armenians; the Jewish Frontier (Vol. 18, No. 1, January 1951) for Philip Friedman "The Extermination of the Gypsies;" the Gypsy Lore Society and the Journal of the Gypsy Lore Society (Vol. 29, Nos. 3-4, July-October 1950) for Jerzy Ficowski, "Part III--The Polish Gypsies of Today"; Commentary Magazine (Vol. 8, No. 5, November 1949 and the estate of Dora Yates, Dr. E. D. Kamm, literary executor, for "Hitler and the Gypsies"; Rene Lemarchand and Society (Vol. 12, No. 2, January--February 1975) for "Ethnic Genocide"; Richard Arens for "Death Camps in Paraguay," American Indian Journal (Vol. 4, No. 7, July 1978); Oberlin College Political Caucus and Alternatives for "East Timor Genocide on the Sly" by Mike Chamberlain; International Commission of Jurists, Geneva, Switzerland, for The Question of Tibet and the Rule of Law, (1959, excerpts); Time, The Weekly Newsmagazine; Copyright, Time, Inc., 1978, for David Aikman, "Cambodia: An Experiment in Genocide," July 31, 1978; Columbia University Press and Rounaq Jahan for Pakistan: Failure in National Integration (1972, pp. 203-204); Society for "Witnessing Survival" by Robert

Jay Lifton (1978); Worldview and Helen Fein for "On Preventing Genocide;" Israel Charny and The Reconstructionist (Vol. 45, No. 7, November 1979) for "A Pilot Project for a Genocide Early Warning System," published by permission of the author and Whole Earth Papers (Global Education Associates, East Orange, New Jersey, Pat Mische, editor, copyright   Israel Charny); The United Nations Publications Board for "The Crime of Genocide" (pamphlet); and the Carnegie Endowment for International Peace for Raphael Lemkin, Axis Rule in Occupied Europe, (Washington, D.C., 1944, pp. 79-95). In some cases footnotes have been eliminated for space considerations and the titles slightly changed or abbreviated.

GENOCIDE AND HUMAN RIGHTS
A GLOBAL ANTHOLOGY
TABLE OF CONTENTS

PREFACE

This anthology is the first of its kind in any language. A deepened awareness of genocide and human rights has produced the need for such a handbook for both scholars and politicians. There are several reasons for this interest: President Jimmy Carter's concern for human rights in the international arena; the rise of neo-Nazism in Germany and the United States; the publicity of Nazi war criminals and collaborators; the impact of the NBC-TV Holocaust special; the rise of Holocaust-related courses in colleges and adult education centers; and the psychological/historical distancing from the tragedies of World War II. All these reasons have propelled people to take a closer look at the problem of genocide.

The more one learns, the more one questions: what exactly is genocide? How does it differ from other massacres and misfortunes? What are the common features in various genocides? What about forgotten and/or non-Western genocides? What factors lead to genocide? Why don't victims fight back? What political, military, and sociological steps can be taken to minimize or even avoid the impact of genocide? How can governmental and non-governmental agencies intervene? Why, as so often is the case, are people apathetic or impotent in responding to genocide--both victims and outsiders?

It may surprise the reader that genocide, so straight-forward a phenomenon, is so difficult to define and apply to particular cases. Yet, a common theme running through this anthology is one of definition. As obscene as it may be, scholars and diplomats often debate the fine distinctions of mass death. This is especially true when using the United Nations definition. Is this genocide racially or religiously based? Then, fine, it is genocide. Is it mass killings based on political ideologies? Then, we are sorry. It is not technically genocide. Genocide is not a value-free term. It is loaded with political and emotional bias. Was the war in Vietnam genocide? The oppression of American blacks under slavery? Is the struggle in Ireland genocide? Cambodia? Biafra? Bangladesh? Timor? Tibet? Ideological and geopolitical issues constantly raise their heads in a discussion of what is and what is not genocide. In fact, some contributors to this anthology were hesitant in being placed in an anthology that attempts comparison among genocides. They felt that "their" genocide was unique and that by comparing it to others, it would be "cheapened." I do not wish to cheapen any mass murder. I had to make a hard decision as to what I called "real" genocide and what I considered to be "questionable" genocide. There will be readers who will quarrel with my choices. I hope they will then write their own typologies. No one will ever be totally satisfied. What I do offer is a description of a wide array of genocides and this, I feel, is important to scholars and students.

To strengthen the book's usefulness as a handbook, I have also included an appendix which contains several key documents on genocide and human rights as well as a listing of resource centers, periodicals, and libraries as well as a bibliography.

My fondest hope is that this anthology will be useful not only in teaching genocide but will become one step in the direction of a full scale comparative study of the subject from a global perspective. For a Ph.D student out there, here is a challenging and virtuous goal.

In preparing this anthology, I would like to thank the following people for their support and criticism through the years: Helen Fein, Leo Chorbajian, Vahakn Dadrian, Hugo Adam Bedau, Erich Goldhagen, Herbert Kelman, Israel Charny, and Henry Tischler. Due to a restructuring of the book's chapters, I have had to delete several important essays. Perhaps future editions of this book will include them. I have tried to tighten the scope of this anthology and, for this, I would like to thank an anonymous referee. Despite all the excellent advice from the people above, (some of it I didn't follow; most of which I did) I of course accept final responsibility for the end result.

Jack Nusan Porter
Brookline, Mass.
July 1, 1981

INTRODUCTION

INTRODUCTION

WHAT IS GENOCIDE? NOTES TOWARD A DEFINITION*

Jack Nusan Porter

Preface

This article is dedicated to the memory of my father, Srulik Puchtik (later changed to Irving Porter). He was a Jewish partisan commander in the Ukraine during World War II. My mother, Faye Merin, was a cook in the same underground unit. They survived the war because they fled into the forests and fought the Nazis and their collaborators. My father died in March, 1979, leaving me and my brother and sister a wonderful legacy. My interest in genocide stems from his concern that the world might forget, as it often does, the horrors and the responsibilities that a Holocaust engenders. I have not forgotten.

The purpose of this essay is to clarify the concept of genocide. Prior to 1944 the term did not exist. It was coined in that year by the Polish legal scholar Raphael Lemkin to describe what was happening to Jews in Nazi-occupied Europe. This paper outlines why the study of genocide is important; discusses the United Nations Genocide Convention and why the United States of America has not signed it; and analyzes the uses and abuses of the term. The paper concludes with a definition of genocide, emphasizing three major components: ideology, technology, and bureaucracy. Future directions for research are also indicated. Massacres and mass murder have occurred on an unprecedented scale in the 20th century, but the topic, until the last few years, has seen very little sociological analysis. I hope this essay will help expand research in this important field.

---

* A previous version of this paper was read at the 1977 American Sociological Association meetings, Chicago, Illinois. My thanks to Hugo Bedau, Leon Chorbajian, I. L. Horowitz, Helen Fein, Abby Solomon, James Pitts, and Henry Tischler for their comments, criticism, and support.

Introduction: Why Study Genocide?

There has been a great deal of interest in genocide in the past few years. The 1978 NBC "Holocaust" TV special has been one contributing factor, but a far more important reason is that enough time has elapsed since World War II to allow people to finally confront this issue without recoiling in horror, disbelief, or guilt. Until recently there has been very little written on the sociology of genocide from a distinctly sociological, as opposed to political, religious, or historical perspective. A general theory of genocide is still in the process of development. The work of Raphael Lemkin, Helen Fein, Irving Louis Horowitz, Vahakn Dadrian, and Raul Hilberg has greatly contributed to such a theory.

Fein (1978; 1979a) with her excellent analysis of the dehumanizing ideologies that lay the foundation for genocide; Horowitz (1976) with his macrosocietal analysis of "genocidal" societies; Dadrian (1975a, 1979) with his typology and theory of genocide; and Hilberg (1961) with his comprehensive description of the bureaucracy of genocide have each added a building block to the foundation of such a theory.

One would assume that genocide is easy to define and apply to various phenomena. One of the ironies of research in this field, however, is that just the opposite is true. Both the definition and the application of the label of genocide have proved problematic. The use of the concept in political rhetoric has added to the confusion. These issues will be addressed later; I would first like to share a few ideas on why I believe this research is important.

Some writers see the dehumanization of life as the most important moral metaphor of this century (Lifton, 1967; Lifton and Olson, 1975; and Des Pres, 1976). One purpose of this essay is to sensitize readers to the issue of genocide, thereby promoting a better treatment of the subject in textbooks and in lectures. (See Friedlander, 1973; Fein, 1979b).

There has also been the realization that we have confronted what one could call a culture of mass annihilation, a culture of death. On the battlefields of two major world wars, in Korea and Vietnam, in Africa and the Middle East, in South America and Cambodia, in numerous concentration camps, and in uprisings, pogroms, riots, and massacres, 110,000,000 people, it has been estimated, have died in this century (Elliot, 1972:1, 247-273). Ths is a conservative figure. We hardly know how to accurately count the dead.

Research into genocide will not only contribute to our knowledge and understanding of violence, power, ethnic hatreds, and collective behavior, but other compelling issues as well. The study of genocide will force scientists to ask the essential question: what is the nature of man and woman? is she/he "closer to the angels or to the beasts?" Genocide forces us to realize that human beings are capable of committing great cruelty as well as attaining great spiritual and cultural heights. Sociologists as well as social scientists have been intrigued by these questions.

Genocide is a part of human history. While it may have occurred as often in the past, today there exists the technology and social organization to carry out worldwide extermination. The study of genocide makes one cognizant of the reality, even the banality, of evil in human existence. Then one will more fully understand the fear of genocide that grips not an insignificant number of Jews, blacks, Armenians, Indians, and other traditionally oppressed groups (Hilberg, 1961; Arendt, 1963, Levin, 1973; Dawidowicz, 1975; and Becker, 1975).

Thousands of ordinary citizens participated in genocidal acts. For the most part they were average human beings. What made them engage in such brutality? What must occur in a society to make genocide possible? How does it become acceptable? Is any society immune? Furthermore what of the "innocent bystanders?" Why do people remain silent or indifferent in the face of atrocities?

The study of genocide is important because ultimately so many sociological concerns are related to it: the process of war and colonialism, the experience of death and extreme deprivation, the meaning of survival and resistance, and the very nature of society itself.

This essay cannot address itself to all of these issues, but I hope it will spur other social scientists to do so. Friedlander (1973:7) maintains that the failure to engage in research on genocide and its implications is due neither to ignorance nor ill will. Rather, he maintains, scholars have been unwilling to

-4-

grasp the enormity of the evil. Genocide is such a delicate and complex subject that many have shied away from it. But this attitude is changing and we will continue to see increased research on the topic. One problem that social scientists face is that the world has become so creative in its modes of killing that they are hardput to keep up with their typologies and theories of genocide. The ingenuity and ubiquity of mass death in the 20th century challenges the ingenuity of social scientists to properly define it.

Despite the theoretical and methodological obstacles, a literature on genocide is available, and it is growing. Hopefully, more and more social scientists will avail themselves of this literature.

The United Nations and Genocide

Genocide is a new word for an old crime. The originator of the term was Raphael Lemkin, a Polish legal scholar. The word first appeared in 1944 in his Axis Rule in Occupied Europe (1973 reprint). Lemkin coined a hybrid word consisting of the Greek prefix genos (nation, tribe) and the Latin suffix -cide (killing). He felt that the destruction of the Armenians during World War I and of the Jews during World War II called for the formulation of a legal concept that would accurately describe the deliberate killing of entire human groups. Lemkin was more than a scholar. He inspired and promoted action on the international level to outlaw genocide. It was largely due to his efforts that the United Nations decided to debate the issue of genocide, to organize a convention to discuss it, and to eventually include it as a part of international law in 1948 (Robinson, 1971: Vol. 7:409).

Before 1944 no dictionary, encyclopedia, or textbook used the term genocide, and even after 1944 there have been some glaring omissions. For example, there is no mention of the term in Webster's International Dictionary until 1961. All three major sociology dictionaries have also ignored the term (Gould and Kolb, 1964; Theodorson and Theodorson, 1969; and Hoult, 1969). Both the earlier Encyclopedia of the Social Sciences (Seligman and Johnson, 1933) and the International Encyclopedia of the Social Sciences (Sills, 1968) have no separate descriptive and analytical listing for "genocide." The Sills' encyclopedia does mention genocide but only under the heading of "international crimes" where genocide is defined in the context of international law, not sociologically or historically (Sills, 1968: Vol. 7:515-519).

On the other hand, the encyclopedias written by minority groups affected by genocide (Armenians and Jews are two examples) have excellent coverage of the topic. For example the new Encyclopedia Judaica has a long and comprehensive account of the Holocaust in Europe by Jacob Robinson, yet, ironically, even in this Jewish publication the actual term "genocide" cannot be found as a major listing. Only "genocide convention" is mentioned (Robinson, 1971: Vol. 7:409).

The United Nations General Assembly, during its first session in 1946, carried out the mandate proposed by Raphael Lemkin and adopted two resolutions: the first affirmed the principles of the charter of the International Military Tribunal in Nuremberg, Germany (the so-called Nuremberg Trials of Nazi leaders) and the second affirmed that genocide was a crime under international law and, if committed, would be punished. The U.N. asked for international cooperation in preventing and punishing genocide and invited member states to enact necessary national legislation.

In a final provision the Assembly called for studies aimed at creating an international legal instrument to deal with the crime. That was the origin of the Convention on the Prevention and Punishment of the Crime of Genocide which was unanimously adopted by the Assembly on December 9, 1948. The Convention, which in international law means an agreement among sovereign nations pledging them to specified obligations, went into effect on January 12, 1951. By January 1973, seventy-six governments had ratified the Convention. The United States, however, has never ratified the agreement, claiming that it has existing legislation that covers genocide; that the wording of the Convention is vague in certain areas; that the Convention violates national sovereignty in its provision for an international tribunal; and that an entire nation cannot be charged with the crime of genocide because of the acts of a few individual citizens. These issues have been raised by United States senators, and the Senate has successfully rejected any efforts to ratify the Convention. (See Ervin, 1971; Goldberg, 1971, and Tischler, 1977.)

Controversy has arisen over several sections of the Genocide Convention. Article II reads as follows:

In the present Convention, genocide means any
of the following acts committed with intent
to destroy, in whole or in part, a national,
ethnical [sic], racial or religious groups
[sic], as such:

(a) Killing members of the group;

(b) Causing serious bodily harm to members of
the group;

(c) Deliberately inflicting on the group conditions of life calculated to bring about
its physical destruction in whole or in
part;

(d) Imposing measures intended to prevent
births within the group;

(e) Forcibly transferring children of the
group to another group.

Sections (b) and (d) have generated the most controversy in the United States Senate. The senators who
voted against the United States' ratifying the Convention were mindful that American blacks had charged the
United States with genocide, basing their accusations
on section (a), (b), (c), and (d) of the United Nations
Convention. For details of these charges see, for
example, Patterson, 1961. Furthermore America was
being charged with genocide in Vietnam in the late
1960s and early 1970s; this was another reason why some
senators were extremely reluctant to ratify and support
the Convention.

While the U.N. does provide for enforcement of the
Genocide Convention by the use of international courts,
the actual implementation has been limited. In essence
the U.N. Convention is more of a symbolic than a legislative contract, and those U.S. senators who voted
against it have little to fear of the United States
ever being brought before a tribunal. Claims of genocide have been made, inter alia, to the United Nations
with regard to blacks in Southern Sudan, Kurds in Iraq,
Nagas in India, Communists and Chinese in Indonesia,
Ibos in Nigeria, and Beharis in Pakistan, but no formal
decision in these cases has been reached by the United
Nations (Robinson, 1971: Vol. 7:410). Because of
political pressures and lack of real opportunity for
enforcement, the United Nations has never formally

applied the Convention to any genocide in the postWorld War II period, though numerous private citizens and groups have.

Furthermore the U.N. Convention is not retroactive. Therefore the United States could not be charged with genocide against the American Indians, the blacks, or the Vietnamese. The legal scholar Cherif Bassiouni (1979:173-181) maintains that the U.S. cannot be charged with genocide regarding the Indian massacres or the Vietnam war because it has never ratified the U.N. Genocide Convention. He also argues that because the Convention states that only individuals can be charged with genocide, it would require an extremely loose interpretation of the Convention text to charge a government with a crime. And, finally, Bassiouni contends that in both the Vietnam and Indian frontier situations, the requisite and specific intent of the United States government to commit genocide has never been established. (See also Bedau, 1974.)

The problems of intent and application of the term genocide to specific cases will be discussed in the next section, but, in summary, the following points should be emphasized. First, the U.N. Convention on Genocide has been charged with controversy from its very inception, and it has never enforced specific punishment for cases of genocide. Secondly, there is a difference between the legal and the sociological definitions of genocide. Genocide has taken place in the past (e.g. the persecution of American Indians), but legally the United States cannot be charged with genocide. There can thus be a number of responses to genocide: the act is committed but the victimizer is never found; the act is committed but the victimizer is never charged; the act is defined as genocide by the victims, but the victimizer does not concur that it is in fact genocide, and therefore will not be charged with the crime. From both a theoretical and a practical point of view, the problem of genocide is confusing and frustrating in definition, application, and enforcement.

My definition of genocide is slightly broader than that of the United Nations. I include the deliberate extermination of political and sexual groups as well as racial, religious, tribal, or ethnic groups. Thus the attempt to exterminate homosexuals in Nazi Germany could be labeled genocide. In the early 1950s, under pressure from Soviet Russia, extermination of groups for political persuasion or beliefs did not fall under the rubric of genocide in the U.N. definition. Thus the elimination of anti-Communist Poles or Ukrainians in the USSR in the 1930s and 1940s and, in recent times, the massacre of anti-Communist Cambodians could not be labeled genocide. Annihilation based on political beliefs is not considered genocide according to the legal definition of the United Nations Convention.

The U.N.'s exclusion of political and sexual groups from its Convention proves that we do not have the conceptual categories to describe all forms of mass violence and murder we have seen in this century. Our sociological concepts are inadequate to cope with the phenomena. The term "massacre" describes mass killings without the intent to kill all members of the groups in question. Since the popular and classical definition of genocide implies the murder or attempted murder of an entire group (be it racial, religious, tribal, sexual, or ethnic), then the killing of anti-Communist Cambodians or Ukrainians would not technically be genocide, because the aim of the victimizers was not to kill all Cambodians or Ukrainians, just those with a particular set of political beliefs. I disagree with this narrow definition and believe genocide can include the extermination of groups for strictly political beliefs.

The Problem of Application and Intention

Recently there has been heated debate about the use and abuse of the terms "racism" and "racist" (Goodrich, 1977). The term "genocide" has been similarly abused. Since "genocide" has become such a powerful catch-word, it is often used in political and cultural rhetoric. It is at least understandable that the term has been abused by political activists. However, even professional scholars have misused the concept. Because of the vague wording in some sections of the U.N. Genocide Convention, some scholars have applied the term genocide to the wrong phenomena.

For example genocide has been applied to all of the following: "race-mixing" (integration of blacks and non-blacks); drug distribution; methadone programs; the practice of birth control and abortions among Third World people; sterilization and "Mississippi appendectomies" (tubal ligations and hysterectomies); medical treatment of Catholics; and the closing of synagogues in the Soviet Union. In other words when one needs a catch-all term to describe "oppression" of one form or another, one often resorts to labeling it "genocide." The net result is a debasement of the concept.

Often the concept is applied to phenomena that are total opposites: integration and lack of integration; drug abuse and programs to curb such abuse. The following are examples of this linguistic abuse:

--The Nazi Party of America, demonstrating in Milwaukee in February 1976, argued at a schoolboard meeting that "integration is genocide for the white race." Before the meeting the Nazis distributed literature that charged the Jews with genocide against whites in America. One handbill read: "Deport Blacks to Africa and Jews to Israel or some other island (sic) except...those Jews who are suspected of treasonable activities such as genocide against whites." Such activities were defined as "race-mixing" and the distribution of obscene movies and magazines by "pornographic Jews." The handbills also condemned those "sick, depraved Jews who monopolize the motion picture industry (and who) can hardly wait to turn America into a mongrel cesspool" because these Jews promote racial integration and harmony. (Quoted in Ellerin, 1974; see also Porter, 1977)

--Regarding government-sponsored methadone programs, Black Panther Party leader Ericka Huggins said: "We don't need methadone. We don't need the government making any more good citizens. Methadone is just genocide, mostly against Black people. What we need is political education." (Dubro, 1977:12)

--At an anti-abortion rally in Washington, D.C. in 1978, Senator Orrin G. Hatch (R-Utah) stated: "I call (abortion) an epidemic and it has to be stamped out now." He noted that federal payments for abortion make it "possible for genocidal programs as were practiced in Nazi Germany." (From literature distributed by the National Abortion Rights Action League, 1979)

--Weisbord (1975) cites numerous instances of blacks viewing birth control as a "diabolical plot." His examples include reaction to the sterilization of the Relf sisters in South Carolina in June 1973, which Black Muslims and other black organizations called "a deliberate act of genocidal sterilization." (Quoted in Weisbord, 1975:169)

--Sociologist Rona Fields (1976), in a study of medical treatment of Catholics in Northern Ireland, charged the Protestants with "psychological genocide." She identified social control mechanisms which produce a mixture of chaos and docility and argued that such mechanisms were established in order to destroy the cultural identity of Catholics.

These examples point out the many ways the term has been used. Which applications of the term can be considered legitimate and which not? To some extent that depends on which definition one follows. Naturally some applications, such as those used by the American Nazis, are blatant distortions of reality. Other applications, however, that may sound exaggerated rest on the definition of genocide used in the United Nations Convention. Rona Fields' application of the term, for example, is based on the clause "...causing serious bodily or mental harm" [Article II, section (b)]. This vague and controversial clause has led to several uses or abuses of the term genocide. To Fields (1976) "psychological genocide" can occur if such "mental harm" is present. The question is what constitutes mental harm? How much mental harm is necessary in order to label it genocidal?

Some sociologists have expressed an abhorrence of the abuse that some terms and concepts take within sociology and in the general society. Dennis Wrong (1976) has called the abuse of the term genocide an example of the "banalization and trivialization of a subject and its exploitation for partisan purposes." He is expecially vehement about using the concept of genocide to describe the treatment of blacks in the United States: "Slavery and color castes were evil institutions to be sure, but by no stretch of the imagination can they be compared to the extermination of 10,000 Jews a day in the death camps of Auschwitz." (Wrong, 1976, personal communication to author)

The issue of intent has also generated controversy. The United Nations Convention specifically uses the phrase "intent to destroy, in whole or in part, a national ethnical (sic), racial or religious groups (sic)..." (Article II). However, it would seem that it is not enough for there to be an intention to destroy, but that the intent be acted upon and in great measure carried out. Thus in the case of the American blacks, there was no intent to commit mass extermination. While repressive acts did occur, mass genocide was not one of them. On the other hand, in the case of the American Indians, there was both the intent to commit genocide and its execution.

In the area of intent and in the area of "causing serious...mental harm," the United Nations definition seems too broad or too vague. The problem confronting scholars in the field will be whether to use a narrow or a broad definition at this stage of research. Will the concept be used so broadly that its meaning and application will become useless? Or will it be used in such a narrow manner that certain genocides will be overlooked because they do not fall within the parameters of the definition? Furthermore should sociologists use only a legal definition of genocide such as that of the United Nations, or should they formulate their own definition? In short do we want definitional precision or phenomenological inclusion at this juncture? I would like to find a golden mean between these extremes if in fact that is possible--that is, to reject overly broad applications while remaining flexible. The next section will attempt to develop this kind of definition.

What Is Genocide?

Genocide is the deliberate destruction, in whole or in part, by a government or its agents, of a racial, sexual, religious, tribal, ethnic, or political minority. It can involve not only mass murder, but also starvation, forced deportation, and political, economic, and biological subjugation. Genocide involves three major components: ideology, technology, and bureaucracy/organization.

Ideology. A key element in the act of genocide is an ideology that the victimizer utilizes in order to exterminate the victim. This ideology, usually based on racial or religious grounds, serves to legitimize any acts, no matter how horrendous. Racist or religious propaganda is used to spread the ideology. Such propaganda defines the victim as outside the pale of human existence and therefore vulnerable to attack. Words such as "sheep," "savages," "vermin," "subhumans," "gooks," and "lice" are commonly used, especially during war or colonialization, to reduce the victims to the level of non-humans, thus making it easier to annihilate them.

Helen Fein has added immensely to theory building in genocide studies by emphasizing this key element of ideology. She describes the role of myth, or what Gaetano Mosca would call a "political formula," which legitimizes the existence of a state of volk as a vehicle for the destiny of the dominant group and, by definition, excludes the victim-group as being outside the realm of the "sanctified universe." (Fein, 1979a: 3-30)[1]

Fein presents a theory to explain the genocide of Jews, Armenians, and Gypsies. Historically these groups have been the victims of repeated collective violence--Jews for nearly 2,000 years; Armenians for 500 years of Turkish Ottoman domination; and Gypsies for nearly a thousand years. For Fein, genocide is a rational, premeditated action with particular goals. She notes that the liberal ideal of 19th-century nationalism justified removing authorities who were deemed illegitimate because they did not represent the people. The 20th-century "formula" justified eradicating people to assure the legitimation of the state's authority. One way to eradicate groups that did not fit into a nation-state was to assimilate them; another way was to expel them; a third was to exterminate them.

Fein also describes the process of placing people "outside the sanctified universe." One example she uses is that of the Armenians. The Muslim Turks regarded the Christian Armenians as dimmis or infidels. For many years the latter were tolerated and protected in exchange for their accommodation to discrimination, subordination, powerlessness, and oppression. Armenians were also labeled rayah or sheep who could be fleeced. The Young Turk movement before and during World War I attempted to establish power and authority in order to fulfill its ideal of forging a new Turkish identity and destiny. In their scheme there was no place for large distinct minorities like the Armenians.

The genocide of Jews and Gypsies during World War II was also based on this "formula." Nasism utilized a pseudoscientific, neo-Darwinian, racist ideology which identified the German people (volk) as possessing a distinct identity and destiny. This identity was based on "blood." Jews and Gypsies (as well as homosexuals) were formally defined as not volk, but aliens to whom the Germans or Aryans would owe no obligation at all. While the Germans belonged to the "greatest, highest race" of Aryans, the Jews and Gypsies belonged to no human race. By definition they were nonhuman. (For more on Gypsies see Nowitch, 1968.)

Jews were to be annihilated because they were "vermin," "lice," "bloodsuckers," "parasites," and "bacilli"; Gypsies, because they were "filthy animals," "rodents," etc. Both were seen as racial "polluters" because they were racially "deformed" and "degenerate" in the first place. Thus laws were passed making illegal sexual relations between Jews and Aryans.

In this ideological schema the Aryan volk had a messianic right to prevail over others and to use any means from war to political deception to do so. The volk demanded not only equality with other nations but room to expand and colonialize (the concept of lebensraum). In its expansion it could subjugate and annihilate any "inferior" races who might "pollute" the volk. As Fein (1976:18) concludes about Armenians and Jews:

> ...in both cases the victims had earlier been decreed outside the universe of obligation by Koranic injunction and by Christian theodicy. However, churches holding out the possibility of conversion to all must assume a common humanity and, therefore, may not sanction unlimited violence. But a doctrine which assumes people do not belong to a common species imposes no limits inhibiting the magnitude of crime permissible.

An ideology based on racism or the "new formula" that Fein describes is a prerequisite for genocide; it stigmatizes and isolates the victims while mobilizing the victimizers in their genocidal pursuits.

Technology. Once the victim is labeled by the prevailing propaganda as being outside the universe of moral obligation, the killing can take place. The technology of death has become more efficient as modern nation-states have become more technologically sophisticated. While primitive means like clubs, spears, and gunbutts have been used in poorly developed nations (for example, the genocide in Burundi-Rwanda in the 1960s), more sophisticated methods like gas chambers, crematoriums, and "killing vans" were used by the Nazis to kill Gypsies and Jews. Today, of course, with modern nuclear systems we have the capacity to kill many more human beings in a shorter time than even the Nazi regime was able to do. Thus technology is an obvious component of genocide.

Bureaucracy. Hilberg (1961) has detailed the
enormous state apparatus that was necessary to undertake genocide in Germany and the conquered territories.
Just as technology has become more sophisticated, so
too have organizational and logistic skills. The
carrying out of genocide necessitates some minimum
organization; optimally effective genocide such as in
Germany necessitated an enormously complex organization. Coordination of various military and civilian
groups, rail transportation, the courts, and the like
is essential. Fein (1979:7) and Horowitz (1976) have
noted that modern premeditated genocide must first be
recognized as organized state murder, and such murder
requires a complex bureaucracy. The human victim is
reduced to an nonhuman entity and, like any merchan-
dise, must be assembled, evaluated, selected, stored,
and ultimately disposed of as efficiently as possible.

When Genocide Takes Place

Historically genocide has taken place under three
conditions: during war or following a defeat in war;
during internal colonialization or external imperialism; and during deep-rooted tribal conflicts.

War. A situation leading to what Mendelson (1973:
189-198) calls victimity is common during wartime.
Victimity, which he defines as the tendency or vulnerability to become victimized, can involve many forms of
collective violence including genocide. For several
reasons wartime is especially favorable for the commission of genocide and other atrocities. First, when
armies are confronting each other, genocide and other
violent acts against civilians can simply be considered
an extension of military warfare. Second, wartime provides an opportunity for utilizing propaganda on a
massive scale to label the enemy as inhuman, to stigmatize the victims as traitors, and to create hysteria
leading to scapegoating.

Wartime also blurs the distinction between attacks
against the military and political leadership of the
state and its civilian population. Thus genocide can
be camouflaged during wartime, only to be discovered
during the last stages of the war or immediately after
the war. Thus the bombing of Nagasaki and Hiroshima
during World War II; the bombing of Vietnam in the
1960s; the My Lai massacre during the Viernam War;
Hitler's murder of thousands of Polish officers during

World War II; and Stalin's extermination of Ukrainian
dissidents have all been ultimately called acts of
genocide.

The definition of genocide during wartime must
include the intent to annihilate an entire people,
race, or tribe and not simply to exterminate political
leadership. Under this strict definition, the above
acts, no matter how horrible, could not be considered
genocidal because there was no intent present to annihilate an entire race, religion, nationality or tribe.

President Harry Truman's goal in dropping the A-
bombs was not to exterminate the entire Japanese people
but to cause them to surrender more quickly. Premier
Stalin's goal was not to destroy the entire Ukrainian
people but to kill dissidents. Hitler's intention was
not to destroy the Polish people but to amputate their
military leadership. American military and political
goals in Vietnam were to win the war as quickly as
possible, not to annihilate the entire Vietnamese
people. These examples are what I call acts of "questionable genocide" where distinctions between military
and civilian targets are blurred. War can provide both
the pretext and the opportunity to commit genocide.
War conditions accentuate the vulnerability of minorities, especially those labeled outside the universe of
moral obligation.

Colonialization. Genocide has frequently been
committed during periods of internal colonialization;
for example, the killing of North American Indian
tribes in the United States and South American Indians
in Brazil and Paraguay. (See Dadrian, 1976; Savon,
1972; Arens, 1977, 1978.) Imperialism, or what could
be called external colonialism, has led to the genocide
of aboriginal Indians like the Tasmanians and Maoris in
New Zealand and Australia. Genocide can become a military and political tool in subjugating the land and its
people in the colonial conquest. Numerous Indian
tribes have disappeared or are in the process of disappearing because of conquest and colonialization.
Genocide can take place either directly through outright murder or indirectly through the transference of
disease (such as smallpox) where the victims do not
possess sufficient immunization.

Tribal Conflict. The third arena for acts of
genocide is intertribal conflict, such as the genocides
of the Hutu-Tutsi tribes in Burundi-Rwanda in 1972.

-16-

While genocide during internecine tribal warfare may be technologically unsophisticated and bureaucratically inefficient, the killings are still at high levels. For example about 80 to 100,000 Hutus and Tutsis died in Burundi Rwanda in the early 1970s. (See Lemarchand, 1975.) An important observation is that the occurrence of genocide during tribal conflict undercuts the Marxist myth that since genocide is an extension of imperialism only Western "fascist" states can commit genocide. Third World nations are just as capable of committing genocide as any "advanced" Western society.

The Prediction of Genocide

The recent upsurge of sociological and historical research on the Holocaust and other genocidal events by Hilberg, Horowitz, Fein, Dadrian, and Porter (1979a, 1979b) has laid the foundation for not only a theory of genocide, but for a means of predicting genocide. Charny and Rapoport (1977) have even established a "genocide early warning system" project at the Henrietta Szold Institute in Jerusalem. By synthesizing the contributions of Fein (1979:3-30), Horowitz (1976), and Dadrian (1974, 1975a, and 1979), we can make these predictive statements about genocide.

In those nation-states where the following conditions were found, the likelihood for genocide occurring increases:

a) Minority groups have previously been and are presently defined outside the universe of moral obligation by the dominant group. Such victims have been labeled "outsiders," "scum," or other epithets in order to stigmatize and dehumanize them.

b) Pervasive racialistic ideologies and propaganda are found in the nation-state's society.

c) There is a strong dependence on military security.

d) Powerful, monolithic exclusionary political parties are present.

e) The leadership has strong territorial ambitions.

-17-

f) The power of the state has been reduced by defeat in war and/or internal strife.

g) The possibility of retaliation for genocidal acts by kin of the victims or of interference by neutral nations is at a minimum.

Conversely the following conditions will reduce the possibility of genocide:

a) Pervasive tolerance and respect for minority groups.

b) Temperate and controlled attitudes toward any external military threat.

c) Democratic political structures and governmental institutions.

d) Weak territorial and imperial ambitions.

e) Strong minorities with ready access to legal and human rights.

f) The possibility of retaliation and/or interference by outside nations or kin is at a maximum.

Factors like a healthy economy and non-involvement in war can also minimize the possibility of genocide. Given the fact that the conditions cited can exist in most societies at least at some time in their history, genocide is possible in any society. Presently some countries are more likely than others to commit genocidal acts. The Union of South Afica, for example, is a prime candidate for committing acts of genocide. Holland, Sweden, and Switzerland are much less likely to do so. The vast majority of the world's nations falls somewhere in the middle. Horowitz (1976) among others has described the variables leading to what he calls "genocidal societies." Most of these variables have been outlined in the previous paragraphs. However, much more research is needed to predict where and when genocide will occur.

Future Directions in Research

The last few years have seen an increase in both governmental and academic recognition for Holocaust and genocide studies. President Jimmy Carter established a national commission to develop a fitting memorial to the Jewish and Armenian victims of genocide. There is discussion of establishing a national research center and museum dedicated to these victims. Several university centers for the study of the Holocaust already exist: a Ph.D. program in Holocaust studies at Temple University and Yeshiva University; a Department of Holocaust Studies at the Institute of Contemporary Jewry at the Hebrew University (Jerusalem); the National Institute on the Holocaust under the direction of Prof. Franklin H. Littell and Dr. Josephine Knopp at Temple University: the Simon Weisenthal Center of Holocaust Studies; the National Jewish Conference Center's projects on the Holocaust; the Center for Holocaust Studies at Brooklyn College; the YIVO Institute for Jewish Research; and others in Europe.

A journal, Shoah, published by the National Jewish Conference Center of New York and the University of Bridgeport (Connecticut), is dedicated solely to intellectual, literary, and commemorative discussions of the Holocaust and genocide. ("Shoah" is Hebrew for "Holocaust.") The Anti-Defamation League of the B'nai Brith has probably done the most--distributing teaching materials and educating teachers and laypeople on the subject; the American Jewish Committee has also been active in the field.

Holocaust studies have been instituted at the 8th grade level in the Brookline school system (see Strom and Parsons, 1977), and at the high school level in New York City, Philadelphia, Atlanta, Milwaukee, San Francisco, and Evanston (Illinois).

In 1976 Byron Sherwin (1978) of the Spertus College of Jewish Studies in Chicago received a large grant from the National Endowment for the Humanities to develop an interdisciplinary curriculum in Holocaust and genocide studies for American colleges, universities, and theological seminaries. The grant was made at an appropriate time as courses on the history and sociology of genocide have sprung up on many campuses in the last few years.

This upsurge of interest on the part of government, academia, and foundations has spurred the production of books and articles on the subject. Future researchers should be cognizant of the following issues:

a) The Problem of Definition. As has been pointed out the term, genocide, has applied to many
different situations. If one follows the
United Nations definition, problems will
arise. Where does a massacre end and a genocide begin? The dilemma of definition and
application of the term may never be fully
resolved, because large numbers of people can
be killed without intent of killing the entire
group. Is this latter situation genocide or
not? Were the events in Vietnam or Cambodia
genocide? Hiroshima? My Lai? The black
American experience? (See Person, 1979.)
Social scientists will have to grapple with
these problems of applicability and definition.

b) Comparative Research. Studies of genocide can
not be confined to simply the Armenian or
Jewish cases. They will have to draw upon
examples from many parts of the world and from
many periods of history. Only then can a
truly international and comparative theory of
genocide emerge. More research is needed on
genocide in Africa and Asia, on South American
Indian tribes, on the history of the gypsies,
and other cases. Furthermore other acts of
genocide are coming to light. For example was
the Nazi execution of homosexuals during World
War II an act of genocide or not? Was the
migration of Irish to the United States in the
19th century an escape from genocide induced
by forced starvation? Will history show that
small aboriginal tribes were annihilated
quietly in several parts of the world? Comparative historical and sociological research
should help ferret out answers to these
questions.

c) Predicting Genocide. We should see increased
research, perhaps with the use of computer
simulation, of those factors that will predict
genocide. Perhaps we will never be as accurate as meteorologists predicting earthquakes,
hurricanes, or cyclones, but increased attention should be paid to those economic, political, and psychological factors that cause
genocide and to the ways in which societies
turn state power into genocidal policies.

d) <u>Resistance to Genocide</u>. Ainsztein (1974),
Porter (1979b, 1979d), Dawidowicz (1975), and
Suhl (1975) have analyzed both passive and
active forms of resistance to genocide. They
have discussed the psychological and military
obstacles to such resistance, and they have
extended the meaning of resistance to include
moral, nonmilitary, nonviolent, and spiritual
forms of resistance.

e) <u>The Role of the "Bystander"</u>. This is a
puzzling phenomenon. How and why do nations
and individuals stay neutral or apathetic
while atrocities are being committed? Arthur
Morse (1975) has described how the United
States government knew about the Auschwitz
death camp yet did not bomb the railroad lines
leading to the camp. The United States could
have allowed more refugees to enter the country but did not, thus forcing many of them to
die in Europe. These and other issues that
Morse raises need to be analyzed further.
Stanley Milgram's (1975) research on obedience
to authority is a cognate issue that needs
further refinement. Milgram's experiments
were shocking; he showed that most people
would commit "murder" (experimentally, of
course) under the direction of a powerful
authority figure. These historical and psychological studies could be transformed into
sociological experiments in imaginative ways.

f) <u>The Impact of Genocide on Survivors and their
Children</u>. Steinitz and Szonyi (1975), Chorbajian (1977), Porter (1979c; 1979e), Fogelman
and Savran (1979), Epstein (1979), and others
have contributed to the growing field of
trauma studies. Is there a "survivor's syndrome"? What are the effects of genocide on
the families of victims and their communities?
Studies in this area will give us a deeper
understanding of Jewish, Armenian, Gypsy,
Indian, and other survivors and their
children.

g) <u>The Rise of Neo-Nazism</u>. The growth of neoNazi
and other progenocide groups in the past few
years has surprised social scientists who
thought that Nazism had died at the Nuremberg
Trials after World War II. Why have neo-Nazi

-21-

groups risen in the United States, Germany, and in England? What are the structure and functions of these groups? What issues do they exploit? This area is ripe for research. (See Ellerin, 1974; Porter, 1977.)

Conclusions

The future looks promising for genocide studies. We will be seeing more comparative research (such as Fein, 1978) and more interdisciplinary theoretical studies (such as Porter, 1979a). We will see more research on the Holocaust and other genocidal events in college textbooks (Freidlander, 1973; Fein, 1979b) and in the mass media (Feingold, 1978), and we will also see more curriculum building and guidelines for teaching genocide (Goldman, 1977; Roth 1978; Friedlander, 1978).

The study of genocide demands sensitivity and precision. While the scientific analysis of genocide has been by and large neglected by sociology and anthropology for nearly thirty-five years, we are finally seeing a scholarly confrontation with these historical events.

* * * * *

Footnotes

1. Leon Chorbajian (1979) employs the term feralization to refer to the process of rendering less than human the targets of genocide. I am grateful to him for suggesting this term to me.

CHART 1. COMPONENTS OF GENOCIDE

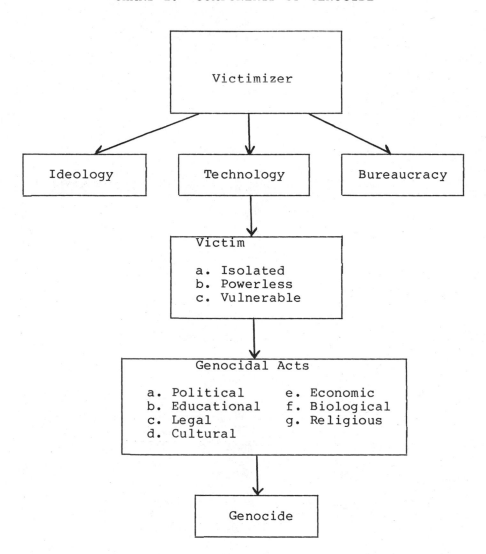

CHART 2. THREE MAJOR FACTORS IN GENOCIDE

I. <u>Ideologists</u>---------<u>Legitimation</u>-------->Genocide

    Agitators   Dehumanization

    Propagandists   Feralization

    Writers   Justification

    Teachers/Scholars

II. <u>Technologists</u>-------<u>Technology of Death</u>--->Genocide

    Army Commanders   Gas/Poison

    Concentration   Guns/Bombs
    Camp Directors

    Engineers   Burning/Cremating

    Doctors   Starvation

    Chemists   Forced Marches

    Soldiers/Guards   Knives/Spears/
                      Blunt Objects

III. <u>Staff</u>--------------<u>Bureaucracy</u>--------->Genocide

    Political Leaders Functionaries

    Inner Circle   Clerks

    Military Leaders   Railroad Personnel

                    Secretaries

APPENDIX - EXAMPLES OF 19TH- AND 20TH-CENTURY GENOCIDE

Victim	Victimizer	Time	Racist Ideology Present	Genocidal Acts
Jews 1933-45 5-6 million	Nazi Regime Axis Allies Collabora- tors, SS	Wartime, World War II	Yes, Quite developed	Extermination Expulsion Relocation
European Gypsies 1939-45 500,000+	Nazi Regime Axis Allies SS and Allies	Wartime, World War II	Yes, developed	Same as for Jews
Armenians 1914-18 1-1.5 million	Ottoman Turks	Wartime, World War I	Yes, but less developed	Same as for Jews
Tasmanian Maoris 1800s 1/4 million	Early British settlers	Period of Colonial- ization	Yes, but crude	Extermination later Prejudice
Brazilian Indians 1960s c.100,000	Portugese Colonizers	Period of Internal Colonial- ization	Yes, but crude	Extermination
Buddhists in Tibet 1950s 100-150,000	Communist Chinese	Invasion Colonial- ization	Uncertain	Killings Pillage Forcible transfer of children
Hutu-Tutsi 1972 80-100,000	Burundi- Rwanda Each other	Tribal Warfare	Yes	Extermination later prejudice
American Indians 1607-1890 c.600,000	U.S. Govt. U.S. Army Colonizers Settlers	Colonial- ization	Yes, but crude	Killings Forced march Expulsion Disease Reservations
S.American Indian Tribes 1960-pres. Many thousands	Government Developers Settlers Army (in Brazil & Paraguay	Period of Colonial- ization	Yes, but crude	Killings Manhunts Slavery Reservations
Hindus in E. Pakistan Bangladesh 1971-72 c. 1-2 million	Pakistani Military Forces	Period of Civil Unrest	Uncertain	Mob Massacres Rape Pillage

References

Ainsztein, Reuben
    1974   Jewish Resistance in Nazi Occupied
           Europe, New York: Barnes and Noble.

Arens, Richard (ed.)
    1977   Genocide in Paraguay, Philadelphia:
           Temple University Press.

    1978   "Death Camps in Paraguay." American
           Indian Journal, 4:2-13.

Arendt, Hannah
    1963 Eichmann in Jerusalem, New York: Viking.

Bassiouni, M. Cherif
    1979   "International Law and the Holocaust," in
           Byron Sherwin (ed.), Encountering the
           Holocaust. New York: Hebrew Publishing
           Company, pp. 146-188.

Becker, Ernest
    1975   Escape from Evil, New York: Free
           Press-Macmillan.

Bedau, Hugo
    1974   "Genocide in Vietnam?" in Philosophy,
           Morality, and International Affairs.
           Virginia Held et al. (eds.), New York:
           Oxford University Press.

Charney, I.W. and Rapoport, Ch.
    1977   "A Genocide Early Warning System: A Pilot
           Project." Jerusalem: Henrietta Szold
           Institute, National Institute for
           Research in the Behavioral Sciences.

Chorbajian, Leon
    1977   "Innocent Odyssey." Ararat: A Quarterly
           18:13-18.

    1979   Personal Communication to the Author.

Dadrian, Vahakn N.
    1974   "The Structural-Functional Components of
           Genocide," in Victimology: A New Focus,
           Violence and its Victims. Israel Drapkin
           and Emilio Viano (eds). Lexington, MA.
           D.C. Heath.

1975a   "A Typology of Genocide," _International Review of Sociology_ 5:2, Autumn, 201-212.

1975b   "The Common Features of the Armenian and Jewish Cases of Genocide: A Comparative Victimological Perspective," in _Victimology: A New Focus: Violence and its Victims_. Israel Drapkin and Emilio Viano (eds.). Lexington, MA: D.C. Heath.

1976   "The Victimization of the American Indian." _Victimology: An International Journal_ 1:4, Winter, 517-537.

1979   "A Theoretical Model of Genocide, with Particular Reference to the Armenian Case." _The Armenian Review_ 31:115-136.

Dawidowicz, Lucy
1975   _The War Against the Jews_. New York: Holt, Rinehart, and Winston.

Des Pres, Terence
1976   _The Survivor_. New York, Oxford University Press.

Dubro, Alec
1977   "Methadone is...." _Liberation_. 20:2, January-February.

Ellerin, Milton
1974   _The American Nazis_. (pamphlet) New York: American Jewish Committee.

Elliot, Gil
1972   _The Twentieth Century Book of the Dead_. New York: Ballantine.

Epstein, Helen
1979   _Children of the Holocaust_. New York: G.P. Putnam's.

Ervin, Sam
1971   United States Senate Hearings. Washington, D.C.: Subcommittee on Genocide Convention of the Committee on Foreign Relations (Wednesday, March 10). Also in _Congressional Record_, May 25, 1970.)

Fein, Helen
1979a   _Accounting for Genocide_. New York: The Free Press.

1979b   "Is Sociology Aware of Genocide? Recog-
         nition of Genocide in Introductory
         Sociology Texts in the United States,
         1947-77," Humanity and Society, 3:3,
         August:177-193.

1978   "A Formula for Genocide: Comparison of
         the Turkish Genocide (1915) and the
         German Holocaust (1939-1945)," Compara-
         tive Studies in Sociology, 1:271-293.

Feingold, Henry
     1978   "Four Days in April: A Review of NBC's
             Dramatization of the Holocaust." Shoah: A
             Review of Holocaust Studies and Commemo-
             rations 1:15-17.

Fields, Rona
     1976   "Psychological Genocide: The Irish Case."
             Paper read at the American Sociological
             Association, New York, New York.

Fogelman, Eva and Savran, Bella
     1979   "Therapeutic Groups for Children of
             Holocaust Survivors." International
             Journal of Group Psychotherapy 29
             (April).

Friedlander, Henry
     1973   On the Holocaust: A Critique of the
             Treatment of the Holocaust in History
             Textbooks Accompanied by an Annotated
             Bibliography. New York: Anti-Defamation
             League of B'nai Brith.

     1978   "Towards a Methodology of Teaching About
             the Holocaust." Social Education 42
             (April):21-25.

Goldberg, Arthur J.
     1971   United States Senate Hearings. Washing-
             ton, D.C.: Subcommittee on Genocide
             Convention of the Committee on Foreign
             Relations (Wednesday, March 10).

Goldman, Martin S.
     1977   "Teaching the Holocaust: Some Suggestions
             for Comparative Analysis." Journal of
             Intergroup Relations 6 (December): 23-30.

Goodrich, H.
1977   "Uses and Abuses of the Terms 'Racism'
        and 'Racist'." ASA Footnotes, 5:4, April,
        4,8.

Gould, Julius and Kolb, William L. (eds.)
1964   A Dictionary of the Social Sciences. New
        York: Free Press.

Hilberg, Raul
1961   The Destruction of the European Jews. New
        York: Quadrangle.

Horowitz, Irving Louis
1976   Genocide: State Power and Mass Murder.
        New Brunswick, Transaction Books.

Hoult, Thomas F.
1969   Dictionary of Modern Sociology. Totowa,
        N.J.: Littlefield, Adams, and Company.

Lemarchand, Rene
1975   "Ethnic Genocide." Society. 12:2,
        January-February, 50-60.

Levin, Nora
1973   The Holocaust. New York: Schocken.

Lemkin, Raphael
1973   Axis Rule in Occupied Europe. New York:
        Howard Fertig. (First published by the
        Carnegie Endowment for International
        Peace in 1944.)

Lifton, R.J.
1967   Death in Life: Survivors of Hiroshima.
        New York: Random House.

Lifton, R.J. and Olson, Eric
1975   Living and Dying. New York: Bantam Books.

Mendelson, Binyamin
1973   "Victimology and the Needs of Contemp-
        orary Society," The Israel Annals of
        Psychiatry and Related Disciplines, 11:3,
        189-198.

Milgram, Stanley
1975   Obedience to Authority. New York: Harper
        and Row.

Morse, Arthur
1975   While Six Million Died: A Chronicle of
          American Apathy. New York: Hart.

Naral
1979   Literature from National Abortion Rights
          Action League. Washington, D.C.

Nowitch, Myriam
1968   Le Genocide des Tziganes sous Le Regime
          Nazi, Paris: Comite pour l'erection du
          Monument en memoire des Tziganes assassi-
          nes a Auschwitz.

Patterson, William L. (ed.)
1961   We Charge Genocide! The Crime of Govern-
          ment Against the Negro People. New York:
          International Publishing Company.

Person, Yves
1979   "D'un Genocide a l'Autre." Pluriel. 19:
          89-94.

Porter, Jack
1977   "A Nazi Runs for Mayor." Present Tense 4
          (Summer): 27-31.

1979a   Genocide and Human Rights: A Global
          Anthology, University Press of America,
          forthcoming.

1979b   Jewish Partisans: Memoirs of Jewish
          Resistance During World War II, Univer-
          sity Press of America, forthcoming in two
          volumes.

1979c   "Is There a Survivor's Syndrome? Some
          Social-Psychological and Political Impli-
          cations." Journal of Psychology and
          Judaism, forthcoming.

1979d   "Some Social-Psychological Aspects of the
          Holocaust: Obstacles to Military Resist-
          ance During Genocide," in Byron Sherwin
          and Susan Ament (eds), Encountering the
          Holocaust, Chicago: Impact Press, 1979,
          pp. 189-222.

1979e   "On Therapy, Research, and Other Danger-
          ous Phenomena." Shoah: A Review of Holo-

caust Studies and Commemorations, 1:3,
(Winter):14-15.

Robinson, Jacob
    1971   "Holocaust" and "Genocide Convention" in
        Encyclopedia Judaica. Jerusalem: Keter
        Publishing Company, Vols. 8 and 7.

Roth, John K.
    1978   "Difficulties Everywhere: Sober Reflect-
        ions on Teaching About the Holocaust."
        Shoah: A Review of Holocaust Studies and
        Commemorations 1 (Spring):1-3.

Sherwin, Byron
    1978   "The Spertus College of Judaica Holocaust
        Studies Curriculum." Shoah: A Review of
        Holocaust Studies and Commemorations 1
        (Spring):9-10.

Sherwin, Byron and Ament, Susan (eds.)
    1979   Encountering the Holocaust. New York:
        Hebrew Publishing Company, and Chicago:
        Impact Press.

Savon, H.
    1972   Du Cannibalisme Au Genocide. Paris:
        Hachette.

Seligman, E.R.A. and Johnson, Alvin (eds.)
    1933   Encyclopedia of the Social Sciences. New
        York: Macmillan Company.

Sills, David (ed.)
    1968   International Encyclopedia of the Social
        Sciences. New York: Macmillan.

Steinitz, Lucy Y. and Szonyi, David M. (eds.)
    1975   Living After the Holocaust. New York:
        Bloch Publishing Co.

Strom, Margo Stern and Parsons, William S.
    1977   Facing History and Ourselves: Holocaust
        and Human Behavior. Brookline, Mass.:
        Brookline Public Schools.

Suhl, Yri (ed.)
    1975   They Fought Back. New York: Schocken
        Books.

Theodorson, G.A. and Theodorson, A.G.
    1969   Modern Dictionary of Sociology. New York:
            Thomas Crowell.

The Crime of Genocide
    n.d.   New York: United Nations Signed the Geno-
            cide Treaty?" Paper read at the American
            Sociological Association meetings,
            Chicago, Illinois.

Weisbord, Robert G.
    1975   Genocide: Birth Control and the Black
            American. Westport, Conn.: Greenwood
            Press.

Wrong, Dennis
    1976   Personal communication to author.

I. THE JEWS

I. THE JEWS

Apart from descriptive accounts of genocide, this anthology has several foci--the problem of defining genocide, the role of the United Nations and its Genocide Convention, and the transformation of the concept into social and political policymaking. At the very center of genocide studies is the Jewish Holocaust in Europe. From the reams of written material, I have selected several essays that probe particularly difficult questions arising out of this annihilation.

First Yehuda Bauer tackles head-on the issue of reconciling the uniqueness of the Holocaust with its universalist meanings. He takes to task both ex-President Jimmy Carter and Nazi-hunter Simon Wiesenthal for "flattening out" the concept of Holocaust by describing it as an event that touched not only six million Jews but five million non-Jews. Bauer not only questions that five million figure but argues that the Holocaust is turning into just another sorry chapter in man's inhumanity to man, and not the unique, supreme event it was. In Bauer's words: "[Jews] stand in danger of having their specific martyrdom...obliterated by their friends."

Alan Rosenberg examines another thorny question: why has it been so difficult for most people to integrate the "greatest crime of our time" into their moral framework or conscience? The answer is so painful that, according to Rosenberg, most people simply avoid the subject. He outlines the reasons for that pain and, in the process, defines more precisely the concepts used to describe genocide.

Historian Henry Feingold raises a third painful issue: how did the United States and other governments allow the genocide in Europe to go on even after they knew about it? The indictment, he notes, grows longer and more damning. His conclusion, European Jewry and other victims were doomed by the indifference and callousness of the Allied powers.

Jack Nusan Porter concludes this section on the Jews with discussion of a fourth painful subject: why didn't the Jews fight back? How did they allow themselves to be killed in such great numbers? Didn't anyone resist? These questions are easy to ask, even smug, but they smack of ignorance of the events. Yet they are continually asked by Jews and non-Jews alike.

WHOSE HOLOCAUST

Yehuda Bauer

The problem of reconciling the uniqueness of the Holocaust with its universalist meaning has been exercising the minds of many people for some time now. In his 1980 State of the Union address, President Jimmy Carter made a statement that bears directly on this issue and takes it out of an academic discussion into the political arena. Referring to the proposals submitted by the President's Commission on the Holocaust in September, 1979, he interpreted them as involving what he termed an "appropriate memorial to the six million Jews and the millions of other victims of Nazism during World War II." In 1979, on Holocaust Remembrance Day (Nissan 27), Carter spoke of 11 million victims of the Holocaust, of whom six million were Jews and five million were non-Jews.

His more recent statement was undoubtedly an improvement on last year's, but even now the meaning of the very careful phrasing used by the President is that the Holocaust memorial should commemorate all victims of Nazism, Jews and non-Jews alike. The memorial, as seen by the President (not by the Commission), would in that case submerge the specific Jewish tragedy in the general sea of suffering caused by the many atrocities committed by the Nazi regime. In the public mind the term "Holocaust" has become flattened in any case. Any evil that befalls anyone anywhere becomes a Holocaust-- Vietnamese, Soviet Jews ("cultural Holocaust"), blacks in American ghettos, women suffering inequality, and so on. The President's statement points in the same direction.

The trouble is that this is done with the best of intentions, as a gesture towards America's Jewish citizens by the only country that now stands by the Jewish people despite political disagreements with the Israeli government. Cynics may point to the internal political motivations of Carter's gestures; but that is immaterial. Only in the U.S. do political motivations for pro-Jewish gestures exist. Carter's appointment of the Commission and his public observance of the Holocaust Memorial Day last year stand out as symbols of deep American feelings of identification with the Jewish contents of the Holocaust. They were preceded all over the United States by a growing recognition of the

Memorial Day by Christian congregations, a movement that, ideally, will spread even more in the future. There is an obvious contradiction between observance and feeling on the one hand, and definitions and cognitive responses on the other hand.

Nor is it difficult to see why the President should have used watered-down definitions of the Holocaust. Pressures from non-Jewish ethnic groups and, possibly, religious denominations had to be taken into account. Any memorial would, it appears, have to be an American memorial, and not a specifically Jewish one. It was unclear how the uniqueness of the Holocaust and its universalist implications could be combined in a way that would be in accord with the American heritage and American political reality. The result is that the Holocaust is in danger of becoming de-Judaized and Americanized. The resulting total misunderstanding of the event is in danger of becoming compounded. It is difficult to undo the damage even now. However, if it is not done immediately, it may be too late, with disastrous consequences for Jews and non-Jews alike.

The most frightening example of this reluctance to face facts, so reminiscent of Jewish attitudes during the early period of Nazi rule in Germany, is the way Jewish and non-Jewish organizations treat the problem of Soviet anti-Semitism. This is usually represented as a case of discrimination related to the anti-Israeli policies of the USSR and to the problem of freedom of emigration. In actual fact, however, we are faced with an organized campaign against supposed Jewish influence in the modern world. The term "Zionism" serves as a thin cover for what really is intended--namely, "Jews" --and the propaganda is no longer directed primarily against Israel as such.

Zionists, the mass circulation Soviet paper Nedelia claimed on November 21-22, 1977, in an article entitled "Gangster Leaders" control 158 out of the 163 largest arms factories in the imperialist West. The author, Lev Korneyev, is one of the specialists in the anti-Semitic Soviet propaganda machine. Korneyev has also claimed, in mass circulation papers in the USSR, that strikes in Israel are suppressed by a Civil Guards Corps consisting of Israeli criminals recruited by the Israeli army for that purpose.

A department recently established within the Soviet Academy of Science directs this type of propaganda. A group of rabid anti-Semites (V. Begun, I. Shevtsov, T. Kichko, Y. Ivanov, and V. Emelianov) receive full backing from the authorities; anti-Semitic propaganda, in fact, is a central facet of quasi-historical and quasi-intellectual semi-official activity. In a lecture entitled "Judaism and Zionism: Emelianov wrote that the principles of Judaism were formulated in the Torah, "the blackest book in mankind's entire history. Its main theses are that the Jews are a chosen people and should seize the territory of others...Jews must not work, work is for the Goyim. That was the origin of the division of humankind into humans proper--the Jews, and two-legged cattle--the Goyim. All nations must become the Jews' slaves. The Zionists have planned to achieve world domination for 2000 years. " Here, it appears, it becomes perfectly clear what is meant by the term "Zionism." It is no longer an attack "merely" on Israel, but on the Jewish people as a whole, and through it, on democratic mankind. Except of course that in contemporary Soviet propaganda it is no longer "Zionist Imperialism" but rather "Imperialist Zionism" that is the target--in this view it is the Jews who run the imperialist camp and who therefore are the real enemies of the Soviets.

This is not only similar to the Nazi ideology based on the "Protocols of the Elders of Zion," but exactly parallel. The blindness of the non-Jewish world to the phenomenon of Soviet anti-Semitism and its implications not only for Jews but for the democratic world as such is matched by the reluctance of the Jewish world to face up to the facts. We have to contend with the spreading of a poisonous revival of potentially murderous Jew-hatred that repeats an increasing number of the elements that characterized the Nazi variety.

All this has a direct connection with the memory of the Holocaust. Even during the war itself, Soviet statements spoke of the mass murder of Soviet citizens, Russians, Ukrainians, Beylorussians, Jews, Georgians, etc., usually in this or a similar order, when dealing with the mass murder of Jews (the first instructive instance of this was Molotov's announcement of Nazi crimes published in Pravda on January 6, 1942). At that time not only was there no active anti-Semitism on the part of governmental bodies, but efforts were made in the partisan movement to eradicate the many instances of anti-Semitism that occurred in it. Yet even then there was a clear reluctance to recognize the special character of the Nazi anti-Jewish murder campaign; a tremendous effort was made to subsume it under universalist slogans that tended to eradicate the particularity of the Jewish fate.

Soviet ideology cannot, to be sure, deal with particular humanity; neither with the individual nor with the autonomous group. Its totalitarianism is evident in its utter incapacity to deal with anything but meaningless generalizations--"the working masses," "monopoly imperialism," "progressive mankind," and the rest.

However, the discussion centering on the Holocaust made things even more difficult for the Soviet official mind. Jews--"Zionists"--were the worst enemies of the Soviet peoples, but they were the victims of Nazism. A solution was therefore found: the Nazis and the Zionists were allies, in fact they were identical with each other. Zionists helped Hitler to destroy the Jewish masses. This, of course, implies that the Jewish masses--a term with a positive connotation--no longer exist, that they were destroyed by the Zionists in league with the Nazis. Ts. Solodar in his book Wild Wormwood writes, for instance, that "the Eichmann trial was designed to conceal the cooperation with the Nazis of such Jewish leaders as Weizmann, Ben-Gurion, Moshe Sharett, Levi Eshkol. It is immaterial how many Jews were killed with the aid of Zionist leaders; it is, in any case, an incontestable fact that the founders of the State of Israel are covered with Jewish blood."

The denial of Jewish particularity in the Soviet case is likely to promote a return to Jew-hatred of the Nazi kind. While the denial of the particularity of the Holocaust is a special hallmark of Soviet propaganda, past and present, in the Soviet Union as in other countries Jews can be found who will defend such an attitude. The denial of the Holocaust as a specifically Jewish tragedy is therefore a worldwide phenomenon connected with dangers of anti-Semitism.

It is apparently no less a man than Simon Wiesenthal, the recent recipient of a well-deserved award for hunting down Nazis, who has invented the "11 million" formula that is a key slogan in the denial of the uniqueness of the Jewish experience. Wiesenthal is going around campuses and Jewish organizations saying the the Holocaust ws the murder of 11 million people--the six million Jews and five million non-Jews who were killed in the Nazi camps.

In purely historical terms this is sheer nonsense.
The total number of people who died in concentration
camps during the war period--excepting Jews and Gypsies
--was about half a milion, perhaps a little more.[1] On
the other hand, the total number of non-Jewish civilian
casualties during the war caused by Nazi brutality cannot be less than 20-25 million (probably close to 20
million Soviet citizens and 3 million Poles alone).
POWs died in speical camps that were not part of the
concentration camp system (though some thousands were
shipped to concentration camps and murdered there).

The vast majority of Jews were not killed in concentration camps proper, but in special death installa-
tions, whether these were located in a concentration
camp complex, as in Auschwitz, or in separate centers
(such as Chelmno, Belzec, Treblinka, Sobibor). Probably up to 1.5 million Jews were killed by machine-
gunning near their homes in Soviet territories occupied
by the Nazis.

Whichever way one looks at it, Wiesenthal's definition just makes no sense at all. His figures are not
comparable: they turn out to be either much too high or
much too low. Needless to say, his mistake is not
arithmetical, but conceptual. Basic to it is his lack
of comprehension for what one might call the gradation
of evil.

When Raphael Lemkin invented the term "genocide"
in 1943, he did not yet fully comprehend the total
planned annihilation of the Jewish people in Europe.
His definition therefore contains a contradiction: on
the one hand, he says quite clearly that "the practice
of extermination of nations of ethnic groups as carried
out by the invaders is called by the author "genocide";
on the other hand, he says that genocide is effected

> through a synchronized attack on different
> aspects of life of the captive peoples: in
> the political field (by destroying insti-
> tuions of self-government...); in the social
> field (by disrupting the social cohesion of
> the nation involved and killing or removing
> elements such as the intelligentsia...); in
> the cultural fields (by prohibiting or
> destroying cultural institutions and cultural
> activities...); in the economic field (by
> shifting the wealth to Germans and by prohi-
> biting the exercise of trades and occupations

by people who do not promote Germanism...);
in the biological field (by a policy of depopulation and by promoting procreation by
Germans in the occupied countries); in the
field of physical existence (by introducing a
starvation rationing system for non-Germans
and by mass killing, mainly of Jews, Poles,
Slovenes, and Russians); in the religious
field (by interfering with the activities of
the Church...); in the field of morality (by
attempts to create an atmosphere of moral
debasement through promoting pornographic
publications and motion pictures, and the
excessive consumption of alcohol).[2]

If Lemkin really meant that genocide was the total
physical annihilation of nations and ethnic groups,
then the second part of his definition made no sense.
If you kill off everybody, then the fact that you
thereby restrict the activity of churches is scarcely
meaningful. If you murder everyone, they are in any
case debarred from the exercise of trades and occupations, or even the consumption of alcohol and pornographic literature. Clearly, what Lemkin meant when he
wrote "extermination" was not total murder, but what
one might call selective mass murder--as, indeed, he
indicates in the second part of his definition.

Ths is entirely in accord, of course, with what
happened to the Polish people, for instance, at that
time. Large numbers of Catholic priests were arrested
and many of them murdered, especially in the German-
annexed western provinces of Poland; about 10,000
members of the Polish intelligentsia were brutally murdered in 1939-40 in the so-called "AB-Aktion"; whole
areas were depopulated (Zamosc, Poznan), and large numbers of their inhabitants killed. The frightful suffering of the Polish nation undoubtedly fits the term
"genocide"--it was the intentional denationalization of
an ancient and proud people by murder and oppression.
It was not a planned total annihilation, because contrary to legends the Nazis never intended to murder all
Poles--they needed them as slaves for the building of
Germany after Hitler's victory. The Poles were Aryans
--subhuman Aryans, to be sure, but Aryans nonetheless.
Genocide was not Holocaust, and the Poles were not
Jews.

The attitude of Nazi Germany to the Jews was motivated by ideological considerations; the economic or

political arguments were mere rationalizations. In Nazi eyes, Jews were a satanic power in the world, and had to be combated as such. Jews were also "parasites," and though the two metaphors do not agree, they formed a very powerful ideological combination.

The picture of the satanic Jew who controls the world or is out to control it stems from Christian imagery (only someone possessed by the devil could have murdered God), as developed and refined, if that is the word for it, by succeeding generations. Early in this century it crystallized in the "Protocols of the Elders of Zion," which effected the transition from a purely religious notion to a modern political one: the Elders of Zion met, according to the Protocols, at the Zionist Congress, and anyone reading the U.N. resolutions on the subject of Zionism today should realize what their origins are.

The other picture, that of a virus, parasite, or a pest of some sort, stems from the misuse of biology and other natural sciences at the hands of a chauvinistic intelligentsia trying to define themselves in terms of race. The Jews, in Hitler's conception, were not a race at all, but an anti-race, a mysterious mixture of nomadic tribes, whose main function was that of parasites on the bodies of healthy nations. Control of Jews inevitably led to decomposition (Zersetzung), collapse, and ultimately to the death of the Jew as well, because as a parasite he could not survive the destruction of the body upon which he fed. Christianity had been the Jews' way of subverting ancient civilizations. Ultimately, in Hitler's view of things, Christianity would have to be eliminated, because it was essentially Jewish. In modern times, the work of destruction begun by Christianity was continued by Bolshevism, another devilish Jewish invention. There was, in Hitler's view, a direct connection between the two.[3]

This concept led Hitler and his central Nazi group to believe that they were threatened with annihilation at the hands of world Jewry. In his dualistic way of thinking, Hitler saw the forces of light--the natural, healthy Germanic nations of the Aryan race, bearers of culture, fulfilling the purposes of the Superior Being --pitted against the forces of darkness, namely the Jews. In his August, 1936, instructions to Goering on the four-year plan, Hitler says quite clearly that unless Germany starts a war that will ensure her domination of Europe within a very short time, the German people will be exterminated by world Jewry.[4]

There, and in other documents we find very clearly the background of the Nazi motive in starting World War II: domination of the civilized world by the Germanic nations, and a fight to the death against Jewry, which controls France, America, and Russia, and is about to gain control over Britian. The war, unbelievable as it may sound, was fought for two reasons: to ensure Germanic supremacy, and to destroy world Jewish domination by defeating te countries controlled by Jewry, east and west. The war against Jews, to use Lucy Dawidowicz's excellent term, was endowed with universalist dimensions. On its success, in Nazi eyes, depended the future existence of the human race. In other words, the Jews were not subhuman, like the Poles: they were not human at all. They had to be destroyed, as vermin would be (hence the Nazi term "annihilation," Vernichtung).

Anyone who is not convinced that this very brief summary of Nazi ideology is not exaggerated, should consult the sources.[5] Anyone who thinks that this ideology is dead, that it disappeared with the demise of the Nazi Reich, is unfortunately struck with the same kind of blindness that afflicted the world at large and the Jews especially less than two generations ago.

The uniqueness of the Holocaust does not therefore lie in numbers. It does not even lie in the method of mass murder (though the very fact that large numbers of victims were murdered with a gas used for the extermination of vermin--Zyklon B--is symptomatic). Not even the fact that gassing was reserved for Jews, with the exception of some Soviet POWs, who served as guinea pigs, and 6,000 Gypsies, is decisive. What makes the Holocaust unique is the existence of two elements: planned total annihilation of a national or ethnic group, and the quasi-religious, apocalyptic ideology that motivated the murder. The fact that the Holocaust took place in Christian Europe, and that its antecedents are clearly connected with the development of Christianity, has been noted by Christian commentators, who argue that the Holocaust is a tremendous credibility crisis for Christianity, and that it poses even more basic problems for non-Jews than it does for Jews.

The universal implications of this unique event are precisely in its uniqueness. In other words, if

one takes away the basic truth that the Holocaust was
the planned total annihilation of the Jewish people and
the actual murder of close to six million of them, then
the whole event becomes completely meaningless. The
terrible warning it contains stems from the attitude of
Western civilization towards the unique situation of
Jewry in Western culture. The victims of this attitude
are first and foremost the Jews, but finally it is
Western civilization that pays the price. Six million
Jews were murdered, but it took a coalition of the
major powers, tens of millions of non-Jewish victims
and wholesale destruction of whole countries to defeat
a regime which was out to rule the world and base
itself on anti-Semitism as one of its two main ideological pillars.

In the final analysis, then, anti-Semitism is not
something that has a great deal to do with Jews, except
that they are its object and victim; anti-Semitism is a
cancer of the body politic of the Gentile nations.
Christianity, which is an attempt to establish moral
guidelines for personal and community life, is ultimately itself a victim of anti-Semitism, as Nazi history
clearly shows.

We have arrived at an interesting conclusion:
Holocaust is both the name for a specific, unique event
in recent history, and also a generic concept: the
planned total annihilation of a national or ethnic
group on the basis of general ideology. There is of
course a connection between Holocaust and genocide,
though the difference, as shown above, is important.
In the process of modern mass brutalization, peaking
during World War II, genocide became a possibility,
then an actuality. Mass brutalization, resulting in
the development of technical means for industrial mass
production of corpses, made for the development of a
possibility of Holocaust as the ultimate conclusion
from genocide. Until now it has happened to Jews only,
but future dangers to others are there: who knows who
the "Jews" will be next time?

The closest parallels to the Holocaust of the Jews
were the mass murder of the Armenian nation and the
Gypsy people. All three, be it noted--Jews, Armenians,
and Gypsies--were ethnic entities lacking a major
territorial concentration in a homeland. But the
differences are as important as the parallels: the
Armenian massacres occurred for nationalistic reasons,
to destroy what in Turkish eyes was a barrier to an

empire of the Turkish peoples. The Gypsies were not murdered for racial reasons (they were about as "pure Aryan" as one could be), but as so-called "a-socials." (Two Gypsy tribes in Germany were protected for racial reasons.) In neither case was the destruction complete. Loopholes were left open (Armenians could convert to Islam and become Turks; Gypsy city dwellers and soldiers were occasionally protected, etc.) But there is no doubt that the parallels are there.

The Wiesenthal-Carter definition appears to reflect a certain paradoxical "envy" on the part of non-Jewish groups directed at the Jewish experience of the Holocaust. This itself would seem to be an unconscious reflection of anti-Semitic attitudes, the other extreme of which is the growing tendency to deny the Holocaust altogether. The Holocaust created a pro-Jewish reaction among large numbers of non-Jews, especially in North America. A reversion back to "normalcy" regarding Jews requires the destruction of the Holocaust caused attitude of sympathy (one remembers the apocryphal story of the British official who defined anti-Semitism as disliking Jews more than is reasonable). This is achieved by claiming that the Holocaust was not really something unique, but rather something that happened to many million of others, including not only Poles and Russians and Serbs, who were indeed victims of Nazi genocides, but many others who were not. The Holocaust then becomes lost, flattened out, a meaningless term, and a "normal" attitude of anti-Jewishness becomes possible again. That this should be helped along by a great and deserving personality such as Wiesenthal is sad. The less said about it the better.

During the war, the Western powers were careful not to make special mention of the Jews in their announcements and their denunciations of the Nazis--with the sole exception of their declaration of December 7, 1942, on the Nazi murder of the Jewish peole. They were afraid of being accused of fighting a Jewish war, of singling out Jews for special favors. Jews therefore became Poles or Frenchmen of the Jewish religion. Today, Carter is in danger of unwittingly repeating the same exercise. In the Holocaust, which was the murder of the six million Jews and nothing else, against the background, it is true, of genocidal actions of the most anti-humanistic regime the world has ever seen, the Jews were murdered without much effective action on the part of the free world; they

-44-

were murdered by their enemies. Today they stand in danger of having their specific martyrdom as Jews obliterated by their friends.

* * * * *

Footnotes

1. Martin Broszat, "Nationalsozialistische Konzentrationslager," in: Hans Bucheim, et al, Anatomie des SS-Staates, Olten und Freiburg, 1965, pp. 9-160 (esp. 159-160).

2. Raphael Lemkin, Axis Rule in Occupied Europe, Howard Fertig, 1973 (reprinted), pp. xi-xii.

3. See Hitler's Secret Book, New York, 1962, pp. 212-214; Dietrich Eckart, Der Bolschewismus von Moses bis Lenin. Zwiegesprach zwischen Adolf Hitler und mir, Munchen, 1924.

4. Wilhelm Treue "Hilters Denkschrift zum Vierjahresplan," Vierteljahreshefte fur Zeitgeschichte 3: 155: 184-210.

5. See Hitler's Secret Book (written in 1928 as a continuation of Mein Kampf); cf. also Andreas Hilgruber, "Die Endlosung und das deutsche Ostimperium," in VfZ, 2:1972: 133-153; Joseph Ackermann, Himmler als Ideologe, Gottingen, 1970.

THE GENOCIDAL UNIVERSE

A FRAMEWORK FOR UNDERSTANDING THE HOLOCAUST

Alan Rosenberg

Why has it been so difficult for most people to integrate the greatest crime of our time into their mental world, their consciousness? Why has it been so difficult for most people to integrate the greatest crime of our time into their moral world, their conscience? Why has the annihilation of at least six million Jews and at least five million non-Jews-- Germans, Poles, Russians, Gypsies and Czechs not become a part of the living history, the context within which we live our everyday lives. It is this question that I would like to explore in this essay.

The question is so important because if we do not integrate the destruction of the Jews and non-Jews that took place during World War II into our mental and moral world, we will not be able to come to grips with the possibility of it happening again. We will be doomed to miss the signs once again, when people, whether Jews or non-Jews, are in the process of being set up as victims of destruction--of genocide. We must also be aware of the fact that if we do not understand how a group of people is processed for destruction, we ourselves may become passive or active participants in this process without any conscious awareness on our part. Germans who were involved in the everyday bureaucratic operations of filling out forms and following what seemed like routine orders, participated in the destructive process without being fully aware of or understanding their involvement and responsibility for maintaining the process of destruction. As I write, genocide is happening to a group of Indians in Paraguay. According to Elie Wiesel, the Ache Indians in Paraguay are being exterminated in almost the same fashion as the Jews were destroyed under the Nazis. A better-known case of contemporary genocide is the situation in Cambodia, where it has been speculated that at least one and a half milion Cambodians have been murdered for no reason other than the fact that they have been labeled as corrupted by the old regime. And, as with the destruction of the Jews, the world has silently sat by, indifferent to the incredible suffering of these people. The reason for our indifference is that the greatest crime of our time has not become a part of either the conscience or consciousness of our time. Because of this lack of integration into our mental and moral world, we have let the signs that should be informing us slip by. And thus, the Ache Indians of Paraguay and the Cambodians become subject to genocide, without any attempts at intervention by the rest of the world.

It is, of course, true that we talk more about the Holocaust and the destruction of other people than we ever did before. It is also true that the Holocaust is being taught more than even before. Finally, it is also true that approximately one hundred million people watched a part of the whole of the TV series entitled "The Holocaust." But this new and incredible upsurge of interest in the Holocaust and other genocides during World War II does not mean that we have, as individuals or as a culture, attempted to understand the meaning of these events for our personal lives and for the society in which we live. Thus, would it be possible for an individual to integrate the greatest crime of our time into his or her mental or moral world and yet be an anti-Semite or a racist? The Holocaust would have been inconceivable without anti-Semitism and racism. While both are, as Hannah Arendt has noted, "outrages to common sense," neither were or are the exlusive property of madmen, amoral technicians, or uncultured primitives. And while both have long histories, about which we still lack sufficient understanding, they are neither incomprehensible nor, what is even more pertinent here, are they like slavery, regrettable episodes of the distant or recent past. Yet racism and anti-Semitism are the essential, if but first, step in the development of the genocidal process which issued in the Holocaust. How is it possible for a culture to sincerely claim that it has reflected seriously on the destructions that took place during the Second World War and stand by while people once again are in the process of being destroyed? Not only do we as a nation stand by while groups of people are being destroyed, we use the same language of indifference that was used by the on-looking nations during the Holocaust. How, I have asked myself, is it possible that the world is letting it happen again?

From the point of view of developing a genuine understanding of the Holocaust and the genocide of other peoples, there seems to be only one good reason to force ourselves to confront so much pain and agony. And that reason is to make ourselves more deeply aware of the conditions and processes that are involved in the destruction of a people; to make our students and ourselves more fully cognizant of the ways in which we can get caught up in the process of destruction. We know that a large number of well-educated people did become enmeshed before they understood what had happened to them. The destruction of eleven million people for no seeming reason is obscene to say the least, but to learn nothing from the event makes us perverse. It mocks the pain of the dead and those still living with the scars of this incredible episode.

But if it is true that after over thirty years, we have not integrated this episode of destruction into either our conscience or our consciousness, we must ask why not? Is it because we are unwilling or because we are unable? Is it because we lack understanding, or because the phenomenon cuts too deeply into our basic beliefs and assumptions? Is it because when we take seriously the Holocaust and the destruction of other people during the Second World War, we are forced as individuals to question almost every major value in which we believe?

In the realm of religion, in the face of so much useless suffering and so much unmotivated evil, we are forced to raise the question of God's existence and the possibility of any principle of intelligibility within the universe? If we can still hold to our belief in a Supreme Being, we are forced to ask what kind of God would allow such perverse evil and suffering to exist? What Deity could co-exist with such demonic forces? How can this be explained? From the point of view of being a Jew, we are forced to ask, is it possible for the Jews to be God's Chosen People in the light of what He allowed to happen to them? This is the plight of Job multiplied and transformed eleven-million-fold. From the point of view of being a Christian, we are forced to ask how it was possible for those who preached a doctrine of love and brotherhood to manifest so much hate or indifference toward their fellow human beings? From the point of view of secular values, we are forced to ask whether the tradition of the Enlightenment, a tradition on which our whole civilization is presumably constructed, can any longer be maintained? When we really step into the world of Auschwitz, is it possible any longer to hold that history is progress? Is it possible to believe that a liberal education has the power to eradicate the evil that human beings do to each other after realizing that the leaders of the

Einsatzgruppen, Hans Frank, and Goebbels had a liberal humanistic education; that they had read Greek tragedy and had studied Kant? These are the kinds of questions, questions for which I have no good answers, that make it extremely difficult for most of us to integrate the Holocaust into our lives. If once one immerses oneself in the genocide of the World War II period, the world is never again the same. I believe that Auschwitz, the symbol of the Holocaust, is a watershed event that when integrated into our lives has transforming effects on us. And these effects are both psychologically and intellectually painful.

Thus, apart from reasons of sloth and self interest, apart from lack of time or just plain callousness, this is the main reason that the event has not been integrated into our mental or moral universe. The effort and the result is as painful as it is transforming. It undermines us as it illuminates us. It shatters us as it frees us from our confident presumptions and comforting illusions.

And yet there is another deep problem. In order for human beings to be able to make an event a part of their world, they need some kind of a conceptual framework that allows them to grasp the meaning of the event; that is, we can only make something ours and make it part of our lives, when we have some kind of symbolic framework that locates it for us, that allows us to feel the event as part of something that has a 'logic' to it, no matter how perverse that logic may be. Not only would the integration of the Holocaust be painful, psychologically and intellectually, but as well, we still would have to construct a logical context for it, in order to fully understand its meaning.

Such an understanding is not easy to acquire. It involves not only identifying the causes and conditions, analogies and disanalogies of an event, but it requires also identifying the meaning and significance of the event or process. Fortunately, in the past several decades, historians, psychologists, philosophers and political scientists have turned in increasing numbers to an examination of various dimensions of what is called "the Holocaust." The work of Arendt, Richard Rubenstein, Yehuda Bauer, Saul Friedlander, Lucy Davidowicz, Raul Hilberg, Karl Schleunes, and Leon Poliakov, comes especially to mind. This body of work, rich in detail, analysis, insight, and provoking hypotheses, nevertheless seems not to have given us sufficient tools for the sort of understanding that is demanded. The main reason is this: we have not yet established an adequate overall framework for understanding. What is required is a synthesizing concept which integrates the event into a totality and thereby renders intelligible its many disparate dimensions. To do this, we must try to grasp what happened to the Jews during the Second World War in relation to what happened to other peoples of Europe. We must see the Holocaust in relation to what was planned for these other people if the war had continued or if it had been won by the Nazis. What is required is a penetration into what Hitler and the Nazi leadership perceived as their total task. Without doing this, there is no way to understand either the Holocaust or the genocide of other peoples during this darkest of periods. The 'logic' of the destructive process that was perpetrated upon the Jews only emerges when we look at what Hitler and the Nazi leadership saw as their total task. It is my belief that when we grasp that the Nazis were attempting to re-create the world, to radically refashion it, and when we realize what this re-creation concretely meant, we will be able to generate the framework that will help us to integrate the greatest crime in history into our moral and mental world. What then was this total task which Hitler and the Nazi leadership conceived?

Hitler and the Nazi leadership were in the process of creating what I shall call "a genocidal universe." This effort had as its ultimate destructive goal, the annihilation of all those people who were classified as members of non-Aryan races. These were so-called "subhumans." It is in this framework of the genocidal universe that the almost total annihilation of European Jews must be understood. The Holocaust must been seen as a unique form of genocide that had a special meaning for Hitler and the Nazis, but this unique genocide, the Holocaust, msut not be separated from the processes of destruction that involved non-Jews, nor from the plans that the Nazis had developed for other peoples, plans which would likely have been implemented had the war continued or had it been won by the Nazis.

Before developing in detail the total of the genocidal universe, it is important for us to become clear as to the meaning of several key concepts as used in this essay. In this way, we may avoid subsequent and needless confusion over the meaning and referents of "Genocide," "Holocaust," and "Final Solution." This is

especially important with regard to the terms "genocide" and "holocaust," since these terms have been used
interchangeably by most writers. This imprecise use of
terms has had the effect of confusing genocide as a
general phenomenon that has occurred a number of times
in history, with the Holocaust, which was a unique form
of genocide, perpetrated by the Nazis upon the Jews.

For our purposes we will define the term "genocide" as it ws originally defined by Raphael Lemkin in
his important book, Axis Rule in Occupied Europe, published in 1944. But before turning to Lemkin's definition, it should be noted that in 1948, the term "genocide" took on a meaning somewhat different from the one
proposed by Lemkin. This change occurred as a result
of the United Nations Convention on Genocide, a convention which had as its explicit task not only the establishment of genocide as an international crime, but of
defining the term "genocide" so that there would be one
clear and globally accepted meaning of the term. On
both these counts, the Convention failed.

This is Lemkin's definition:

This new word [is] coined by the author to
denote an old practice in its modern development...Generally speaking, genocide does not
necessarily mean the immediate destruction of
a nation, except when accomplished by mass
killings of all members of a nation. It is
intended rather to signify a coordinated plan
of different actions aiming at the destruction of essential foundations of the life of
national groups, with the aim of annihilating
the groups themselves...Genocide is directed
against the national groups as an entity, and
the actions involved are directed against
individuals, not in their individual capacity, but as members of the national group.

The following points in Lemkin's definition should
be emphasized:

First, the term "genocide" is used to denote an
old practice in its new form. This implies that genocide was not unique to the Second World War period and
therefore not unique to what happened to the Jews under
the Nazis.

Second, the term refers not only to the immediate
destruction of a nation or a group of people, as was

the case with the Jews of Europe, but also to the systematic underlining or destruction of the essential foundations of a nation or a group of people with the ultimate aim being their annihilation. Here we see that genocide can refer to a long-term process. For example, the Nazi annihilation of the Polish elite was from Lemkin's point of view an act of genocide, part of a long-range process and plan to eliminate the Poles as a people.

Third, genocide can be carried out without directly killing anyone. This can be done, according to Lemkin, by undermining the social and political institutions or by causing the decline of the population by regulating the rate of birth through such methods as sterilization and regulation of marriage.

Fourth, as regards the meaning given "genocide" by the U.N. Convention on genocide, it departs from Lemkin's in the following way: it used the term to refer to "the intent to destroy in whole or in part (emphasis is mine), a national, ethnic, racial or religious group." For Lemkin, only the attempt to destroy a group in its biological totality can be referred to as genocide.

In the early 1960s the term genocide became part of our everyday language; that is, it went from being a technical term to being a popularly, and less carefully used term. Moreover, its popular meaning corresponds to neither Lemkin's careful definition nor to the definition prepared by the U.N. Convention. In general, the term "genocide" has come to be used to denote any mass murder, whether there was intent to destroy a whole people or part of people. In the public mind, any large killing becomes a bit of genocide. Unfortunately, the broad meaning helps confound and confuse crucial issues. Indeed, it importantly contributes to our inability to grasp the destructive events of the World War II period. In this essay, we shall consistently employ the Lemkin definition of "genocide."

The term "Holocaust" presents us with an even more formidable problem than the term "genocide." Unlike genocide, the term "Holocaust" has not found an authority with the stature of Lemkin to fix the contours of its meaning, nor has there been an international convention that had as one of its main purposes the task of developing a definition that could be accepted throughout the world. It is true that in 1953, when

the Knesset met to establish Yad Vashem as a memorial
to the Jews under the Nazis, they chose "Shoah" (destruction or catastrophe) _instead_ of "Holocaust" to
name the event. But this managed only to further comp-
licate matters, since those who seem to have been most
affected by the event identified it with a term which
has not made its way into popular usage. Besides these
difficulties, there are two other specific historical
problems with the term "Holocaust" that should be
considered.

First, the term had not been used to refer to what
happened to the Jews under the Nazis by either Jewish
or non-Jewish writers who wrote during the period immediately after the War. The terms that were used included "Catastrophe," "Great Catastrophe," "Jewish Catastrophe," "Disaster," and "Permanent Pogrom." It was
not until the years 1957 to 1959 that the term "Holocaust" started to be used in reference to the destruction of European Jews. At this time, it was used mainly by Jewish writers who felt the need to define the
event for themselves as Jews. The term took root in
the mid-60s and today, it is the dominant term. In
fact, most people do not know the event by any other
name.

The second, specifically historical problem with
the term "Holocaust" regards its religious origins.
From the point of view of Judaism the term means "burnt
offering" and implies a sacrifice to God. But this
religious connotation stands in the way of allowing us
to grasp the event which it denotes. Indeed, it is
clear why the Knesset rejected the term. Jews in
Israel do not choose to see themselves as sacrifices to
God. Unfortunately, it does not now seem possible to
abandon the term "Holocaust." It is now well ensconc-
ed, both in the popular vocabulary of the world and of
the scholarly community. And we must acknowledge the
insight that the destruction of European Jews had
unique and important qualities which separate it from
other genocides. It seems that the best strategy is to
define the term "Holocaust" in such a way that it
allows us to best penetrate the event it denotes. I
will thus define the term "Holocaust" as a unique form
of genocide that was perpetrated against the Jews by
the Nazis during World War II. We will think of it as
having primarily a referential meaning, referring as it
does to a unique event. But as a _kind_ of genocide, it
shares some features with other genocides (as defined
above) and differs from them in others. Thus:

The Holocaust is unique since the destruction of six million people represents the largest genocidal attempt in world history;

The Holocaust is unique insofar as it was the first time in history that a legally constituted government pursued a policy of bureaucratically organizing the annihilation of a people;

The Holocaust is unique insofar as it was the first time in history that a people were "reduced" to their physical qualities so that they could be annihilated in an efficient manner through the latest machines of modern mass murder--death camps;

The Holocaust is unique with regard to the Second World War since the annihilation of the Jews as a whole was to be immediately carried out while the annihilation of other groups, equally "subhuman," was to take place at a later date;

The Holocaust is unique because of the Nazi attempt to transform the Jews literally into the image that the Nazis had of them before killing them.

These dimensions of the episode seem to have no historical precedent and they demand serious attention with regard to the development of any comprehensive theory of genocide.

The effort to clarify terms may help to eliminate two major problems which have plagued the study and understanding of genocide and of the Holocaust. First, it allows us to avoid the confusions which arise when every mass murder that has happened in history, or is now happening, is labelled an act of genocide or a holocaust. The importance of identifying these types of events correctly has nothing to do with the politics of who suffered more or whose tragedy was worse, but with the fact that the different types of mass murder develop in different ways and with different "logics." What must be understood is the different forms they take. In fact, I believe that these kinds of distinctions allow us to study the Holocaust as a particular phenomenon, to see the destruction of the Jews of Europe as unique in a fundamental way without playing down, or minimizing in any way, the suffering that Jews and other people who have been victims of genocide or mass murder have undergone.

Second, and more important from the point of view of the main thesis of this paper, Hitler and the Nazi leadership were in the process of developing a genocidal universe; the clarification of the terms "genocide" and "Holocaust" allows us to see clearly what the Nazis did and planned to do to all those non-Jewish groups who were also slated for destruction. And it allows us to do this without eliminating or de-emphasizing the fact that Jews were at the center of their genocidal universe by labelling what was going to happen to them as the "Final Solution." No other group that had been chosen for genocide was given the "honor" of being labelled with such a grandiose phrase.

"Final Solution" the last of our three key terms, had also two historical meanings. When it was originally used in 1938, its meaning related to all those immigration schemes, whether voluntary or coerced, which were developed to solve the so-called "Jewish Question." But from the end of 1941 on, the term referred to the physical destruction of the Jews. In this essay, we use the term in its post-1941 meaning, to refer to the annihilation of the Jews as a people.

One final comment regarding the problem of definition may be in order here. Writers, of course, are at liberty to introduce new terms, and to define both them and old terms in new ways. Sometimes, as we have seen, such changes soon become conventional and well established in standard usage. Sometimes, of course, they do not. But from the point of view of understanding, the ultimate test of a concept is its ability to help us to comprehend the phenomenon it denotes and distinguishes. In this sense, this essay is an effort to show that Lemkin's notion of genocide is both useful and important, and to show that the event referred to as the Holocaust, while unique in significant regards, is not fully comprehensible until it is placed in its proper context.

What were, then, some further dimensions of what I called "the genocidal universe?" As we have said, the Nazi leadership had as its ultimate goal of destruction the annihilation of all those groups that were considered, or were to be considered, sub-human or non-Aryan. At the same time as the annihilation of the sub-humans was in progress, the Nazi leadership was attempting to reconstruct the world in an image which was being fashioned from materials which must be identified.

The rough picture is clear enough. The problem was one of forming a world populated by a pure Aryan race. This meant that there had to be a constant process of purification of the race in terms of an abstract definition of the concept of Aryan. This process of purification was never-ending, since the Nazis believed that it was part of nature's law that through struggle and destruction, the race as a whole was weeding out those that were unfit, and was thereby creating, gradually but inexorably, a more perfect species.

It is thus crucial to see that "Aryan" did not refer only or necessarily to some actual national or racial group or that it was intended to have a clear meaning. The concept was abstract and open in precisely the sense that it could refer to a changing sub-group of an ever-changing population.

While, to be sure, "Nordic," "German," "Germanic," were taken as points of reference in defining "Aryan," a persistent theme is the "bastardization," "negroization," "degeneration," and "uprooting" of Aryan "spirit" and "blood." As "spirit" and "blood" suggest, this "bastardization" was both racial and cultural. One text might here suffice:

> Racial history is thus at the same time natural history and soul mystique. The history of the religion of blood is, conversely, the great world-narrative of the rise and decline of peoples, their heroes and thinkers, their inventors and artists.

Accordingly

> Either through a new experience and cultivation of old blood, coupled with an enhanced fighting will, we will rise to a purificatory action, or the last Germanic-Western values of morality and state-culture shall sink away in the filthy masses of the big cities, become stunted on the sterile burning asphalt of a bestialized humanity, or trickle away as a morbific agent in the form of emigrants, bastardizing themselves in South America, China, Dutch East India, Africa...

Since the struggle for the perfection of the race was literally never-ending, there would always be a non-Aryan enemy. Accordingly, it was not merely that the Nazis undertook a program of genocide. Rather, they undertook a program of genocide which constituted but a stage in the construction of a new world; hence, the concept of a "genocidal universe."

This can't be emphasized strongly enough. The total task of Hitler and the Nazi leadership required that there would <u>always</u> be racial victims who would need to be annihilated. Startling as it may seem, for the Nazi leadership, the struggle for perfection could <u>never</u> end, so that the annihilation of this group or <u>that</u> could not be the end of the program of genocide. This was the first time in world history that a government has conceived of genocide as central to its total task.

A second reason why an enemy or victim was necessary in the Nazi scheme of things is that the criteria for who is a member of the Aryan race is not defined in a formal way, but only in relation to its opposite, the non-Ayran. For example, not one member of the Nazi leadership, with the exception of Heydrich, had any of the physical features that supposedly describe the Aryan.

What we discover when we analyze the fact that the Aryan is only defined in relation to its opposite, is that, for Hitler and the Nazis, there are only two races of people, Aryan and non-Aryan, and <u>both</u> are <u>constructions</u>, fabricated from whole cloth. Then, within the non-Aryan race, there is a hierarchy of racial enemies. At the top of the racial hierarchy of inferiors is the Jew, enemy number one. For the Nazi, this meant that Jews were the embodiment of <u>absolute</u> evil. Thus it was required that they be annihilated first and immediately. The Jew was the major obstacle standing in the way of ultimate perfection, but it is important to see that while Jews had a special place in the hierarchy of inferiors, they were to be but the first group to be processed for destruction. Within the Nazi genocidal universe, the destruction of the Jewish people was but the beginning of the process of genocide planned against all those groups of peoples which were conceived as standing in the way of Aryan perfection.

After the Jews, were the Gypsies, who must be destroyed. And after them, the Slavs who were then needed for labor. But as the need for their labor decreased, they too could be eliminated. There were the Russians, Poles and the Ukrainians who were all doomed for destruction as soon as it was feasible. And, lest we forget, there were Germans who did not fulfill the Aryan image. They too were also programmed to be annihilated. And even after these destructions were accomplished, the kingdom of death would not have stopped. There could be no end of victims that must be destroyed in a universe tht makes genocide central to its toal task, the development of a "pure" race of humans, the Aryans.

WHO SHALL BEAR GUILT FOR THE HOLOCAUST ?

THE HUMAN DILEMMA

Henry L. Feingold

A simple searing truth emerges from the vast body of research and writing on the Holocaust. It is that European Jewry was ground to dust between the twin millstones of a murderous Nazi intent and a callous Allied indifference. It is a truth with which the living seem unable to come to terms. Historians expect that as time moves us away from a cataclysmic event our passions will subside and our historical judgment of it will mellow. But that tempered judgment is hardly in evidence in the historical examination of the Holocaust. Instead, time has merely produced a longer list of what might have been done and an indictment which grows more damning. There are after all six million pieces of evidence to demonstrate that the world did not do enough. Can anything more be said?

Given that emotionally charged context, it seems at the least foolhardy and at the most blasphemous to question whether the characterization of the Holocaust's witnesses as callously indifferent does full justice to the historical reality of their posture during those bitter years. There is a strange disjuncture in the emerging history of the witnesses. Researchers pile fact upon fact to show that they did almost nothing to save Jewish lives. And yet if the key decision makers could speak today they would be puzzled by the indictment, since they rarely thought about Jews at all. Roosevelt might admit to some weakness at Yalta, and Churchill might admit that the Italian campaign was a mistake. But if they recalled Auschwitz at all it would probably be vague in their memories. The appearance of three articles dealing with the reaction to the Holocaust in America in this issue of _American Jewish History_ offers an opportunity to rethink the assumptions underlying our research. Perhaps, it is premature to do so.

Historical research in the area of the Holocaust is beset with problems of no ordinary kind. It seems as if the memory of that man-made catastrophe is as deadly to the spirit of scholarship as was the actual experience to those who underwent its agony. The answers we are receiving are so muddled. The perpe-

trators have been found to be at once incredibly demonic but also banal. The suspicion that the victims were
less than courageous, that they supposedly went "like
sheep to the slaughter," has produced a minor myth
about heroic resistance in the Warsaw Ghetto and the
forests of eastern Europe to prove that it wasn't so.
Like the resistance apologetic, the indictment against
the witnesses is as predictable as it is irresistible.

That is so because in theory at least witnessing
nations and agencies had choices, and there is ample
evidence that the choices made were not dictated by
human concern as we think they should have been. In
the case of America the charge of indifference is heard
most clearly in the work of Arthur Morse, who found the
rescue activities of the Roosevelt administration insufficient and filled with duplicity, and Saul Friedman, who allowed his anger to pour over into an indictment of American Jewry and its leadership.[1] One ought
not to dismiss such works out of hand. And yet it is
necessary to recognize that they are as much cries of
pain as they are serious history.

The list of grievances is well known. The Roosevelt admistraton could have offered a haven between the
years 1938 and 1941. Had that been done, had there
been more largess, there is some reason to believe that
the decision for systematic slaughter taken in Berlin
might not have been made or at least have been delayed.
There could have been threats of retribution and other
forms of psychological warfare which would have signaled to those in Berlin and in the Nazi satellites
that the final solution entailed punishment. Recently
the question of bombing the concentration camps and the
rail lines leading to them has received special attention.   The assumption is that physical intercession
from the air might have slowed the killing process.
American Jewry has been subject to particularly serious
charges of not having done enough, of not using its
considerable political leverage during the New Deal to
help its brethren.   Other witnesses also have been
judged wanting. Britain imposed a White Paper limiting
migration to Palestine in the worst of the refugee
crisis, the Pope failed to use his great moral power
against the Nazis, the International Red Cross showed
little daring in interpreting its role vis-a-vis the
persecution of the Jews.   The list documenting the
witnesses' failure of spirit and mind could be extended; but that would take us away from the core problem
faced by the historian dealing with the subject.

He must determine what the possibilities of rescue actually were. Failure cannot be determined until we have some agreement on what was realistically possible. There is little agreement among historians on what these possibilities were, given Nazi fanaticism on the Jewish question. Lucy Dawidowicz, for example, argues compellingly that once the ideological and physical war were merged in the Nazi invasion of Russia in June 1941, the possibilities for rescue were minimal. That, incidentally, was the position also taken by Earl Winterton, who for a time represented Britain on the Intergovernmental Committee, and Breckinridge Long, the Undersecretary of State reponsible for the pot-pouri of programs which made up the American rescue effort during the crisis. Other historians, including myself, have pointed out that the Nazi <u>Gleichshaltung</u> on the Jewish question was nowhere near as efficient as generally assumed. The war mobilization of their economy, for example, was not achieved until 1944. Opportunities for rescue were present especially during the refugee phase, when the final solution had not yet been decided upon and possibilities of bribery and ransom existed. It was the momentum of this initial failure during the refugee phase which carried over into the killing phase.

The point is that in the absence of agreement on possibilities, historians are merely repeating the debate between power holders and rescue advocates which took place during the crisis. The latter group insisted that not enough was being done and the former insisted that the best way to save the Jews was to win the war as quickly as possible. Nothing could be done to interfere with that objective--including, ironically, the rescue of the Jews. When Stephen Wise pointed out that by the time victory came there would be no Jews left in Europe, he exposed what the argument between rescue advocates and their opponents in fact was about. It concerned priorities, and beyond that, the war aims that ordered those priorities. What rescue advocates were asking then, and what the historians of the role of witness are asking today, is: why was not the Jewish question central to the concern of the witnesses as it was to the Nazis who spoke about it incessantly? But we cannot solve that question of priorities until we have some answer to the question of what World War II was all about, and what role the so-called "Jewish question" played in it.

Clearly, Allied war leaders were wary of accepting the Nazi priority on the Jewish question. The war was not one to save the Jews, and they would not allow war strategy and propaganada to be aimed in that direction. None of the conferences that worked out war aims and strategy--the Argentia meeting which produced the Atlantic Charter (August, 1941), the several visits of Churchill to Washington, the Casablanca Conference (January, 1943), the Quebec conference (August, 1943), the Moscow Conference (October, 1943), the Teheran Conference in November, and finally the Yalta and Potsdam conferences in 1945--had anything to say about the fate of the Jews. The silence was not solely a consequence of the fact that Allied leaders did not remotely fathom the special significance of what was happening to Jews in Nazi concentration camps. Even had they understood, it is doubtful that they would have acknowledged the centrality of the final solution. To have done so would have played into Nazi hands and perhaps interfered with a full mobilization for war. Hence Roosevelt's insistence on using a euphemistic vocabulary to handle what Berlin called the Jewish problem. There was distress in the Oval Office when George Rublee, who had unexpectedly negotiated a "Statement of Agreement" with Hjalmar Schacht and Helmut Wohlthat in the spring of 1939, spoke of Jews rather than the "political refugees," the preferred euphemism. The two agencies concerned with Jews, the intergovernmental Committee for Political Refugees which grew out of the Evian Conference, and the War Refugee Board carefully avoided the use of the word Jew in their titles. When the American restrictive immi- gration law was finally circumvented in the spring of 1944 and a handful of refugees were to be interned in Oswego outside the quota system, just as had been done for thousands of suspected Axis agents active in Latin America, Robert Murphy was cautioned to be certain to select a "good mix" from the refugees who had found a precarious haven in North Africa. Undoubtedly what Roosevelt meant was not too many Jews. The crucible of the Jews under the Nazi yoke was effectively concealed behind the camouflage terminology conceived by the Nazi bureaucracy and the Allies. Even today in eastern Europe unwillingness persists to recognize the special furor the Nazis reserved for the Jews and the relation- ship of the Jews to the Holocaust. The Soviet govern- ment does not acknowledge that it was Jews who were slaughtered at Babi Yar; and in Poland the Jewish vic- tims have become in death what they were never in life, honored citizens of that nation. In the East it became the Great Patriotic War and in the West it was ultima- tely dubbed the Great Crusade, never a war to save the

Jews. Those who examine the history text books continually note with despair that the Holocaust is barely mentioned at all.

The low level of concern about the fate of the Jews had a direct effect in strengthening the hands of those in Berlin responsible for implementing the final solution. They became convinced that the democracies secretly agreed with their plan to rid the world of the Jewish scourge. "At bottom," Goebbels wrote in his diary on December 13, 1942, "I believe both the English and the Americans are happy that we are exterminating the Jewish riff-raff." It was not difficult even for those less imaginative than Goebbels to entertain such a fantasy. Each Jew sent to the East meant, in effect, one less refugee in need of a haven and succor. Inadvertently the final solution was solving a problem for the Allies as well. Nazi propaganda frequently took note in the early years of the war of the reluctance of the receiving nations to welcome Jews. They watched London's policy of curtailing immigration to Palestine, American refusal to receive the number of refugees that might have been legally admitted under the quota system, the Pope's silence. Goebbels' impresson was after all not so far from the truth. Smull Zygelbojm, the Bundist representative to the Polish Government-in-Exile, came to much the same conclusion shortly before his suicide.

Yet Zygelbojm, who was very close to the crisis, was bedeviled by the dilemma of what to do. He was dismayed by the assumption underlying a request for action that he received from Warsaw in the spring of 1943. The message demanded that Jewish leaders "go to all important English and American agencies. Tell them not to leave until they have obtained guarantees that a way has been decided upon to save the Jews. Let them accept no food or drink, let them die a slow death while the world looks on. This may shake the conscience of the world." "It is utterly impossible," Zygelbojm wrote to a friend, "they would never let me die a slow lingering death. They would simply bring in two policemen and have me dragged away to an institution." The bitter irony was that while Zygelbojm had come to have grave doubts about the existence of a "conscience of the world," his former colleagues in Warsaw, who were aware of the fate that awaited Jews at Treblinka, could still speak of it as if it was a reality.

Once such priorities were in place it proved relatively easy for State Department officers like Breckinridge Long to build what one historian has called a "paper wall;" a series of all but insurmountable administrative regulations, to keep Jewish refugees out of America. "We can delay and effectively stop for a temporary period of indefinite length," he informed Adolf A. Berle and James C. Dunn on June 26, 1940, "the number of immigrants into the U.S. We could do this by simply advising our consuls to put every obstacle in the way and resort to various administrative advices [sic] which would postpone and postpone." That is precisely what was done; only in the year 1939 were the relevant quotas filled. During the initial phase the mere existence of strong restrictionist sentiment reinforced by the Depression proved sufficient. After the war started, the notion that the Nazis had infiltrated spies into the refugee stream was used. The creation of a veritable security psychosis concerning refugees triggered the creation of a screening procedure so rigid that after June 1940 it was more difficult for a refugee to gain entrance to the neutral United States than to wartime Britain. During the war a similar low priority for the rescue of Jews might be noted in the neutral nations of Latin America and Europe, the Vatican and the International Red Cross. There was no agency of international standing which could press the Jewish case specifically. But that is a well known story which need not be retold here.

The question is, why did not the witnessing nations and agencies sense that the systematic killing in the death camps by means of production processes developed in the West was at the ideological heart of World War II, and therefore required a response? Why were they unable to fathom that Auschwitz meant more than the mass destruction of European Jewry? It perverted the values at the heart of their own civilization; if allowed to proceed unhampered, it meant that their world would never be the same again. Roosevelt, Churchill and Pius XII understood that they were locked in mortal combat with an incredibly demonic foe. But as the leaders of World War I sent millions to their death with little idea of the long-range consequences, these leaders never had the moral insight to understand that the destruction of the Jews would also destroy something central to their way of life. Even today few thinkers have made the link between the demoralization and loss of confidence in the West and the chimneys of the death camps. The Holocaust has a relatively low priority in the history texts used in our schools. It is merely another in a long litany of atrocities. Today as yesterday, few understand that a new order of events occurred in Auschwitz, and that our lives can never be the same again.

Yet how could it have been different? If the key decision makers at the time were told what Auschwitz really meant, would it have made a difference? They would have dismissed the notion that they could make decisions on the basis of abstract philosophy even if the long-range continuance of their own nations were at stake. They were concerned with concrete reality, with survival for another day. Until the early months of 1943 it looked to them as if their enterprise would surely fail. And if that happened, what matter abstract notions about the sanctity of life? The sense that all life, not merely Jewish life, was in jeopardy may have been less urgently felt in America, which even after Pearl Harbor was geographically removed from the physical destruction wrought by the war. In America it was business as usual. What was being done to Jews was a European affair. Roosevelt viewed the admission of refugees in the domestic political context, the only one he really knew and could control to some extent. He understood that the American people would never understand the admission of thousands, perhaps millions, of refugees while "one third of the nation was ill housed, ill fed and ill clad." In case he dared forget, Senator Reynolds, a Democrat from North Carolina in the forefront of the struggle to keep refugees out, was there to remind him, and did so by using the President's own ringing phrases.

That brings us to one of the most bitter ironies of all concerning the role of America. The Roosevelt administration's inability to move on the refugee front was a classic case of democracy at work, the democracy which American Jewry revered so highly. The American people, including its Jewish component before 1938, did not welcome refugees. So strong was this sentiment that it would have taken an act of extraordinary political courage to thwart the popular will. Had Roosevelt done so there was a good chance, as Rep. Samuel Dickstein, the Jewish Chairman of the House Committee on Immigration and Naturalization pointed out, that there would have occurred a Congressional reaction of even more restrictive laws in the face of the crisis. Roosevelt was occasionally capable of such political courage, especially on a major issue. Witness his action on the Destroyer-Bases deal which he implemented by Executive Order in September, 1940. But in the case of refugees, even Jewish refugee children, he chose to be more the fox than the lion. He settled first for a politics of gestures. That is perhaps the key to the mystery of the invitation of thirty-two nations to Evian extended in March, 1938 to consider the refugee problem. The invitation was carefully hedged. It stated that the United States would not alter its immigration regulations and did not expect other states to do so. That of course consigned the Evian Conference to failure.

Soon the "politics of gestures" became more elaborate. It featured among other things an enthusiasm for mass resettlement schemes. That usually amounted to tucking away a highly urbanized Jewish minority in some tropical equatorial rainforest or desert to "pioneer." The Jews predictably could not muster much passion for it. Resettlement imposed on the Jews, whether conceived in Berlin or Washington, they understood as a concealed form of group dissolution, and they would have little to do with it. Thus it was doomed to failure.

By the time Henry Morgenthau Jr., Roosevelt's Secretary of the Treasury and perhaps his closest Jewish friend, was enlisted in the rescue effort, it was already late in the game. Morgenthau did succeed in convincing the President to establish the War Refugee Board in January, 1944. He prepared a highly secret brief which demonstrated that the State Department had deliberately and consistently sabotaged efforts to rescue Jews. It was a devastating document, and the WRB which it brought into existence did play an important role in saving those Hungarian Jews in Budapest who survived the war. But it was created too late to save the millions.

Similar practical concerns dictated the response of other witnessing nations and agencies. Pressed unwillingly into a life-and-death struggle for survival, British leaders predictably viewed German anti-Jewish depredations within the context of their own national survival. It was a foregone conclusion that in balancing the needs of the Jews against their own need for Arab loyalty and oil should there be a war, the latter would win out. Within that context they were, according to one researcher, more generous to Jewish refugees than the United States. Apparently moral considerations did bother some British leaders after the betrayal of the White Paper. It was partly that which led to the hedged offer of British Guiana for a small resettlement scheme. That colony had been the scene of two prior resettlement failures, and posed many other problems, so that except for some territorialists like Josef Rosen, Jews did not welcome it with enthusiasm and Zionists certainly did not see it as a substitute for Palestine. The indifferent response of Jewish leaders exasperated Sir Herbert Emerson, chairman of the Intergovernmental Refugee Committee. The subtle anti-Semitism in his reaction was not uncommon among middle echelon bureaucrats in London and Washington: "The trouble with the refugee affair was the trouble with the Jews and most eastern people," he complained in Washington in October, 1939, "there was always some other scheme in the background for which they were prepared to sacrifice schemes already in hand."

The problem with assessing the role of the Vatican as witness is made more complex by the fact that such power as it had was in the spiritual rather than the temporal realm; and yet the Pope faced a problem of survival which was physical, involving as it did the instition of the Church. Just as we expected the leader who introduced the welfare state in America to demonstrate a special sensitivity to the plight of the Jews, so the Pope, who ostensibly embodied in his person the moral conscience of a good part of the Christian world, was expected to speak out, to use his power. He did not, and it does not require a special study of Church politics to realize that its priorities were ordered by crucial requirements in the temporal rather than the spiritual sphere. During World War II it also sensed that it faced a struggle for mere survival. The Vatican probably possessed more precise information on the actual workings of the final solution than any other state. And while the Pope had none of the divisions Stalin later sought, he had an extensive, brilliantly organized infrastructure which might have been brought into play for rescue work and a voice that had a profound influence with millions in occupied Europe. Yet the Pope remained silent, even while the Jews of Rome were deported "from under his window." That posture contrasted sharply with the activities of certain Dutch and French Bishops and some lesser officials like Cardinal Roncalli, later Pope John, who were active in the rescue effort. But these did not bear the responsibility for the survival of the institution of the Church itself.

One need not search out the reason for the Pope's silence in his Germanophilia or in his oversensitivity to the threat the Church faced from the Left. The latter had been demonstrated under the Calles and Cardenas regime in Mexico and during the Civil War in Spain. But observing that the Church genuinely felt the threat of "Godless Communism" is a long way from concluding that therefore Pius XII accepted the Nazis' line that they were the staunchest opponents of a Communist conspiracy which was somehow Jewish in nature. The immediate threat to the Church during the years of the Holocaust emanated from Berlin, and we know today that Hitler did indeed intend to settle matters with the Church after hostilities were over.

The Nazi ideology posed not only a physical threat, but also divided the Catholic flock. Over 42% of the SS were Catholic, and many top-ranking Nazi leaders, including Hitler, Himmler, Heydrich and Eichmann, were at least nominally so. The war itself had placed the Vatican in a delicate position since Catholics fought on both sides. The Pope's primary problem was how to walk that delicate tightrope. The determination not to speak out on Jews, which was at the very center of Nazi cosmology, should be viewed in that light. His choice was not basically different from that of the British in the Middle East or of Roosevelt on refugee policy.

The International Red Cross also thought in terms of its viability as an agency whose effectiveness was based on its ability to maintain a strict neutrality. It faced a legal dilemma, for while the Nazis spoke endlessly about the threat of "international Jewry" the Jews of Germany were legally an "internal" problem during the refugee phase. After the deportation and internment in camps began, their status became even more difficult to define. When Denmark requested the Red Cross to investigate the fate of Danish Jews deported to Theresienstadt, it could not do so since the request indicated that Denmark continued to recognize them as Danish citizens. But such requests were not forthcoming from other occupied countries. And the Danish request set the stage for one of the cruelest hoaxes of the war. The Red Cross delegation which visited Theresienstadt to carry out that charge apparently was totally taken in by the Potemkin village techniques, and gave the "model" camp a clean bill of health even while inmates were starving to death and being deported to Auschwitz behind the facade. Overly sensitive to the fact that it was a voluntary agency whose operation depended on the good-will of all parties, it did not press the case concerning Jews with determination. Food parcels were not delivered to camps until 1944, nor did it press for a change of classification of certain Jewish inmates to prisoners of war. That tactic, suggested by the World Jewish Congress, might have saved many lives. It was for that reason that Leon Kubowitzki, the leading rescue proponent of the World Jewish Congress, found that "the persistent silence of the Red Cross in the face of various stages of the extermination policy, of which it was well informed, will remain one of the troubling and distressing riddles of the Second World War." Yet here too one can observe how the integrity and well being of the agency took precedence over the rescue of the Jews. It may well be that the priorities of nations and international agencies are directed first and foremost to their own well-being and cannot be readily transferred for altruistic reasons to a vulnerable minority facing the threat of mass murder.

We come next to a question which embodies at once all the frustrations we feel at the failure of the witnesses and is for that reason posed with increasing frequency in Holocaust symposia and in publications on the catastrophe. The question of bombing Auschwitz and the rail lines leading to the camp raises the twin problems of assessing the failure of the witnesses and of determining the range of possibilities and their relationship to strategic priorities. The assumption is that interdiction from the air was, in the absence of physical control of the death camps, the best practical way to interrupt the killing process.

A recent article in Commentary by Professor David Wyman and another by Roger M. Williams in Commonweal demonstrate beyond doubt that by the spring of 1944 the bombing of Auschwitz was feasible.[2] Thousands of Hungarians and Slovakian Jews might have been saved had the American 15th Air Force, stationed in Italy and already bombing the synthetic oil and rubber works not five miles from the gas chambers, been allowed to do so. Moreover, by the fall of 1944 Auschwitz was well within the range of Russian dive bombers. Given that context, the note by Assistant Secretary of the Army John J. McCloy that bombing was of "doubtful efficacy" and the Soviet rejection of the idea are the most horrendously inhuman acts by witnesses during the years of the Holocaust. All that was required was a relati-

vely minor change in the priority assigned to the rescue of Jews.

Yet a perceptive historian cannot long remain
unaware of the seductive element in the bombing alternative. All one had to do, it seems, was to destroy
the death chambers or the railroad lines leading to
them, and the "production" of death would cease or at
least be delayed. Things were not that simple. Jewish
rescue advocates were late in picking up the signals
emanating from Hungary for bombing, and even then there
was little unanimity on its effectiveness. It was the
World Jewish Congress which transmitted the request for
bombing to the Roosevelt administation; but its own
agent, A. Leon Kubowitzki, held strong reservations
about bombing since he did not want the Jewish inmates
of the camps to be the first victims of Allied intercession from the air. There was then and continues to
be today genuine doubt that, given German fanaticism on
the Jewish question and the technical difficulties
involved in precision bombing, bombing the camps could
have stopped the killing. The Einzatsgruppen, the special killing squads which followed behind German lines
after the invasion of Russia, killed greater numbers in
shorter order than the camps. The Germans were able to
repair rail lines and bridges with remarkable speed.
And, of course, Auschwitz was only one of the several
camps where organized killing took place.

Most important, the bombing-of-Auschwitz alternative, so highly touted today, does not come to grips
with the question of the fear that the Germans would
escalate the terror and involve the Allies in a contest
in which the Germans held all the cards. In a recent
interview, McCloy cited this reason rather than the
unwillingness to assign war resources to missions that
were not directly involved in winning the war as the
reason uppermost in Roosevelt's mind when the bombing
alternative was rejected. An almost unnoticed sub-
theme in McCloy's August 14th note spoke of the fear
that bombing might "provoke even more vindictive action
by the Germans." Survivors and rescue advocates might
well wonder what "more vindictive action" than Auschwitz was possible. But that views the bombing alternative from the vantage of the Jewish victims--which,
as we have seen, is precisely what non-Jewish decision
makers could not do, given their different order of
priorities and sense of what was possible. The people
who conceived of the final solution could in fact have
escalated terror. They could have staged mass execu-

tions of prisoners of war or of hostages in occupied countries or the summary execution of shot-down bomber crews for "war crimes." Their imagination rarely failed when it came to conceiving new forms of terror, nor did they seem to possess normal moral restraints as one might find in the Allied camp. That was one of the reasons why the final solution could be implemented by them.

Nevertheless, one can hardly escape the conclusion that bombing deserved to be tried and might conceivably have saved lives. The failure to do so, however, is best viewed in the larger framework of the bombing question. It began with a collective demarche delivered by the governments-in-exile to the Allied high command in December, 1942. That request did not ask for the bombing of the camps, but for something called "retaliatory bombing." That notion too was rejected because of the fear of an escalation of terror, and rescue advocates did not pick up the idea until it was all but too late. There is good reason to believe that retaliatory bombing offered even greater hope for rescue than the bombing of the camps themselves.

In 1943, when the death mills of Auschwitz and other death camps ground on relentlessly, bombing was in fact not feasible but retaliatory bombing of German cities was in full swing. In one sense the bombing of Hamburg in July, 1943 and the savaging of other German cities, including the bombing of Dresden, which many Germans consider a separate war atrocity, make sense today only when considered in the context of the death camps. Albert Speer and our own post-war evaluation of saturation bombing inform us that it had almost no effect on curtailing German war production. Not until one industry, fuel or ball bearings, was target-centered did the Nazi war machine feel the pinch. Yet it might have furnished rescue advocates with an instrument to break through the "wall of silence" which surrounded what was happening to Jews. Even bombing interpreted as retaliatory could have remarkable effects, especially in the satellites. When Miklow Horthy, the Hungarian regent, called a halt to the deportations on July 7, 1944, he did so in part out of fear that Budapest would be subject to more heavy raids as it had been on June 2nd. It was the bombing of Budapest, not Auschwitz, that had the desired effect. We know that Goebbels in his perverse way fully expected such a quid pro quo and had even taken the precaution of planning a massive counter-atrocity campaign should the Allies make a connection between bombing and the death camps. Himmler also had already made the link. We find him addressing his officers on June 21, 1944 on the great difficulties encountered in implementing the final solution. He told the gathered group that if their hearts were ever softened by pity, let them remember that the savage bombing of German cities "was after all organized in the last analysis by the Jews."

Yet the natural link between bombing and the final solution made by Nazi leaders was not shared by Allied leadership or by Jewish rescue advocates. Had they done so, it is not inconceivable that the fear of disaffection and the terrible price the Reich was paying might have led more rational-minded leaders in the Nazi hierarchy to a reevalution of the final solution, which was after all a purely ideological goal. Not all Nazis were convinced that the murder of the Jews was worth the ruin of a single German city. We do not know if such a rearrangement of Nazi priorities was possible; the theme of retaliatory bombing was not fully picked up by rescue advocates, and by the time the notion of bombing the camps came to the fore in March, 1944, millions of Jews already were in ashes. That is why the twelve-point rescue program which came out of the giant Madison Square Garden protest rally in March, 1943 is as startling in its own way as McCloy's later response to the plea to bomb Auschwitz. It was silent on the question of bombing. It seems clear the researchers into the role of the witnesses in the future will have to place failure of mind next to failure of spirit to account for their inaction during the Holocaust.

I have saved the discussion of the role of American Jewry for the end because it is the most problematic of all. For those who remain convinced that American Jewry failed, how the problem is posed does not really matter, since the answer is always the same. Still, how did it happen that American Jewry possessing what was perhaps the richest organizational infrastructure of any hyphenate group in America, experienced in projecting pressure on government on behalf of their coreligionists since the Damascus blood libel of 1840, emerging from the Depression faster than any other ethnic group, boasting a disproportionate number of influential Jews in Roosevelt's inner circle, and chairing the three major committees in Congress concerned with rescue,[3] despite all this was unable to appreciably move the Roosevelt administration on the rescue question?

Stated in this way, the question provides not the slightest suggestion of the real problem which must be addressed if an adequate history of the role of American Jewry during the Holocaust is ever to emerge. For even if all of these assets in the possession of American Jewry were present, one still cannot avoid the conclusion that American Jewry's political power did not match the responsibilities assigned to it by yesterday's rescue advocates and today's historians. We need to know much more about the character and structure of American Jewry during the thirties, the political context of the host culture in which it was compelled to act, and the ability of hyphenate or ethnic groups to influence public policy.

The political and organizational weaknesses of American Jewry during the thirties have been amply documented. It seems clear that the precipitous shift of the mantle of leadership of world Jewry found American Jewry unprepared. A communal base for unified action simply did not exist. Instead there was fragmentation, lack of coherence in the message projected to policy makers, profound disagreement on what might be done in the face of the crisis, and strife among the leaders of the myriad political and religious factions which constituted the community. It may well be that the assumption of contemporary historians that there existed a single Jewish community held together by a common sense of its history and a desire for joint enterprise is the product of a messianic imagination.

One is hard-pressed to find such a community on the American scene during the thirties. Even those delicate strands which sometimes did allow the "uptown" and "downtown" divisions to act together vanished during the crisis. The issues which caused the disruption stemmed from the crisis and seem appallingly irrelevant today. There was disagreement on the actual nature of the Nazi threat, the efficacy of the antiNazi boycott, the creation of a Jewish army, the commonwealth resolution of the Biltmore Conference, the activities of the Peter Bergson group, and the way rescue activities were actually carried out around the periphery of occupied Europe. There was something tragic in the way each separate Jewish constituency was compelled in the absence of a unified front to go to Washington to plead separately for its particular refu-

-73-

gee clientele. In 1944 Rabbi Rosenheim, director of
the Vaad Ha-Hatzala, the rescue committee of the
Orthodox wing, explained why he found it better to act
alone. He observed that the rescue scene "was a dog
eat dog world [in which] the interest of religious Jews
[is] always menaced by the preponderance of the wealthy
and privileged Jewish organizations especially the
Agency and the Joint." Clearly for Rosenheim the Nazis
were not the only enemy. It did not take long for the
unfriendly officials in the State Department to learn
about the strife within the community. In 1944 we find
Breckinridge Long writing in his diary: "The Jewish
organizations are all divided amidst controversies ...
there is no cohesion nor any sympathetic collaboration
[but] ... rather rivalry, jealousy and antagonism." It
was a fairly accurate observation.

Yet one can have doubts whether the Administration's rescue policy would have been appreciably
changed had the Jews had a Pope, as Roosevelt once
wished in a moment of exasperation. In the American
historical experience the ability of pressure groups to
reorder policy priorities has been fairly circum-
scribed. The Irish-Americans, perhaps the most politically astute of all hyphenate groups, tried to use
American power to "twist the lion's tail" in the 19th
and 20th centuries. Yet with all their political
talent they were unable to prevent the Anglo-American
rapprochement which developed gradually after 1895.
During the years before World War I the German Americans were a larger and more cohesive group than American Jewry during the thirties. Yet they failed to
prevent the entrance of America into war against their
former fatherland. And adamant opposition of Polish-
Americans did not prevent the "Crime of Crimea," the
surrender of part of Poland to the Soviet Union at
Yalta.

There are more examples which could be cited to
establish the fact that hyphenate pressure has not been
distinctly successful in pulling foreign policy out of
its channels once it has been firmly established that a
given policy serves the national interest. Despite the
rantings of the former head of the Joint Chiefs of
Staff and others, Jews have done no better than other
groups in this regard. That it is thought to be otherwise is part of the anti-Semitic imagination, which has
always assigned Jews far more power and importance
behind the scenes than they possessed. It is one of
the great ironies of our time that many Jews share the

belief that they possess such secret power. It is a comforting thought for a weak and vulnerable people. It should be apparent to any Jew living in the time-space between Kishinev and Auschwitz that such can hardly be the case. A powerful people does not lose one third of its adherents while the rest of the world looks on.

The charge that American Jewry was indifferent to the survival of its brethren during the Holocaust is not only untrue, but would have been highly unchar-acteristic from a historical perspective. Much of American Jewry's organizational resources in the 19th and 20th century--the Board of Delegates of American Israelites, the American Jewish Committee, the Joint Distribution Committee and the various philanthropic organizations which preceded it, the American Jewish Congress, the various Zionist organizations and appeals --was structured in relation to Jewish communities and problems abroad. From its colonial beginnings, when American Jewry welcomed "messengers" from Palestine, it has consistently demonstrated a strong attachment to Jewish communities overseas. The Holocaust years did not mark a sudden change in that pattern. A close perusal would indicate that virtually every means of public pressure, from delegations to the White House to giant public demonstrations--techniques later adopted by the civil rights movement--were initially used by American Jewry during the war years to bring their message to American political leaders. They were not terribly effective because leaders were not fully attuned to Jewish objectives, and because the war itself tended to mute the cry of pain of a group trying vainly to convince America that its suffering was inor-dinate and required special attention.

Given the circumstances, American Jewry seemed bound to fail. Sometimes one is tempted to believe that such was the case with everything related to the Holocaust, including the writing of its history. Those who despair of the role of American Jewry forget that throughout the war years the actual physical control of the scene of the slaughter remained in Nazi hands. Wresting that physical control from them, the most cer-tain means of rescue, required a basic redirecting of war strategy to sve the Jews. Even under the best of circumstances, military strategists never would have accepted such restrictions. British historian Bernard Wasserstein, searching through recently declassified British documents, discovered that at one point, as the

-75-

war drew to a close, Churchill and Eden actually favored a direct military effort to save the Jews. But they did not succeed in breaking through the middle echelons of the bureaucracy and the military command to effect it. That is the reason why the American failure during the refugee phase (1938-1941), and the bombing of the camps and rail lines leading to them looms so large today. Such steps were impossible without a massive redirecting of strategy and without great sacrifice of lives and material. Aside from the possibility of ransoming proposals, which came at the beginning and end of the Holocaust, there seemed to be no other way to rescue appreciable numbers.

Besides the lack of precedent for responding to such a situation, American Jewry was plagued by its inability to get the fact of systematized mass murder believed. Few could fathom that a modern nation with a culture that had produced Goethe, Heine, Bach and Beethoven, the German Kulturgebiet which Jews especially linked to progress and enlightenment, had embarked on such a program. It beggared the imagination. The immense problem of gaining credibility was never solved during the crisis and contributed notably to the failure to activate decision makers to mount a more strenuous rescue effort. The role of the State Department in deliberately attempting to suppress the story of the final solution, a now well-known and separate tragedy, made breaking through the credibility barrier even more difficult.

It is in that context that the role of Rabbi Stephen Wise in asking Sumner Welles to confirm the Riegner cable, which contained the first details of the operation of the final solution, is best viewed. American Jewish leadership might be accused of ignorance, ineffectiveness, or just sheer lack of stature, as Nahum Goldmann recently observed, but the charge of betrayal is unwarranted and unfair. The contents of the Riegner cable, which spoke of the use of prussic acid and the production of soap from the fat of the cadavers, was so horrendous that to have publicized it without confirmation would have resulted in widening the credibility gap. Middle echelon State Department officials were not remiss in accusing Jewish leaders of atrocity mongering. In the context of the history of the thirties that charge was far from innocent. The notion that Americans had been skillfully manipulated by British propaganda into entering World War I was common fare in the revisionist history which made its debut in the thirties. A warning that British and Jewish interests were plotting to bring America into World War II had been a major theme in a speech delivered in September, 1941 in Des Moines by Charles Lindbergh, a greatly esteemed national folk hero. It was but a small jump for the isolationist-minded American public to believe that it was happening all over again. The neutrality laws passed by Congress in the thirties were based on the same supposition.

Although the delay in several months in publicizing the Riegner report was probably costly, it was necessary to gain credibility. Moreover, a duplicate cable had been forwarded to the British branch of the World Jewish Congress, so that there was little danger that the story could have been permanently suppressed by the State Department. Evenually even the Department's attempt to cut off the flow of information at the source was discovered and used to remove its hand from the rescue levers.

The inability to believe the unbelievable was not confined to Washington policy makers. It plagued Jewish leaders who were right on top of the operation and had every reason to believe it. The strategies developed by the Jewish Councils in eastern Europe, "rescue through work" and "rescue through bribery," and eventually the surrender of the aged and the infirm in the hope that the Nazis did not intend to liquidate useful Jews, was based on the assumption that the Nazis did not intend to kill all the Jews.

Even after the press made public news of the final solution, most Americans including many Jews, simply did not absorb the fact of what was happening. A poll of Americans in January, 1943, when an estimated one million Jews already had been killed, indicated that less than half the population believed that mass murder was occurring. Most thought it was just a rumor. By December, 1944, when much more detail was available, the picture had not drastically altered. Seventy-five percent now believed that the Germans had murdered many people in concentration camps. But when asked to estimate how many, most answered one hundred thousand or less. By May, 1945, when Americans already had seen pictures of the camps, the median estimate rose to one million, and 85% were now able to acknowledge that systematic mass murder had taken place. But the public was oblivious to the fact that the victims were largely Jewish. The inability to understand the immensity of the crime extended to the Jewish observers around the periphery of occupied Europe. They underestimated the number who had lost their lives by a million and a half. The figure of six million was not fully established until the early months of 1946.

The credibility problem was at the very core of the reaction of the witnesses; they could not react to something they did not know or believe. The problem of credibility takes us out of the realm of history. We need to know much more about how such facts enter the public conscience. How does one get people to believe the unbelievable? Rescue advocates did not succeed in solving that problem during those better years; and that, in some measure, is at the root of their failure to move governments and rescue agencies. In democracies it requires an aroused public opinion to move governments to action. Without that there is little hope that governments who are naturally reluctant to act would do so.

Thus far no historians have probed the role of Jewish political culture, those assumptions and qualities of style and habit which shape relationships to power and power holders, in accounting for the Jewish response. To be sure there are some untested observations in Raul Hilberg's The Destruction of European Jewry and Lucy Dawidowicz's The War Against the Jews. But no systematic study of its workings during the Holocaust years has been published. It is such an elusive subject that one can seriously wonder if it can be examined by modern scholarship. Yet it is precisely in that area that one of the keys to our conundrum regarding the Jewish response may lie.

Underlying the response of Jewish victims and witnesses at the time is an assumption about the world order so pervasive that we tend to forget that it is there at all. Jews believed then that there existed somewhere in the world, whether in the Oval Office or the Vatican or Downing Street, a spirit of civilization whose moral concern could be mobilized to save the Jews. The failure to arouse and mobilize that concern is the cause of the current despair regarding the role of the Jewish witness, and which leads to the search for betrayers. It is an assumption that continues to hold sway in Jewish political culture, despite the fact that there is little in recent Jewish experience that might confirm the existence of such a force in human affairs.

To some extent that despair is present in most literary works dealing with the Holocaust, especially in the speeches and works of one of the leading spokesmen for the victims, Elie Wiesel. It is a contemporary echo of what the Jewish victims felt before they were forced to enter the gas chambers. Emmanuel Ringelblum and others recorded it in their diaries. They wondered why no one came to their rescue and often assumed that the civilized world would not allow such a thing to happen. It can be heard most clearly in the message sent to Smull Zygelbojm which asked Jewish leaders to starve themselves to death if necessary in order "shake the conscience of the world." The assumption was and continues to be that there is a "conscience of the world."

American Jewry continued to hold that belief. Most of them were convinced that Roosevelt's welfare state, which reflected their own humanitarian proclivities, was a manifestation of that spirit of concern. That is why they loved him so; after 1936, even while other hyphenates began to decline in their political support, American Jewry raised the proportion of its pro-FDR vote to over 90%. Yet if they searched for deeds which actually helped their coreligionists, they would have found only rhetoric. That and their support of FDR's domestic program proved sufficient to hold them even after he had passed from the scene.

It may be that the Jewish voter had not resolved in his own mind the problem of possibilities of rescue or even the need for it. He assumed in his private way that the "authorities" were doing all that could be done. American Jewish leaders who were aware of the previous dismal record of government intercession in the Jewish interest nevertheless were hard-pressed for an alternative. They might have recalled how hard Jews had fought for an equal rights clause in the Roumanian Constitution at the Congress of Berlin in 1878, only to see it almost immediately thwarted by the Roumanian government. They surely were aware that dozens of diplomatic intercessions on behalf of Russian Jews at the turn of the century had come to nothing. Surely they knew that the most successful single effort to bring better treatment for their coreligionists, the abrogation of the Treaty of 1832 with Czarist Russia in 1911, had come to nothing. They might have recalled that when Louis Marshall turned to the Vatican in 1915 with a request that it use its influence to halt the anti-Jewish depredations in Poland, the response had been indifferent. The League of Nations, which many Jews imagined would house the spirit of humanity and even amplify it, had become a dismal failure by the thirties. They must have noted Roosevelt's niggardly response to the refugee crisis and Britain's reneging on the promise contained in the Balfour Declaration. They must have seen how drastically the situation had deteriorated even since World War I. At that time one could at least hint that Berlin would do for Jews what London would not and gain concessions. In short, they could not have failed to understand that for Jews living in the thirties the world had become less secure and benevolent than ever. But living with the knowledge of total vulnerability in an increasingly atavistic world is a reality almost too painful to face. One had to choose sides, and clearly Roosevelt with all his shortcomings was still better than the alternatives. There were in fact no alternatives, not on the domestic political scene and not in the international arena. The truth was that during the years of the Holocaust Jewish communities were caught in the classic condition of powerlessness which by definition means lack of options. That was true of American Jewry as well.

In that context the central assumption of pre-Holocaust Jewish political culture becomes understandable. It was based as much on powerlessness as on residual messianic fervor, or the universalism of democratic socialism which large numbers in the community adhered to. As a general rule it is precisely the weak and vulnerable who call for justice and righteousness in the world. The powerful are more inclined to speak of order and harmony. It is in the interest of the weak to have a caring spirit of civilization intercede for them. That may explain why Jews especially called on a threatened world to be better than it wanted to be.

For American Jewry the notion of benevolence and concern in the world was not totally out of touch with reality. Bereft of specific power, they did in fact make astounding economic and political advances in the 18th, 19th and 20th centuries. Despite occasional setbacks, the idea that progress was possible, even inevitable, was deeply ingrained in American Jewry's historical experience. More than other Jewries who lived in the West, they had to some degree been disarmed by their history so that they never fully understood the signs that all was not well in the secular nation-state system. The most important of these signs was the relative ease with which the nations ordered and accepted the incredible carnage of World War I. That experience contained many of the portents of the Holocaust, including the use of gas and the cheapening of human life. The rise of totalitarian systems in the inter-war period which extended further the demeaning of individual human dignity was not part of their experience, so they did not understand what the massive bloodletting in the Soviet Union signified. They did not understand that the nation-state was dangerously out of control, that all moral and ethical restraints had vanished and only countervailing power held it in check.

Many Jews still looked to the nations for succor; they sought restraints. "We fell victims to our faith in mankind," writes Alexander Donat, "our belief that humanity had set limits to the degradation and persecution of one's fellow man." The countering facts were of too recent a vintage to seep into their historical consciousness and alter their visions and assumptions about the world in which they lived. Jewish leaders and rank and file blithely disregarded the mounting evidence that states and other forms of human organization, even those like the Holy See which professed to a humanizing mission through Christian love, were less than ever able to fulfill such a role. The behavioral cues of states came from within and were determined by the need of the organization to survive at all costs. With a few notable exceptions the rescue of Jews during the years of the Holocaust did not fit in with such objectives, and they were allowed to perish like so much excess human cargo on a lifeboat.

The indictment of the witnesses is based on the old assumption that there exists such a spirit of civilization, a sense of humanitarian concern in the world, which could have been mobilized to save Jewish lives during the Holocaust. It indicts the Roosevelt administration, the Vatican, the British government and all other witnessing nations and agencies for not acting, for not caring, and it reserves a special indignation for American Jewry's failure to mobilize a spirit which did not in fact exist. It is an indictment which cannot produce authentic history. Perhaps that cannot really be written until the pain subsides.

Footnotes

1. Arthur D. Morse, While Six Million Died (New York: Random House, 1965); Saul S. Friedman, No Haven for the Oppressed (Detroit: Wayne State University Press, 1973).

2. Commentary, LXV, 5 (May, 1978), 37-46; Commonweal, Nov. 24, 1978, 746-751.

3. Rep. Sol Bloom, House Foreign Affairs Committee; Rep. Samuel Dickstein, House Committee on Immigration and Naturalization; Rep. Emmanuel Celler, House Judiciary Committee.

WHY DIDN'T THE JEWS FIGHT BACK?

Jack Nusan Porter

Introduction

The Holocaust, the attempted genocide of the Jews by the Nazis during World War II, presented social scientists with an extraordinary case history. In the years following World War II, social scientists produced an overwhelming quantity of research in areas that either directly related to the period or to issues raised by it.

World War II was massive in its scale of death and power, towering and complex in its elemental balance of good and evil, majestic and stirring in its multi-leveled meaning, overwhelming in its simplicity. Almost anything can be found within its confines--if one wishes to look for it. At times, the questions become so profound that only poets, novelists, and mystics can provide "answers." Every scholar feels impotent, overwhelmed, and disillusioned by the enormity of the event. Social scientists have attempted to grapple with the questions raised by the Holocaust and they continue to do so. Various research techniques have been used, including philosophical discourses, intensive interviews and case studies, laboratory stimulation, historical analysis, psycho-history, participant observation and survey research.

Almost any good introductory psychology textbook will indicate those topics that seem to have received their impetus from the Holocaust (for example, Krech, et al, 1962). They include the human struggle for freedom and the need to escape from freedom by embracing totalitarian systems (Fromm, 1941), the susceptibility of individuals for mass movements (Hoffer,

* Funding for this research came from a grant of the Wein Foundation of Chicago under the direction of Dr. Byron Sherwin of Spertus College. My thanks to Dr. Robert Ravven, and the staff of the Countway Medical Library of Harvard University for their support and counsel. This paper was read at the 2nd International Symposium on Victimology, Wednesday, Sept. 8, 1976, Boston, Mass.

1951); psychoanalytic and sociological studies of anti-Semitism and racism (Adorno, et al, 1950; Ackerman and Jahoda, 1950), and the structure and dynamics of prejudice (Bettelheim and Janowitz, 1950; Allport, 1958). These topics in turn have led to enumerable studies of race, racism, and race relations most particularly Black-White relations (Myrdal, 1944); the impact of group pressure on individual judgment (Asch, 1955); the question of conformity, attitude formation and attitude change, the sub-field of small-group research and in particular, the influence of various types of leadership on group efficacy (Haythorn, 1956).

The entire field of collective behavior, stimulated by the Holocaust, would come to include: the analysis of crowd behavior, rumors, and political revolution (Turner and Killian, 1972); the art and science of propaganda and the impact of the mass media on popular opinion (Cantril, 1941; Hovland et al, 1949, 1957; Kracauer, 1947), and the new field of psychohistory which began with a psychosociological analysis of the mind of Adolf Hitler (Langer, 1972).

World War II ushered in an era of large-scale research that for the first time was funded by governmental agencies. Some of these funds went to university institutes and departments; others were funneled directly to the social scientists themselves. The Office of Strategic Services, the Department of Labor, as well as the specific research institutes of the Army, Navy and Air Force were all responsible for the dramatic increase in research during and after the War. (One quick glance by the reader at the dates of the books referred to in the notes will verify this fact.)

Pioneering efforts were made to apply the latest techniques of modern psycholgy, sociology, and history, not to distant nor abstract issues, but to the most pressing issues of the day. The old adage is correct: "necessity breeds creativity", and there are few forces as compelling as World War. Many of the studies made during and within a decade following that War are today considered classics in the field.

The confines of the present article do not provide the opportunity to enter into a discussion of all the socio-psychological "spin-offs" that the Holocaust engendered. The present task is more modest--to briefly introduce and clarify one specific area of research--the social and psychological obstacles of resistance to genocide.

The Question of "Sheep to Slaughter"

Until the Eichmann trial of 1961, most people assumed that the Jews "went like sheep to slaughter" to the death camps without putting up the least bit of resistance. This passivity in the face of large-scale extermination raised a storm of controversy throughout the Jewish communities of the world and especially in Israel where the "tough" machismo sabra model was idealized. Subsequent research has shown that resistance did in fact take place on many fronts, the Jewish ghettos, the concentration camps, and the forests. An entire literature exists describing this resistance. (Suhl, 1975; Ainsztein, 1974; Foxman, 1968; Friedman, 1960; Barkai, 1962; Porter, 1981; Suhl, 1975).

Whether this resistance was effective from a strictly military point of view is debatable, but that is not the present concern. What is of interest are the obstacles to resistance in the face of genocide. One may agree with Elie Wiesel's observation that "the question is not why all Jews did not fight, but how so many of them did. Tormented, beaten, starved, where did they find the strength--spiritual and physical--to resist?" (Quoted in Suhl, 1974:4).

Spiritual and moral forms of resistance will also be discussed in this chapter but our concern is to define "resistance" in terms of military and physical resistance. Only a small percentage of Jews physically resisted. Our goal is to try to determine why?

First of all, one must understand that the same obstacles to resistance held true for many non-Jews as well, though the obstacles were more stringent for Jews. Some of these obstacles can account for the fact that in some case, entire nations were paralyzed into inaction. By its very nature, resistance is engaged in by only a small minority of the total population. One is speaking here of armed resistance, yet other forms of resistance are available to a larger segment of the population. Each person resisted according to his/her abilities. One cannot include the very young, the very old, the lame, the sick, and those who were executed so quickly that they had no time to resist. While spiritual and moral resistance was available to them, physical resistance was not.

The first and foremost barrier was simply the incomprehensibility of the Holocaust itself. The audacity of the phenomenon psychologically overwhelmed many Jews. One's first reaction was denial; to dismiss the entire idea as a cruel hoax. In fact, even most of the Allied nations and their leaders simply rejected early atrocity reports as wartime "propaganda" (See Morse, 1968).

Greuelpropaganda

Bruno Bettelheim describes three separate psychological mechanisms that were most frequently used in dealing with the horrors of genocide (Bettelheim, 1966). These mechanisms are based on the assumption that an allegedly civilized nation could not stoop to such inhumane acts. The implication that modern man had such inadequate control over his cruel impulses was perceived as a threat to the psyche.

According to Bettelheim, the following defense mechanisms emerged. First, the atrocity report's applicability to mankind in general was denied by asserting that such horrible acts (if in fact they did exist) were committed by a small group of insane or perverted persons. The Eichmann trial of 1960-61 in Israel demonstrated just the opposite: that these acts were carried out with scientific and bureaucratic precision by hundreds of ordinary people (soldiers, guards, railroad engineers, chemists, physicians, etc.). Social psychologist Stanley Milgram (1973a, 1973b) has verified in his research that most people will harm their fellow human beings rather than disobey authority figures.

Second, the truths of the atrocity reports were further denied by ascribing them to deliberate propaganda. In fact, the Germans themselves, masters of the art, called it greuelpropaganda (horror propaganda), and were quite aware that the more outrageous the atrocity, the more difficult it was for the world to believe. The Germans also understood that the bigger the lie, the more it would be believed. Such lies had to exist within the realm of possibility and had to be based upon already manifested myths and prejudices. Thirdly, the reports were believed, but this knowledge was repressed as soon as possible. In addition to the individual's psychological mechanisms, the Germans were experts in un-nerving their victims, in bewildering them, and in thwarting any plans for escape. The ploys used are well-known. They had code words which camou-

flaged their real intent--"relocation," "Jewish problem," "final solution." They made people believe that
the death camps were work camps. The victims were met
by an orchestra at the train station; they were given
bars of "soap" when they entered the gas chambers, the
SS sent postcards back to the victim's friends and
relatives describing how "wonderful" the situation was
and how "well" they were being treated. It is not an
exaggeration to say that it was a time in which morality was placed on its head: right was wrong, wrong was
right, true was false, and false was true. This same
thought was echoed by the French partisan leader
Dominique Ponchardier in his book Les Paves de L'Enfer
(from Ehrlich, 1965:272):

> ...It was by definition the era of the false;
> the false combatant, the false decent man,
> the false patriot, the false lover, the false
> brother, the false false. In a world of
> false noses, I was one of those whose nose
> was real and it seemed to me, as it did to
> all the "reals" that in reality we were all
> real cons.

This sense of existential un-reality and dubious
authenticity plagues survivors to this day.

Collective Retaliation

The principle of collective responsibility carried
out by the Nazis baffled the Jews, prevented their
escape from the ghettos, and helped suppress resistance. In many ghettos when an escaped fighter was
caught, not only he but his entire family, his neighbors, and even his work-unit were killed. When a man
or woman decided to resist, he/she knew that it would
endanger not only his/her life, but that of parents,
children, spouse, brother, sister, and acquaintances.
Resistance could also be defined by the authorities as
escape either from ghetto or concentration camp. Leon
Wells, in his memoir The Janowska Road, tells the
following tale (from Wells, 1963:190 and also see
Foxman, 1968:94-95):

> Now the Untersturmfuhrer (SS officer) begins
> his speech, directing it at us: "One of you
> escaped. Because of him these people will be
> shot. From now on for anyone who tries to do
> the same, I will shoot twenty of you. If I

find out that you are planning an escape, all of you will be shot." After his speech, he turns to the chosen six, and shoots one after another...when finished he calls for four of us to pick up the corpses and toss them into the fire.

The Jews in the ghetto faced a severe dilemma. If they left the ghetto to fight, they might save themselves but leave their families behind. If too many fighters left the ghetto, the remaining population would be vulnerable. But if they did not resist in some way, they would be denied the privilege of avenging themselves. The late historian of the Holocaust, Philip Friedman, succinctly summarized this dilemma in the following quote (from Glatstein et al, 1973:276):

In the Jewish underground of Warsaw, Bialystok, and other ghettos, a passionate discussion was going on: What were they to do? Stay in the ghetto or leave it for the woods? It was primarily a moral issue: Were they entitled to leave the ghetto populace to face the enemy alone or did they have to stay on and to take the lead in the fight when the crucial moment of the extermination actions arrived? After heated debates, the opinion prevailed to stay in the ghetto as long as possible despite the disadvantages of the position, and to leave only at the last moment when there was no longer any chance to fight or to protect the ghetto populace.

The Nazis understood the Jewish psyche quite well, and knew where the Jew was most vulnerable. Closely connected to the Nazi principle of collective retaliation was their awareness of the strong family ties among the Jews. Ironically what had been a great strength to the Jewish people now became a pernicious trap. The close-knit family structure made it difficult for one or two members to leave the rest behind and it became extremely difficult for an entire family to escape the ghetto together. To elect to leave the village or escape from the ghetto or camp in the hope of reaching the partisans required a painful decision to leave a wife, mother, father, and child.

In an interview that the author had with his own father, a partisan leader in the Ukraine, this theme is constantly emphasized. The reminiscences are permeated with guilt, even though his leavetaking opened the opportunity to take revenge against the Nazis:

> Am I no different from my parents or my daughters that I lived and they died? No, we were the same. Why, then, did I remain alive? I may not have been able to have helped them if I had stayed but at least we would have been together to the end.

The Hope of Survival

Above and beyond all the concealed tricks, half-truths, and devious ploys used by the Nazis in their "final solution" of the Jews, perhaps the most effective tool was the utter magnitude of the actual killings. This led, as was shown, to numerous ways of adapting to the incomprehensibility of these atrocities. One of the most elemental drives of the human being is to try to survive. Many Jews felt they were not going to be killed; that they were too valuable; that the Germans needed their labor, their talents, or even their money.

Many believed that if they obeyed the law, they would be spared. In short, resistance to them meant suicide; not to resist meant the possibility of life. Why then take the risk? Hold onto life for as long as possible. This was the attitude of many Jews in Europe. (See for example, Miller, 1971:283-342.)

Orthodox Jews, furthermore, refused to take part in military resistance (with some exceptions) because to them resistance was seen as contrary to God's law. It was equivalent to a suicide mission, and suicide was considered a sin. Better to trust in God and His judgment. To the very end, they felt, one must do God's bidding, stay alive, and not risk death. One's goals should be Kevod Hashem (Hebrew term for "religious honor") and Kiddush Hashem ("sanctification of God's name, "religious self-sacrifice").

This form of non-violent resistance (almost Gandian in certain ways) has become a very controversial topic. Some readers will say that this form of passive resistance is not resistance at all but cowardice, that it led to the deaths of many Jews who might have saved themselves if they had not listened to the rabbis. A Russian-Jewish partisan, Moishe Flash, whom the author has interviewed, echoed these sentiments:

Because of God and the religiously orthodox,
many Jews died because it kept the people
from fighting. The rabbis had a strong hold
on the people. Because of that I had to
leave my religion for awhile and fight.

Non-violent resistance took many forms. There
were prayer groups and Hebrew classes that would con-
gregate in ghettos and camps despite heavy penalties.
There were attempts to rescue Torah scrolls from burning synagogues although some people were killed in the
process. There are stories of Hasidim who literally
prayed and danced in religious ecstasy until the last
minute of their lives. Are these acts of bravery or
cowardice? Is there an answer to such value-laden,
emotional questions?

Lack of Arms, Lack of Leadership, Lack of Trust

The most serious obstacles to resistance once the
psychological, theological, and family barriers were
overcome, were lack of arms, lack of communication
between Jews and outside partisan groups, and lack of
trained leadership. Resistance comes down to basics.
In any revolt, only a small minority are able to resist
and these few must have something to fight back with.
Even here the Jews were not always successful.

As Philip Friedman (in Glatstein et al, 1973:277)
states in his article "Jewish Resistance to the Nazis":

A steady uninterrupted supply of arms is a
condition sine qua non for resistance operations. Most of the non-Jewish underground
movements had received vast supplies of arms
and other material from their governemnts-in-
exile and from the Allied governments. But
in no country was the Jewish underground
treated on an equal footing with the recognized national organizations.

Whatever the Jewish underground was to receive had
to pass through unfriendly national channels. Often
the requests were refused outright (e.g. the Vilna and
Bialystok ghettos), or came too late and in very small
quantities (e.g. the Warsaw ghetto). During the Warsaw
ghetto revolt led by Mordechai Anilewicz, the Jewish
partisans, after prolonged negotiations with the Polish
underground, received only fifty revolvers, fifty hand

grenades, and four kilograms of explosives. These meager weapons were all the Jews had to fight off entire artillery regiments and air-attacks--and even some of the revolvers were defective and useless. One of the major reasons the Jews received so little aid from the Armia Krajowa, the Polish Land Army, the largest underground movement in Poland, was because its leadership was rife with anti-Semitism (Suhl, 1975:6).

Each gun, each grenade, each rifle was worth its weight in gold. Quite often, each piece had to be literally purchased in gold on the black market from illegal arms dealers and army deserters, or had to be stolen from guards, soldiers, and peasants, or made in small clandestine factories and repair shops (Glatstein et al, 1973:277).

Aside from the lack of arms, there was often a lack of trust and communication between Jews and the surrounding communities, especially in Poland, the Ukraine, Latvia, Lithuania, and Hungary. Some of this mistrust was due to anti-Semitism; but much of it was due to outright fear of the Germans who would retaliate for collaborating with the enemy (defined as Jews, Communists, and partisans). In the words of Harvard professor Erich Goldhagen (1978), Jews lived not only like fish lived in hostile sea, but like fish upon hostile dry land. All of these factors hampered the effective coordination between Jewish and non-Jewish fighting groups. With regards to trained leaders, the Nazis had killed off the Jewish leadership in the first phases of the genocide, and therefore leadership posi- tions fell to the young adults, to women, and to the inexperienced.

Conclusions

The above discussion has attempted to define the major social, familial, and psychological obstacles to resistance. These obstacles were effective in con- founding the Jews and their sympathizers. The myth of total Jewish compliance and cowardice must not however be replaced with a new myth, the myth of the Jewish superman. The true picture of this tragedy lies beyond the myths that people have developed.

I hope that this analysis has made a contribution to the study of victimology. Too often the victim is blamed for his or her inability to counter an attack.

The tendency to blame the victim is as true for victims of the Nazi genocide as it is for victims of rape or poverty. What has been described here are a few of the barriers to resistance. While there was resistance, both organized and unorganized, passive and active, effective and ineffective, one must underscore the formidable obstacles that lay in the way of such resistance. Value-laden terms such as "cowardice" and "heroism" should be reserved for poets, propagandists, and politicians. They should be used with the utmost caution by scholars.

References

Ackerman, N.W., and Marie Jahoda, <u>Anti-Semitism</u> and <u>Emotional Disorder: A Psycholanalytical Interpretation</u>, New York: Harper, 1950.

Adorno, Theodor, et al, <u>The Authoritarian Personality</u>, New York: Harper, 1950.

Ainsztein, Reuben, <u>Jewish Resistance in Nazi-Occupied Eastern Europe</u>, New York: Barnes and Noble, (Harper and Row), 1974.

Allport, Gordon, <u>The Nature of Prejudice</u>, New York: Doubleday, (Anchor Books), 1958.

Asch, Solomon, "Opinions and Social Pressure", <u>Scientific American</u>, Vol. 193, 1955, pp. 31-35.

Barkai, Meyer (ed.), <u>The Fighting Ghettos</u>, Philadelphia: Lippincott, 1962.

Bettelheim, Bruno and Morris Janowitz, <u>Dynamics of Prejudice</u>, New York: Harper, 1950.

Bettelheim, Bruno, <u>The Informed Heart</u>, New York: The Free Press, 1966.

Cantril, Hadley, <u>The Psychology of Social Movements</u>, New York: John Wiley, 1941.

Ehrlich, Blake, <u>Reistance: France 1940-1945</u>, Boston: Little Brown, 1965.

Foxman, Abraham H., "Resistance: The Fight Against the Many, in Judah Pilch, (ed.), <u>The Jewish Catastrophe in Europe</u>, New York: American Association for Jewish Education, 1968.

Friedman, Philip, "Jewish Resistance to Nazism" in <u>European Resistance Movements</u>, 1939-1945, London: Oxford Pergamon Press, 1960.

Fromm, Erich, <u>Escape from Freedom</u>, New York: Farrar and Rinehart, 1941.

Glatstein, Jacob, et al, (eds.), <u>Anthology of Holocaust Literature</u>, New York: Atheneum, 1973.

Goldhagen, Erich, Speech given at Harvard University, April, 1978.

Haythorn, W., "The Effects of Varying Combinations of Authoritarian and Equalitarian Leaders and Followers", Journal of Abnormal and Social Psychology, Vol. 52, 1956, pp. 210-219.

Hoffer, Eric, The True Believer, New York: Harper, 1951.

Hovland, C.I., et al, Experiments on Mass Communications, Princeton, N.J.: Princeton University Press, 1949.

_____, The Order of Presentation in Persuasion, New Haven, Conn.: Yale University Press, 1957.

Kracauer, Siegfried, From Caligari to Hitler: A Psychological History of the German Film, Princeton, N.J.: Princeton University Press, 1947.

Krech, David, et al, Individual in Society, New York: McGraw-Hill, 1962. There are also later editions.

Langer, Walter C., The Mind of Adolf Hitler, New York: Basic Books, 1972.

Milgram, Stanley, Obedience to Authority, New York: Harper and Row, 1973a.

_____, "The Perils of Obedience", Harpers Magazine, December, 1973b.

Miller, Arthur, "Incident at Vichy", in The Portable Arthur Miller, New York: Viking Press, 1971, pp. 283-342.

Morse, Arthur, While Six Million Died, New York: Random House, 1968.

Myrdal, Gunnar, An American Dilemma, New York: Harper, 1944.

Porter, Jack Nusan (ed.), Jewish Partisans: Jewish Resistance in Eastern Europe During World War II, Washington, D.C.: University Press of America, 1981.

Suhl, Yuri (ed. and trans.), _They Fought Back: The Story of the Jewish Reistance in Nazi Europe_, New York: Crown, 1967; reissued in paperback by New York: Schocken Books, 1975.

Turner, Ralph and Lewis Killian, _Collective Behavior_, New York: Prentice-Hall, 1972 (second edition).

Wells, Leon, _The Janowska Road_, New York: Macmillan, 1963.

II. THE ARMENIANS

II. THE ARMENIANS

On August 22, 1939, on the eve of World War II, Hitler silenced some of his commanders who were having guilty feelings about the mass killings they were about to undertake with the following words: "Who, after all, speaks today of the annihilation of the Armenians...? The world believes in success alone."

The Armenian genocide has "died several times." Not only during Hitler's era was it forgotten; it is still overlooked by most of the world today. The Jewish Holocaust too often oversahdows it and all other genocides. The Armenian genocide was well-known during its time but through historical distortion and political machinations, it was buried "in the pit of history." The Turks were guilty of burying this crime because the Armenians were, as Marjorie Housepian explains, "few, dispersed, and without a public platform to plead their case..." This "burial" continues up to this day.

Leon Chorbajian, a young Armenian sociologist and a son of survivors of that tragedy, poignantly discusses his personal anguish coming to grips with this silence. As a political activist he saw in Vietnam a repetition of genocide by his own government, and this was particularly disturbing to him. Marjorie Housepian takes a less radical, yet quietly indignant, position on this "unremembered" genocide in her fine essay.

James H. Tashjian, a Boston editor and writer, looks at the events of the past from an historical perspective and interweaves the role of Raphael Lemkin and the United Nations Genocide Convention. He criticizes both the Soviet Union and the United States for their equivocation regarding this treaty. In his view the Convention will remain an ineffective document "until those who have been victimized ... are given the fullest redress for the wrongs done them." That this has never been done in the nearly thirty-five years since the treaty was founded only shows how millions of others face the threat of extinction in the future; the U.N. does little to help. Tashjian's pamphlet appeared in 1967 and, while the years since have added new facets to the story, his basic conclusion about the U.N. is still sound.

THE UNREMEMBERED GENOCIDE

Marjorie Housepian

The Armenian people--some 250,000 in the United States and about four million throughout the world-- consider themselves to have been the victims of a geno- cide perpetrated almost thrity years before that term was coined. They insist that the murder of over a million Armenians in Turkey during 1915-1916 was the result of a deliberate and methodical government policy aimed at the extermination of an innocent minority and not, as the Turkish apologists have claimed, a wartime security measure against a treasonous group. Convinced that the universal indifference to this "solution" of the "Armenian question" later encouraged Hitler to ven- ture on a similar "solution" of the "Jewish question," Armenians feel a tragic kinship with the Jewish people and have sought, in vain, for a sign of acknowledgement of this bond.

There have, of course, been Jews who showed con- cern for the fate of the Armenian people, among them Henry Morgenthau, Sr., who was the American ambassador to Turkey during the first year of the fateful "massa- cre." Within the limits of his power--and sometimes, it seemed to the State Department, beyond these limits --Morgenthau made the Armenian cause his own, proclaim- ing the Turkish crimes to be unparalleled "in the whole history of the human race." There was also Franz Werfel, whose novel Forty Days of Musa Dagh (1934), remains the sole literary testament to the Armenian catastrophe--a dramatization of one of the rare, iso- lated instances of heroic resistance against the Turks, and at the same time a portrayal of hundreds of thous- ands of people marching to their death, silent and unprotesting.

Werfel became familiar with the events through the reports of Armenian escapees, as well as through the eyewitness accounts of foreign missionaries, journal- ists, and officials who had managed to see exactly what was happening, despite the efforts of Ottoman authori- ties to hide their deeds from public view. As the first of these accounts filtered out of Turkey, James Bryce, the English statesman, historian, and author of The American Commonwealth, began collecting documentary evidence, which was later summarized in his British Blue Book, The Treatment of the Armenians in the Ottoman Empire (edited by Arnold J. Toynbee). Lord Bryce took pains to have the evidence examined--and to have his verdict corroborated that the Turks were committing what would now be called genocide--by such figures as Gilbert Murray, H. A. L. Fisher, and Moorfield Storey, president of the American Bar Association.

American consuls throughout Turkey were simultaneously sending detailed accounts of the systematic massacres to the State Department, and such humanitarians as Johannes Lepsius, a leading German Protestant, were also gathering evidence. At great risk to his life, Lepsius even visited Turkey on several occasions and pleaded with the Turkish rulers on behalf of the Armenians. His efforts were unsuccessful, as was his attempt to apply pressure on his own government. As Turkey's wartime ally, Germany had no intention of pressing the Turks to desist; in fact, according to Morgenthau in Ambassador Morgenthau's Story, Germany gave its tacit encouragement to the policy of extermination.

Thus--though the world was in a position to know what was happening--that policy proceeded to run its course. As will be seen, the events left no mark in history; indeed, today there are few who even know they occurred.

II

The Armenians are an ancient people who converted to Christianity about 300 C.E., a number of years before the conversion of Constantine. Fatally located at the crossroads between East and West, the Armenian kingdom was stormed by all the invading hordes: Saracens, Seljuks, Mongols, Tartars, and lastly the Ottoman Turks. Yet the Armenian Church--independent both of the Greek Orthodox and the Roman Catholic--preserved the national identity through this long series of invasions, through the subjugation of the kingdom by a succession of pagan and Moslem powers, and finally even through the dispersion of about half of the Armenian people to every corner of the globe.

Under the Ottoman Empire, the Armenians became a subject race, forbidden to bear arms and prey to the semi-barbarous Kurds who roamed among their towns and periodically beset them, with the encouragement and approval of the Turkish authorities. By 1908, when the "Young Turks" overthrew the oppressive Sultan Abdul

Hamid, the more fortunate among the Armenians had fled the country, or else had settled in the large cities, where they improved their position considerably; indeed, along with Ottoman Greeks, they controlled much of Turkey's six northeastern provinces; there they comprised the bulk of the craftsmen and tradesmen, and tilled the soil in what, at the time, was Turkey's breadbasket.

The new Turkish leaders were greeted with jubilation by the Armenians, who were promised equality under law and even permitted to elect deputies to parliament. But the new regime soon shattered their hopes. Encouraged by the Germans to the notion of pan-Islamism, inflamed with nationalism and thwarted--by minority deputies who were taking the new doctrine of equal rights seriously--in its attempt to "ottomanize" all the minorities of Turkey, the Young Turk revolution rapidly degenerated into chauvinism and fanaticism.

Hardly had the new rulers gained power when they became embroiled in the disastrous Balkan Wars and proceeded to lose virtually all of Turkey's vast European territory to their former slaves: the Bulgarians, the Greeks, and the Serbs. Thus, in 1914, as Turkey was becoming immersed in World War I, thousands of destitute and disgruntled Moslem refugees from the Balkans were encamped on her doorstep. Desperately in need of capital, the government was faced with the fact that much of Turkey's trade was in foreign hands, while the rest was controlled by Ottoman Greeks and Armenians. The Armenians, whose compatriots outside Turkey were voicing their enthusiasm for the Allies, provided the most logical and defenseless minority on which to turn --despite the fact that Armenians wihthin Turkey were doing their utmost to demonstrate their loyalty to the state.

"For years it had been Turkish policy to provoke the Christian population into committing overt acts, then seizing upon such misbehavior as an excuse for massacre," Morgenthau writes. "The Armenian clergy and political leaders saw [in 1914] many evidences that the Turks...were [provoking rebellion] and they went among the people cautioning them to be quiet and bear all insults and even outrages patiently, so as not to give provocation. 'Even though they burn a few of our villages,' these leaders would say, 'do not retaliate, for it is better that a few be destroyed than that the whole nation be massacred.'" As time went on, however, the provocations increased. One ruse adopted by the authorities was to requisition a certain number of fighting men from an Armenian town. These were then taken away and slain, and their bodies left where they could be readily found. When the citizens of Van--a town near the Russian border--organized a defense and held siege rather than submit their men to the slaughter, their "revolution" was made a pretext for subsequent "punitive" actions.

It soon became evident that the Turks were out to do more than burn a few villages. During the night of April 24, 1915, the intellectual and religious leaders of the Armenian community in Constantinople were seized from their beds, imprisoned, tortured, and ultimately put to death on charges of sedition. (The Turkish reply to Ambassador Morgenthau's protest was to hang fourteen men in the public square the following day.) Simultaneously, all Armenians serving in the Turkish army--these had already been gathered into separate "labor battalions"--were taken aside and killed. Then, when the leaders and fighting men were disposed of, the final phase began. Lord Bryce describes the opening procedure as follows:

> At one Armenian center after another throughout the Ottoman Empire, on a certain date (and the dates show a sequence), the public crier went through the streets announcing that every male Armenian over 15 must present himself forthwith at the Government building ...The men presented themselves in their working clothes, leaving their shops and work-rooms open, their ploughs on the field, their cattle on the mountain side. When they arrived, they were thrown without explanation into prison, kept there a day or two, then marched out of the town in batches, roped man to man along some southerly or southeasterly road...They had not long to ponder over their plight for they were halted and massacred at the first lonely place on the road.

After a few days' interval, the Armenian women and children, as well as any remaining men, were ordered to prepare themselves for deportation. Many were turned out on the road immediately, but in some towns they were given a week of grace which they spent in a frenzied attempt to sell their personal possessions for whatever was offered. Government orders forbade them from selling real property or stocks, as their banishment was supposed to be temporary. Scarcely were they out of sight, however, when Moslem refugees from Europe, who had been gathered nearby, were moved into their homes. Since the Turks of the interior were almost totally unskilled, a representative Armenian craftsman in each area--a shoemaker, a tailor, a pharmacist--was permitted to remain. All the rest were set upon the roads leading to the deserts. According to Morgenthau, hundreds and thousands "could be seen winding in and out of every valley and climbing up the sides of nearly every mountain." In the first six months alone, over 1,200,000 people joined this unearthly procession.

By now the story bears a chillingly familiar quality, the more intensified when one remembers that the victims of this last, most hideous phase were almost exclusively women and children. They were marched south from the plains of Anatolia, through a region that is a no-man's land of treacherous ravines and craggy mountains forbidding to the most hardened traveler, and finally into the bleak Syrian desert, fiercely hot by day and frigid by night. On the way, they were beset by all the Moslem populations they encountered. First there were the Turkish villagers and peasants who robbed them of their few provisions, their clothes, and took such of their women as they pleased; then the Kurds, who committed blood-chilling atrocities, first butchering any males in the convoy, then attacking the women. According to the Bryce Report: "It depended on the whim of the moment whether a Kurd cut a woman down or carried her away into the hills. When they were carried away their babies were left on the ground or dashed against the stones." Then came the "chettis", savage brigands who had been loosed by the thousands from prisons and set in the victims' path, and dervishes who roared down from their convents in the hills and carried off children "shrieking with terror." And always there were the gendarmes, prodding the exhausted and terror-stricken figures with whips and clubs, refusing them water when they passed wells and streams, bayonetting those who lagged behind, and committing increasingly perverted atrocities.

Apologists have claimed that these atrocities were simply the work of barbaric and fanatic tribesmen, but Morgenthau has shown that they were a matter of deliberate policy. Thus, an educated state official told him with some pride that "all these details were mat-

ters of nightly discussion at...headquarters...Each new
method of inflicting pain was hailed as a splendid
discovery, and the regular attendants were constantly
ransacking their brains in an effort to devise some new
torment. He told me that they even delved into the
records of the Spanish Inquisition and other historic
institutions of torture and adopted all the suggestions
found there.

Nor can there be any doubt that the policy of
extermination as a whole was planned by the central
government. The official record includes the following
orders, sent on cipher telegrams and in all but one
case addressed to the provincial government of Aleppo
(the lightning advance of Allenby's forces prevented
the Turks in Aleppo from destroying these compromising
documents):[1]

> September 3, 1915
> We recommend that the operations which we
> have ordered you to make shall first be
> carried out on the men of the said people,
> and that you shall subject the women and
> children to them also. Appoint reliable
> officials for this.
> > (signed), Minister of the Interior
> > Talaat.

> September 16, 1915
> It was first communicated to you that the
> Government, by order of the Jemiet, had
> decided to destroy completely all Armenians
> living in Turkey. Those who oppose this
> order and decision cannot remain on the offi-
> cial staff of the Empire. An end must be put
> to their existence, however criminal the
> measures taken may be, and no regard must be
> paid to age, or sex, or to conscientious
> scruple.
> > (signed), Minister of the Interior
> > Talaat.

> November 15, 1915
> From interventions which have recently been
> made by the American Ambassador at Constan-
> tinople on behalf of his Government, it
> appears that the American consuls are obtain-
> ing information by secret means. In spite of
> our assurances that the Armenian deportations
> will be accomplished in safety and comfort,

they remain unconvinced. Be careful that events attracting attention shall not take place in connection with those who are near the cities or other centers.[2] From the point of view of the present policy it is important that foreigners who are in those parts shall be persuaded that the expulsion of the Armenians is in truth only deportation. For this reason it is important that, to save appearances, for a time a show of gentle dealing shall be made, and the usual measures be taken in suitable places. It is recommended as very important that the people who give such information shall be arrested and handed over to the military authorities for trial by court-martial.

>(signed), Minister of the Interior
>Taalat.

January 10, 1916
Enquiries having been made, it is understood that hardly ten per cent of the Armenians subjected to the general transportation have reached their destinations; the rest have died from natural causes, such as hunger and sickness. We inform you that we are working to bring about the same result with regard to those who are still alive, by using severe measures.

>(signed), Abdullahad Nouri.

As a result of Turkey's policy, over one million Armenians died.

III

During World War I, the French government originated the phrase "crimes against humanity" to describe Turkish acts against the Armenians, but the war was hardly over when the world proved itself eager to forgive Turkey its crimes. There was a reason for this, though not necessarily a good one. To put it in the simplest terms, after Kemal Ataturk's victory in the Greco-Turkish war of 1920-22, every Western power, in its haste to beat its rivals to his favor--among other things, there were his lush Mosul oil fields to consider--found one reason or another to absolve, and even to exalt, the Turkish nation.

If the United States lagged behind a year or two in this, it was not because of any pangs of conscience felt by those in charge of the Harding administration's foreign policy (among them Allen Dulles, then the Chief of the State Department's Near Eastern Division). It was rather because the American Protestant leadership, much to its later dismay, had created a certain amount of public antipathy toward Turkey in the course of wartime fund appeals for the "starving Armenians." The starving ones were those who had escaped into nearby countries, as well as a number of emaciated orphans whom the missionaries had managed to rescue from the deserts. But when the time came to save Protestant missionary "investments" in Turkey--investments both of real estate (schools, hospitals) and of a century of futile efforts to gain a foot-hold among the Moslems-- the professional moralists joined forces with American business interests and hastened publicly to exonerate Turkey.

Having arrived in the Near East in the 1840s to convert Moslems to the Protestant Christian faith, the missionaries had quickly discovered that for a Moslem the penalty for such conversion was death, as sanctioned by Koranic law. The Armenians, however, in their eagerness to partake of the educational benefits, were "converting" in considerable numbers from their established Church to the more evangelical brands of Protestantism. The missionaries therefore remained in Turkey, justifying the expenditure of funds and energy with the long view that "if it were possible to... instill them (the native Christians) with a lively missionary spirit, they would be...the best and most effectual missionaries because native to the soil."[3] They had no doubt that the indirect approach would take hundreds of years. Then, quite suddenly, and in one unbelievably simple stroke, Ataturk dissolved the Caliphate and secularized the nation in the early 1920s. The missionaries no longer had any need for the Armenians, and indeed there were few Armenians left. Subsequently, all the churchmen had to do in order to remain in Turkey and prepare to serve Moslems directly was to procure Ataturk's favor. This, however, required considerable public-relations work in revising opinion in the country toward Turkey, and various Protestant leaders plunged into the task with true missionary zeal.

We believe in America for the Americans, why not Turkey for the Turks?" wrote one of these leaders, George A. Plimpton, in 1923. He was not, to be sure, referring to the extermination of the Armenians but to the expulsion from Turkey of the Greek population following the Greco-Turkish war. His excessively pro-Turkish attitude was, however, both typical and instructive. Thus, he expressed the thought that the loss of the Greeks (and presumably of the unmentioned Armenians) "has cost great suffering and involved great financial sacrifice to Turkey," in the sense that she had lost her merchants, businessmen, and major taxpayers. And he added some words that sound strange coming from a Trustee of Union Theological Seminary: "Whether it was right or wrong is not for us to decide."

Having articulated these sentiments in a letter to the New York Times Plimpton also proceeded to include them in The Treaty With Turkey, a volume compiling "statements, resolutions and reports in favor of the ratification of the Lausanne Treaty," brought out jointly by some significantly interested individuals and institutions, the foremost being the American Board of Commissioners for Foreign Missions and the United States Chamber of Commerce. The burden of their combined task was to praise Turkey, to dismiss, and at the same time to justify, its actions against the Armenians, and to demonstrate that if the Turks were in any way antagonized--such as by the failure of the United States to sign the treaty--both American business and American philanthropy would suffer. A proposed clause in the treaty, providing safeguards for the minorities left in Turkey, was denounced as an unreasonable intrusion into Turkey's internal affairs. It was deemed essential, however, to include a clause "to protect foreign corporations and individuals from the retroactive application of new and possibly excessive taxes."

IV

While the American Protestant movement was cementing relations with Turkey, it was at the same time helping to draw a veil over the historical record. In effect, it was dismissing the word of its own missionaries, whose eyewitness reports had provided the bulk of the testimony about the genocide.

The record of events was further distorted by the Turks themselves, who lost no time in putting forth their own version of the Armenian story. One or two, like Djemal Pasha, third-ranking of the Turkish leaders, attempted to absolve themselves of responsibility by professing that they were only following orders. Soon, however, more skillful Turkish dialecticians took up the argument, protesting that the Armenians, as traitors to the Turkish war effort, had constituted a menace to the very existence of the Turks in 1915, and thus had to be liquidated. No concrete evidence was offered by the Turkish apologists for this contention, nor for the secondary argument that Armenians themselves had been massacring Turks in 1915, and even before.

Already in 1916, shortly before the publication of Bryce's documents in England, the Young-Turk government--doubtless with world opinion in mind--had jumped the gun by publishing an official pamphlet, "The Truth About the Armenian Revolution and the Governmental measures." Lord Bryce had apparently seen this document, for he meticulously refuted every argument contained in it. Andre Mandelstam, the first Dragoman of the Russian Embassy in Constantinople from 1898 to 1914, and later a professor of international law in Paris, also pointed up the speciousness of the argument contained in the pamphlet.

At the beginning of the war, according to the Turks, Armenian secret societies provoked revolts and committed massacres. Since, however, there were no eyewitnesses to these alleged acts, the only "proof" the Turks could offer consisted of three documents. The first was a manifest addressed by the Russian Czar to the Armenians in Turkey inviting them to revolt (a document that never existed, Mandelstam insists, but that would hardly have justified genocide even if it had); the second was an alleged report on the massacres from the Russian Consul in Bitlis, dated December 24, 1912, and addressed to M. Tcharykov, his ambassador in Constantinople. (According to Mandelstam, Tcharykov had been replaced as ambassador six months earlier: "Could the Russian Consul in Bitlis have been unaware of who his own ambassador was? What a strange Russian diplomat, or else, what a clumsy Turkish fabrication!") Finally, there were some alleged resolutions and publications of the Huntchag (Armenian) party urging Armenians to fight against Turkey. The pamphlet also stressed the existence of a corps of Russian-Armenian volunteers in the Russian army. This corps was made up of Armenians who were citizens of Russia, of course, but to the Turks it somehow constituted proof of the disloyalty of the Armenians living in Turkey, even though the latter had served faithfully in the Turkish army from the time they were conscripted to the time they were put to death.

The Young Turks who devised this pamphlet were well on their way to oblivion when it was issued, but while those who succeeded them lost no time in denouncing the former regime, they continued to defend the Young-Turk policy toward the Armenians with identical arguments, albeit with certain modifications in tone. The authors of the earlier efforts were discredited failures, but during Kemal Ataturk's regime there appeared far more sophisticated and--to the West--more credible advocates of Turkey's case, among them the eminently respected Halide Edib, a lady whose word carried much weight.

Mme. Edib was the first Moslem graduate of the Constantinople Women's College, a woman with undeniable gifts of imagination and intellect. She was a famous novelist in her own country, as well as a journalist, statesman, social worker, and soldier. She was also Ataturk's chief propagandist (until her break with him later in the 20s), and an avowedly passionate Turkish nationalist. Moreover, she was a source of wonder to the West as the first emancipated specimen of her race. Upon coming to America in 1927, she taught at Barnard College, wrote extensively and in excellent English, and became one of the most popular lecturers in the United States.

Halide Hanum, as she called herself, was none too incisive in writing about her attitude toward the defunct Young Turks. Like almost everyone else in Turkey she had welcomed their accession and had then become disillusioned. She never made clear why she became disenchanted, although one may assume that failure does not sustain admiration. Whatever her reasons, they did not include the Young Turks' solution to the "Armenian question." Talaat remained for her "an idealist...modest, charming, a true democrat...However one may criticize him, one is obliged to admit that he was the truest of patriots." She did profess to having once been opposed to his measures against Armenians, and having gone so far as to tell Talaat so, but, "I saw the Armenian question quite differently from the way I see it today. I did not know about the Armenian crimes, and I had not realized that in similar cases others could be a hundred times worse than the Turks. So I spoke with conviction against bloodshed...The next day I received a great volume about the massacre of the Turks by the Armenians."[4] Unfortunately, despite her meticulous documentation of the relatively obvious, Mme. Edib did not cite this "great volume." One is tempted to surmise that it was the aforementioned pamphlet, published at just about the time to which she refers.

Although Mme. Edib's tone is quite often passionate, she deftly modulates it when she refers to human suffering, toward which she continually protests her sensitivity. Once or twice she even refers to Armenian suffering, as when she remembers seeing (in 1918) "a poor Armenian in Syria who had lost his speech and wandered in the night crying like a dumb tortured animal because he _imagined_ (italics mine) his two boys, who were separated from him, had been shot. I know --never mind what I know." She does not care to dwell on these things, she writes, for "of the massacres and violences it is best not to speak much--the sooner they are forgotten, the better."

V

Western historians applauded these sentiments of Mme. Edib's and lost no time in echoing them. By the 20s the world was sick to death of violence and no one was much interested in the Armenians. Furthermore, Arnold J. Toynbee, the editor of the best known primary source on the genocide, Lord Bryce's Blue Book, had reversed his previous views about Turkish responsibility, and emerged a stalwart defender of the Moslem world. Unfortunately for history, Lord Bryce himself died in 1922.

Toynbee's part in the historical distortion of the Armenian case cannot be overestimated. After completing his editorship of The Treatment of the Armenians, he published a summary of its contents, The Murderous Tyranny of the Turks, in which he inserted a plea that the world remember these "unprecedented crimes" after the war, and insure against their recurrence. But then, in 1920, Toynbee covered the Greco-Turkish war as a reporter for the Manchester Guardian. Viewing the hostilities from the Turkish side, he beheld the astonishing vision of Turks as suffering human beings, and of Greeks (and even an occasional Armenian) as the actual inflictors of suffering. This revelation, by his own admission, led him to reverse his former views. (Arnold Toynbee to his son, Philip, in A Dialogue Across a Generation: "It was quite an influential thing in my life [seeing that war]. I always try to see things from the unpopular point of view, the point of view that isn't represented. I think that's a very strong urge in me." Philip Toynbee: "Of course, it has been said that there's a certain perversity in this, and that in your anxiety to be fair you sometimes exaggerate the merits of the unpopular case." Arnold Toynbee: "I'm sure I do. Leaning over backwards."

By now convinced of the positive value of suffering and the negative nature of anger (Arnold Toynbee to Philip Toynbee: "Anger I do feel is a sin--we're all angry with somebody sometimes, and when I find it in myself I am horrified with myself..."), Toynbee must have had little sympathy for Armenians who continued to feel resentment toward the Turks. Equating all violence by denying qualitative differences in motives, he reasoned that one side was no better than the other--"The Near Eastern people do not differ in kind from one another", he wrote in 1923--but he clearly implied that Moslems were less bad than the rest. And so in the bibliography of his new book, The Western Question in Greece and Turkey, he saw fit to list his previous writing, The Murderous Tyranny of the Turks, as an example of the sort of "prejudice" for which he would henceforth atone.

It is not difficult but merely time-consuming to pinpoint the fallacies in Toynbee's work. Experts have done so in the case of his treatment of the Arab Israeli question, but no experts have emerged on behalf of the Armenians to refute Toynbee; and judging by the line subsequent historians have taken, he continues to be considered the greatest living authority on the Near-Eastern area. Thus Toynbee's dismissal of the Armenian case, his repudiation of his own and Bryce's Blue Book, exercised an incalculable influence. Despite his protest (in an article written in July 1923 in Current History) that he still believed in "the truth of the evidence" presented in the Blue Book, he went on to say that "Equally dark deeds have been inflicted by Greek soldiers...during the War for Greek independence..." This was the same man who in 1917 had been so forthright in condemning the Turkish extermination of the Armenians: "Turks will say (after the war), 'We were at war. We were fighting for our existence. The Armenians were traitors at large in a war zone.' But such excuses are entirely contradicted by facts. These Armenians were not inhabitants of a war zone. None of the towns and villages from which they were systematically deported to their death were anywhere near the seat of the hostilities."

The attitude that prevails today toward recent
Turkish history can be illustrated by a passage from
Richard Robinson's The First Turkish Republic (1963), a
popular reference book in American universities:

> The problem of Armenians living in Eastern
> Anatolia drew down much popular condemnation
> on the head of the Turk. Although Armenians
> numbered at most not more than 40% of the
> population in any single province save two,
> the bulk of their numbers was concentrated in
> that area adjoining Russia, thereby enabling
> the Russian army to draw recruits out of
> Anatolia. The Armenian community let it be
> known that it would not support the Ottoman
> war effort, and encouraged by President
> Wilson's principle of self-determination,
> moved to create an independent Armenian
> state. To the Ottoman authorities, these
> activities constituted wartime treason and
> they reacted violently. Most of the Armenian
> population was forced to flee and large num-
> bers perished at the hands of the Turks.
> These Turkish reprisals recharged the racial-
> religious animosity of the earlier period of
> Armenian troubles before 1900. Though the
> fact does not in the least excuse Turkish
> behavior on this occasion, the Turks did con-
> sider the Armenian defection as treason, a
> stab in the back that was all the more pain-
> ful because of Turkish military reverses. It
> is also quite clear that the Armenians reci-
> procated in kind, and many Turks lost their
> lives violently.

Though Professor Robinson is not primarily a
historian--he is a Harvard economist and business-
administration specialist on Turkish and Near Eastern
affairs--his writing is typical of most bona fide historians on the Armenian "massacre," when and if they
trouble to mention the "incident" at all. The above
paragraph contains an amazing number of inaccuracies.
To begin with, there is no evidence, and Robinson's
sources offer none, that "the Armenian community let it
be known that it would not support the Ottoman war
effort." Nor has Robinson studied the deportation
routes, which show that Armenians were being uprooted
not only from the relatively small area by the Russian

border, but also from such vastly dispersed towns and villages as Ismid, a few miles from Constantinople, and Musa Dagh, near the Mediterranean sea, not to mention all the scattered towns in between. That "the Russian army drew recruits out of Turkish Anatolia" has not been established, but Robinson may be referring to the fact that many male Armenians who escaped into Russia during the genocide subsequently enlisted in the Russian army. Obviously, this was a result, and not a cause, of the exterminations. Since President Wilson did not reveal his principle of self-determination until 1918, it could not have encouraged the Armenians to create anything in 1915. It is true that an independent, and short-lived, Armenian state was created in 1920 by the Western powers who signed the Treaty of Sevres. Its creation, however, was again a result, and not a cause, of genocide. If the Armenians were ever guilty of "reciprocating in kind," it was while they were defending this state several years after they had experienced genocide. Finally, that "the Armenian population was forced to flee," is merely Dr. Robinson's euphemism for a deliberate uprooting.

Accuracy, then, is hardly the strong point of the above writing, and since this is the only kind of writing in which Armenians currently find themselves discussed at all, their resulting cynicism is not surprising. Nor was that mood diminished last year when, on the eve of the Fiftieth Anniversary of the genocide, the New York Times suggested editorially that it was high time for the Armenians to forgive the Turks. Few Armenian readers of the Times missed the grim irony of the fact that this editorial appeared only a few weeks after the same newspaper had been decrying Germany's proposed statute of limitations on Nazi murderers. But then it is common practice to refuse to recognize the meaning of the Armenian fate. In Eichmann in Jersualem, Hannah Arendt dismissed their case as a "pogrom;" and this February, as the Fiftieth Anniversary year drew to a close, Karl Jaspers was quoted in the pages of Commentary as denying any pre-Hitler precedent for genocide.

Public commemorations of the Fiftieth Anniversary were not without effect, however; they caused a somewhat hysterical reaction in the Turkish press. Editorials flayed in various directions, but found one point of agreement: the unforeseen spurt of Armenian activity in recalling "alleged," "so-called," "supposed" masacres was obviously engineered by Cypriote provocateurs.

-113-

In an editorial in the Ankara newspaper _Oulous_, in March, 1965, Jehad Baban, a member of the Turkish parliament, was both incredulous and indignant. "It is very strange that after so many years the Armenians resort to such agitations," he wrote, referring to the public commemorations in Lebanon. "The only result of this kind of behavior will be to strain relations between Turkey and Lebanon, which allows the organization of this kind of commemoration on its own territory."

Sometimes the tone was almost mellow, as when one Turkish author chose to remember the Armenians as "Turkish-Armenian brothers [who] for one thousand years lived together with the Turks as inseparable as flesh and fingernail." And a Mr. Kabakji pleaded gallantly that the whole thing be forgotten. "Let us bury the old stories in the pit of history. Let us live together as humans with brotherly love."

It is not brotherly love, but the burying of history that Armenians oppose. The question remains whether one can feel forgiveness, and therefore bury the dead, when the world has too readily done so on one's behalf. One may grant that there are few Turks left alive who can be accounted personally responsible for the murders, but the fact remains that a nation guilty of genocide did indeed succeed in burying the story "in the pit of history." In part it succeeded because the Armenians are few, dispersed, and without a public platform to plead their case--from which astute and dangerous men can draw the conclusion that the world cares little for the fate of those who are politically impotent.

There is evidence, at any rate, that Hitler drew this conclusion. As he announced his own plans for genocide to his Supreme Commanders on August 22, 1939, he noted confidently: "Who, after all speaks today of the annihilation of the Armenians? The world believes in success alone."[5]

Footnotes

1. First published in the London *Daily Telegraph*, May 29, 1922.

2. This statement explains why all but the community leaders in Constantinople and Smyrna were spared in 1915.

3. From Julius Richter's *A History of the Protestant Mission in the Near East*, London, 1910.

4. From *The Memoirs of Halide Edib*, New York, 1925.

5. Quoted in Louis Lochner's *What About Germany?*, New York, 1942.

MASSACRE OR GENOCIDE:

AN ESSAY IN PERSONAL BIOGRAPHY AND OBJECTIVE EXPERIENCE

Leon A. Chorbajian

My parents and their friends were born around the turn of the century, and as fate would have it they became survivors of what the Turkish government decided upon as its final solution to the Armenian question. In kitchens, living rooms and backyards I would sometimes be privy to their experience as they would relate tales of murder, narrow escape, revenge, and the fate of erstwhile kinsmen. They would dip into their minds and describe, filling in gaps in one another's memories, sometimes with emotion, but mostly with surprising dispassion. While they spoke freely of what polite people call unspeakable horrors, they seldom had a name by which they called these events. They knew what it meant to them and names did not matter. They just talked. Of course, there was a name, and as I grew older I came to understand that it was the Armenian massacres. A hated name--stark and irrevocable. It spoke of unseen grandparents, a lost homeland, sad eyes, and in the world outside our home, an unknown history.

Today this history contains a number of possibilities. Some suggest that it be forgotten. The past is past, they say, and it has gotten to be a long time ago. Do we forever need to go on discussing these things? Can't we get on with something better? Something nice? At the opposite extreme are those who vow never to forget. The prospect frightens them, and with clenched fists and tense muscles they exhort the young that these evil deeds should never be forgotten.

While forgetting cannot be a conscious act, the once vivid past will lose its sharp edges through time, and a people will fall victim to a social amnesia. It is in this sense of a collective forgetting that I speak. This forgetting can soothe since it allows a people to rid themselves of a great deal of emotional unpleasantness. There is, however, a price to be paid, and that price is the alienation of the self from the historical experience. The forgotten past will beget the impoverished future.

Any history will touch its children if they let it. The question is how should one be touched. Some

of the old men and women of my childhood were very
touched indeed. Staring back into murder, they were
paralyzed, and that was all that the trauma of their
lives allowed them to do. Today we have greater distance, and therefore, more choices about what we think
and do. This has, therefore, not so much made the past
irrelevant as it has made our understanding of the past
as significant as the events which make it up. The
understandings we come to have bear upon our image of
ourselves and others, and upon the ways we choose to
live our lives in the contemporary world. How we think
about the past and relate it to our present are the
central issues of this essay. Our vehicles are the
concepts of massacre and genocide. Each can be a name
for the early twentieth century experience of the
Armenian people, and because each is different in its
meanings and its subtleties, it comes to bear upon the
larger issues of what we think and how we carry ourselves as actors in the larger world.

Aftermath of an Experience

A good place to begin is with Michael J. Arlen's
Passage to Ararat. It is a book of personal reconcili-
ation, Arlen's coming to terms at once with Armenians
and his deceased celebrity father who had complex and
mixed feelings about being an Armenian. Arlen's book
is useful because it was undertaken when its author was
well into adulthood. Arlen had married, fathered children, authored books, and turned forty before he sought
to unravel for himself the meaning of the Armenian
experience. The significance of Arlen's belated inquiry is that he could experience and reflect upon that
experience at the same time. Thoughts which would be
closed to a child or lost to him as an adult were there
for Arlen to experience and to expand upon, and as a
result he is there, open and exposed, for us to learn
from.

The elder Arlen began his publishing career in
1915 with a series of protest articles in Ararat: A
Searchlight for Armenia. The genocide was his subject
matter. Shortly thereafter he began publishing short
stories and novels to become a best selling author of
the 1920s. Writing of dashing men and liberated women,
their loves and betrayals, Arlen titillated the reading
public of his day. After his initial work, he never
again wrote seriously of Armenians. His son, Michael
J. Arlen, knew his father was Armenian, but Armenians

were rarely so much as mentioned in the household and
then only with disparagement. The skeleton lay in the
closet for years, only to be awakened when Arlen is
invited to give a talk at an Armenian gathering in New
York. After the talk an elderly Armenian asks Arlen to
his home, and eventually Arlen finds himself in an
apartment with two old men. One of them begins to
talk:

> ...in an intense low voice about his family's
> experiences with the Turks. He described the
> killing of his father and his elder brother.
> He described the flight of his mother and his
> two sisters, one of whom was captured and
> never heard from again...He began to weep...
> The man on the couch began to speak again,
> this time more softly--in a kind of croon--
> about his boyhood, long ago...He talked of
> running, fleeing, as a boy, across the
> desert. Of hiding in a cave for days. There
> were dead bodies in a cave. A camel driver
> befriended him and hid him for three weeks--
> or months. The story was true, I knew--a
> true and moving story, and one so far beyond
> my own experience. But I found I wished his
> arm away from mine, wished away his frail
> hand, his tears. "My father had committed no
> crime--can you believe it? He had done
> nothing wrong."[1]

The old man's story makes Arlen very uncomfort-
able. He believes what he hears but cannot wait to
leave. Once out on the street he is relieved though
shaken and shaken most of all by the old man's insistence that his father was innocent and had done nothing
wrong.

> As I thought about it, there seemed to be
> something terrible buried in that admission,
> although whether the negative electrical
> charge I felt lay in the statement or in me I
> couldn't tell. Only that I hated it.[2]

Arlen does not tell us why he hated it. He does
not seem to know, at least, at that point. Later in
the book we notice that he has taken up the study of
Armenian history. He is very attracted to accounts of
bravery by ancient Armenian warriors and generals. He
recounts an exploit to his wife. To her it is all
matter of fact while to him there is an intense, though

-118-

unclear, attraction. His wife asks, "But what are you looking for? Of course the Armenians are brave." Arlen tells her that is not the point. He is sharp and abrupt, but the point eludes him.[3] The odyssey continues. In Soviet Armenia Arlen is befriended by Sarkis who tells him the Armenians did nothing and were slaughtered innocents. Arlen writes:

> I thought, it keeps coming back to that. The Armenian refrain: "We were murdered. We were innocent. We were slaughtered. We did nothing." It was supposed to evoke compassion, I knew, and each time I willed the compassion forward, but it would not come. I felt shame before Sarkis and myself. I also felt, there is something amiss with that refrain."[4]

In his quest for an answer Arlen inadvertently finds it in the daily life of Soviet Armenia.

> ...here was Arak, and here were how many others of his generation, and older, whom we saw every day on the street, overheard in cafes, observed standing upright on the buses returning from work, upright and proud. That was it! Not only had they survived the terror and persecution but now they were on their feet: building soccer stadiums, pink stone apartment houses, statues, refrigerators, computers, fashioning fine tall children; and talking of the past without that coloring of lamentation and self-pity which so many Armenians elsewhere seemed to employ when they talked about the Turks.[5]

To sum up Arlen we can say the following: he started out with a curiosity about Armenians and soon learned that all roads somehow led back to the genocide. More so than the brutality and tragedy of these events, Arlen found himself struck by the context in which they were framed and presented. The claim to total innocence and martyrdom spoke to Arlen of weakness and submission. He was repelled and searched for another Armenian, "...a prosperous, robust type of Armenian, who does not live in dark rooms and weep about the past."[6] Arlen responds to tales of ancient Armenian warriors becasue they offer him glimpses of another Armenian, not a helpless, massacred Armenian, but one who is strong and fights to defend family and

homeland. Finally the attraction of Soviet Armenia is
not so much ideological as it is a setting where people
live constructive and vibrant lives free of a debili-
tating legacy from the past. It is Arlen's answer to
the sad laments of old men.

If Arlen's experiences were merely eccentric I
would not have bothered with them. Rather it struck me
while I was reading him that I always hated this kind
of martyred innocence when I heard my elders speak of
their experiences. It was not the horror of the stories since at some level I had gotten used to them.
What I hated was this tone of passive acquiescence and
martyrdom. I would sometimes ask, "Why did you let it
happen?" or "Didn't you do <u>anything</u>?" I thrilled on
those rare occasions when someone told of a guerrilla
combat by a group of Armenians or of an isolated act of
revenge carried out against some Turk. It excited me,
not because a Turk had been killed, but because it
spoke to me of some kind of action on the part of
Armenians. In these moments, Armenians were no longer
the passive instruments of other people's actions.
These stories said to me that instead of Armenians
letting it happen to them, they had struggled and lost.
That always made me feel better.

Massacre and Genocide

Action as the means by which people define their
lives and their worlds has been an important theme in
modern literature. A central concept in Marxism is
that of the working class mission to define and make
its own history. Feminist writers, students of mental
illness, and researchers of slave rebellions are among
the many others who have stressed the importance of
people acting upon their worlds rather than stagnating
to be molded and acted upon by forces larger than
themselves. Being acted upon, without power, control
or a voice over your fate is to be deeply alienated
from the life experience. Arlen was not entirely clear
on why he could not abide by the old man's tears and
Sarkis' martyred innocence, but at some level he understood these definitions of history to be destructive.

Oppression and injustice are hardly new to the
world, nor are the Armenians alone in having experienced them in recent history. Yet it is the case that
no other people have so singlemindedly focused upon
their innocence as their defense. Blacks say they were

enslaved for their labor, and the Jews say that they were the scapegoats of Hitler's quest for world empire. The Irish and the American Indians were brutalized for their land, and the Vietnamese and the Biafrans were the victims of liberation struggles. While all claim innocence, none falls back on the Armenian refrain: "We were innocent, we did nothing, and we were slaughtered." Yet when it is considered that at the time there were Armenian political movements engaged in the struggle to create an independent Armenian homeland, it cannot be said that the Armenians were totally innocent. To be sure the cause was a just one, and it could in no way justify the Turkish response. But the question remains: why should history be distorted to claim passivity and total innocence for the Armenians? Not only is it inaccurate, but it places Armenians at the mercy of others who must be impressed with the overwhelming justice of their cause. Willingly, it seems, the Armenians have abdicated their role as agents of their history and chosen to view themselves as the victims of unbridled evil. Of all the victims of modern inhumanity, the Armenians claim to have been supremely acted upon. This is the void from which Arlen is repelled, and rightly so since such view represents the cul de sac of history and emotion. There is no where to go, and the Armenian can only weep or forget. Boxed in, it proves difficult to embrace one's self as an Armenian, and as a result to become open to embrace the experience of others.

This bring us to the concepts of massacre and genocide. Although the terms are sometimes employed synonymously, there are established differences in meaning. Massacre speaks of savage and indiscriminate killing while genocide refers to the planned, systematic extermination of a people. It is a difference of scale and sometimes of intent. Genocide is necessarily large scale and planned. There is abundant evidence to prove that the last rulers of the Ottoman Empire and their successors knew exactly what they were doing. The killings of the Armenians were planned and intended to be total. It was a genocide.

It has become somewhat popular to refer to the killings as a genocide, and they are now occasionally called "The Forgotten Genocide" or "The First Genocide of the Twentieth Century." This is quite recent, however, and for the most part massacre has been the more frequently employed term. But why should this have been the case when genocide was the more historically apt?

To answer this question we need to consider that victims are seldom in a position to distinguish between massacre and genocide. A genocide may be made up of what are a series of massacres, yet to the victims the distinction is irrelevant, and in any case they may not have the means to gain information on an overall plan of extermination. Many Jewish intellectuals fled fascist Germany before World War II and helped to publicize Hitler's final solution to the Jewish question. In the Armenian case, the writers, poets, journalists, and Church and business leaders of Constantinople were arrested and killed before the terror was unleashed in the countryside. This left the Armenian masses without spokesmen while other factors exacerbated their isolation. Anatolia, particularly in the central and eastern regions, was far removed from the centers of Western power. The absence of talented and well placed spokesmen and the isolation of the killings at a time when distance meant a great deal more than it does today placed the Armenians in the hands of sympathetic outsiders. Among these the most important were missionaries and foreign diplomats, and they became the major articulators of the mass deportations, murders, and property seizures. The message they sent out was a clear cut and unequivocal one of Turkish brutality and Armenian innocence. There was certainly a great deal of both and coupled with the specific historic circumstances, this type of communique became the basis of the reporting in the popular press. At the height of World War I the political issues of Ottoman decay and Armenian nationalism were far from the immediate concerns of Westerners, and far too few people had the inclination or the means to learn. In this situation publicizing brutality became the simplest and most direct kind of appeal which could be made to arouse attention and to raise money for relief efforts, and so it was that the "Starving Armenian," decimated and helpless, became the symbol of the holocaust.

Circumstances forced most of the survivors to acquiesce to this understanding of wanton, savage killing carried out without reason. That is certainly the way the survivors experienced it. Most were uneducated peasant people, and they did not have the means to learn more about the genocide. Many of the survivors came under the care of missionaries in relief centers, and these factors along with the savagery of the experience led to a victim mentality and favored the concept of massacre. And so the pattern was set. Why were the Armenians killed? Because the Turks are beasts and savages. What did the Armenians do? They did nothing. The Turks came and killed them and drove the rest out into the deserts to starve. It is the imagery of pure good and pure evil.

Genocide Reconsidered

We have traced back the origins of the massacre concept to particular features of the mass killings themselves: their horror, the murder of the Armenian intelligentsia, and the physical, psychological and political dependence of surviving Armenians upon outsiders. These outsiders had to be impressed with the overwhelming justice of the Armenian cause, and this was done by stripping the killing of its political context and presenting the Armenians as the victims of unharnessed evil. This style of thinking served a generation of survivors to comprehend their experience and to offer them a measure of comfort. While this framework for understanding may have been useful in its time, there is ample reason today to question its value.

How can people come to terms with mass murder? In Passage to Ararat Arlen raises questions about the Armenian reponse to the killings:

>...the response of the Armenians to the
>bygone brutalities of the Turks seemed of a
>different nature from the response of other
>groups to massacre. It was as if a particu-
>lar poison had entered the system several
>generations back, and had remained within
>it...[7]

What is the nature of this "particular poison"? Elsewhere Arlen refers to a "hot lump of coal" stuck in the Armenian belly, and he writes of "...the particularly shrill and wounded quality of the Armenian response to the trauma of the Turkish massacres."[8] These are the images of seared emotions and deep, frustrated anger, feelings barely conscious and held inside. It has a good deal to do with the image of "massacre," and the self-doubt, self-pity and shame to which it has inevitably given rise.

In 1915 the Armenian peole prostrated themselves before the world and asked for help. This is what their circumstances forced them to do. Today many

Armenians are content to never speak of the killings or if they do, it is most often in the mold of the 1915 appeals. This is especially true in the United States where the Armenians constitute a small percentage of the population. Most other Americans have not so much as heard of Armenians, and the Armenian community has been as assimilated into American culture as the members of any other ethnic group. The result has been a reticence about the genocide and a pressure to forget the past. The other alternative to forgetting has been the re-creation of the 1915 appeals. Since outsiders do not know, Armenians become shy about talking about their history. If the killings come up, the old pattern is repeated. We run down a few of the major events, claim innocence, condemn brutality and fall back on the sensibilities of the listener to gain sympathy. This approach is uninformed by history, and it allows no connection to be made between the events of 1915 and the contemporary world. It also casts the Armenian into the role of an emotional beggar. "Look," the Armenian says, "I am an Armenian and this is what happened. Please feel badly for me and extend me some sympathy." The Armenian will usually get his sympathy, but it is a poor psychological triumph.

The concept of massacre grew out of a plea for mercy, and for this it was well suited. Massacre, however, is not easily compatible with informed dignity and pride. There are too many nagging questions. Why did it happen to us? What did we do to make it happen? Were there bad Armenians? Good Turks? Why did we let it happen? Are we weak? Helpless? These are among the questions I have asked myself, and so long as they are asked in the framework of massacre, there are no satisfactory answers.

Massacre is a profoundly isolating concept which divorces people from the historical experience. This isolation removes from one's hands the very tools for intelligent understanding. The mass murder of Armenians was not a mere tragic quirk on the periphery of history. The past two hundred years of Western history can be viewed as the struggle of peoples for national liberation. This was a struggle ushered in by the American Revolution and recently played out in Vietnam. Today the struggle continues in Rhodesia and the Union of South Africa. The Armenian Genocide came out of the tragic interplay of Ottoman decay and Armenian nationalism, and while it was to be a nationalism manque, the Armenian struggles were part of a major theme in modern world history.

The Armenian Genocide can also be considered as the beginning of modern history. The twentieth century has been a century of horrors: wars, genocides, and conflicts fueled by technology and modern communications to unprecedented scales. Decisions to exterminate entire peoples have been possible throughout history, but it is only in this century that such plans could come close to being carried out within short periods of time. Since the Ethiopian and Spanish Civil Wars of the 1930s, wars have brought with them the aerial bombardment of civilians. The possibility of raining death from the skies had not previously existed yet within decades it came to be carried out on a massive scale by the Armenians in Southeast Asia. Similarly the concentration camps of fascist Germany and Stalinist Russia involved tens of millions of people, a scale unknown in previous history. The twentieth century has also been the century of atom and hydrogen bombs. The primitive nuclear weapons employed on Japan in 1945 have been supplanted by arsenals of vastly more powerful weapons. Tied to sophisticated delivery systems, these weapons mean that hundreds of millions of people in the northern hemisphere live with the enormous and perpetual threat of nuclear apocalypse. The list can be easily expanded. Suffice it to say that whatever may have been the problems of earlier periods, the issues of our own time are great in number and intensity, and they will make enormous claims upon the human intelligence if they are to be justly resolved.

This is where the Armenians have a contribution to make. If massacre is an isolating concept, genocide is an expansive one which weaves the Armenian experience onto the history of the century. The Armenian Genocide can be called the first of the century because it has sadly not been the last. The most common comparison is with Hitler's plan to exterminate European Jewry, and there are many lesser known examples such as the current policies towards the Indians of Brazil and Paraguay. Moreover, the power of modern weaponry has allowed the large scale carnage of civilians to become an integrated facet of modern warfare. If there are not outright policies of genocide, we can nevertheless speak of military efforts which are genocidal. There are numerous instances such as the Nigerian Civil War and most notoriously the American military effort in the last years of the Vietnam War.[9] Being an Armenian can mean that you are informed and, at a basic moral level, equipped to deal with these issues. The problem

of good and evil with regard to the Armenian experience
cannot be that of the good Armenian and the bad Turk,
but that of justice and injustice and the point at
which the means cease to justify the ends.   In the
history of the modern Armenian there are tools, the
moral armaments if you will, for grappling with these
issues.   Rather than allow them to be lost they should
be seized and employed for the intelligent living of
daily life.

Conclusion

I have tried to appraise the meaning of the Armenian experience, and inevitably I have done so from my
perspective as a second generation, Armenian-American.
The Armenian Genocide is not an event which I experienced first hand, but it is an experience which has
deeply touched and influenced my life.   The 1960s were
a period of turbulence in the United States.   Centuries
of oppression turned to massive political struggles for
racial equality and justice.   A rapacious foreign policy serving the interests of the multinational corporations led to the Vietnam War.   It is well documented in
Senate testimony and elsewhere that the American military effort led to the deaths of over 1,000,000 Southeast Asians.   Most of the dead were civilians who
happened to be in our way, and one had to wonder if the
American "solution" was not far more horrible than what
even government officials predicted would happen if we
had chosen never to enter the conflict.   As more and
more Americans began to ask such questions the basis
for a large scale anti-war movement was established and
the war was eventually brought to an end.

It was a long process for me to integrate these
diverse familial and political influences.   Born to
parents who had survived a genocide, it was a particularly jarring experience for me to understand that my
government was practicing a genocidal foreign policy.
I came to spend a part of my life working in the civil
rights and anti-war movements.   These were choices
which enormously broadened and enriched my life, and I
am convinced that it was through these struggles that I
was able to fully become an Armenian.   I saw that my
parents and their generation had experienced a horror
and violence which was shared by other people in the
modern world.   It was from this realization that my own
political activity during the 60s was inspired, and
this why I have advocated that the Armenian experience

be understood in the larger context from which it stems. This is the foundation of pride, dignity and action which is faithful to the history of our people.

In advocating this approach I am not unmindful of the dangers which it contains. By stressing the similarities in such historical experiences as genocide, slavery, war and other forms of oppression, the history of any people may become blurred and indistinguishable from that of others. This would be a tragedy of understanding, and it is not what I advocate. Historical events are as much the products of unique historical circumstances as they are of general social processes. There are pressing political questions which stem from the Armenian Genocide. The questions of Armenian nationalism and Turkish reparations call for the attention of all Armenians, and it would be a serious error to view any phase of the Armenian question as a dead issue. My intent is simply to correct what I have experienced as an insular and sectarian attitude among Armenians which has too often prevented people from fully comprehending and embracing the implications of their own history.

Footnotes

1. Michael J. Arlen. Passage to Ararat. New York (Farrar, Straus & Giroux), 1975; pp. 23-24.

2. Ibid, pp. 24-25.

3. Ibid, p. 74.

4. Ibid, p. 126.

5. Ibid, p. 156.

6. Ibid, p. 24.

7. Ibid, p. 186.

8. Ibid, p. 185.

9. For a concise and able summary of American strategic planning for Southeast Asia during the middle and later years of the war see Noam Chomsky. "After Pinkville," New York Review of Books. January 1, 1971, pp. 3-14.

GENOCIDE, THE UNITED NATIONS AND THE ARMENIANS

James H. Tashjian

The international crime of <u>genocide</u>, a neologism coined to connote the destruction "in whole or in part [of] a national, ethnic, racial or religious group,"[1] is as old as mankind itself yet, tragically, its prevention or punishment has only in our day become the purpose of the peoples of the world.

In the words of Begum Ikramullah of Pakistan, at the United Nations General Assembly in 1948:

> Genocide has been committed through the ages. While it has always shocked the conscience of mankind, nothing has been done to punish the crime...[2]

Because the history of genocide is the history of man's inhumanity to man, it is a considerable history. Said Lemkin:

> Genocide has repeated itself with the regularity of a biological law.[3]

It seems that whether as initiators or as the victims of the crime of mass annihilation, mankind has been powerless either to stay its own phylogenic passion to kill or to prevent others from the wholesale extirpation of those who stand in the path of their ambitions.

A cursory glance through the pages of history is sufficient to uncover evidence <u>ad nauseam</u> that genocide has been practiced almost traditionally as a weapon of international or domestic political warfare. There is scarcely a nation today with a centuries-old history (and a few of later vintage) which can aver that its escutcheon is unstained by the blood of genocidal events.

The Pharoahs of early Egypt conquered, slew or enslaved as national policy, and the "wolflike" Assyrians threw up their mounds of bones to memorialize the awful scenes of their aggressions and of their conquests.

Alexander, sublimated astonishingly as "The Great", butchered the Persians to impress on them the

real design of his suzerainty, while Xerxes the Persian
systematically slaughtered and destroyed to extend his
empire. He boasted that the sea alone dared disobedience to his power--and he had the waters flailed for
it. Herod's "Massacre of the Innocents," portrayed
graphically by the genius of Delacroix, was calculated
to do away with the male offspring of his realm--simply
because it had been soothsaid that one among those
children would challenge his royalty and his madnesses.

It remained for Rome however to perfect the art of
genocide in its diverse forms. A hundred European and
Asian nations and cultures were ground to memories
under the relentless blows of the Legions and of Rome's
civil adminstrators; the philosophers and poets of
Greek were scotched, the scholars and prophets of
Israel were eliminated; once mighty Egypt's architects
and scientists vanished; the craftsmen of Carthage fell
with their city and their civilization in answer to the
summons, "Delenda est Carthago;" and the Pax Romana
proclaimed by the "benevolent" Octavianus did not
pacify but reduced the world to the service of Rome
and, indeed, made the world Rome alone. Children were
impressed into servitude, the young "barbarian" manhood
were trained to amuse the people of Rome as gladiators
in the arena, while the Christians were fed to the
lions. Dea Roma!

But Attila the Hun came to Italy and sacked and
murdered, and the abominations of Alaric and his Goths
shamed the world. While unfurling the banners of
Christ, the Crusaders entered the Holy City and
consigned the Arabs to the sword and the other non-
Christians to the torch. The unlettered Charlemagne
employed religion as the pretext of his unsatiable
appetite for lands and for riches. Ferdinand of Aragon
lived out a bloody career of genocide, the Inquisition
erased the sect of the Albigenses, and thousands of
others and their ideas. 50,000 Huguenots were destroyed in France, victims of the Chambre ardente and of the
White Terror, to prove finally that Louis XIV had all
the right in the world to boast, "L'etat est moi."

Tartar and Mongol incursions eastward, southward
and westward of those Asiatic reaches terrorized the
world. Genghis Khan blotted out the city of Kiev and
Timurlane threw up his grim monument of Armenian skulls
in the precincts of Erzerum. In their career of conquest, the Mongols alone slew, as state policy, 10,000
human beings.

Cortez and Pizzaro took the word of civilization to the New World. The smoke of the hecatombs of the Aztecs filled the sky, and the conquistadores pulled down the ancient monuments of the Incas in their search for the gold of those who would not abnegate their gods.

The Scots were reduced at Rathlin, the Elizabethan conquest of Ireland, emphasized finally by the draconian laws of Cromwell, reduced the population of that island. The Boers were sent on their trek.

The military adventures of the prophet Mohammed were followed by the genocidal tyranny of the Caliphs. The Osmanli Turk came into Asia Minor and seized the Seljuk throne, turned on the ancient nationalities of that area and made them "giavours" and "pariahs." Sultan Abdul Hamid slew 300,000 Armenians because they dared to hope for reforms--that is internationally-administered measures to halt the genocidal policies of Turkey. Hamid was deposed by the Ittihad Party which promptly produced such figures as Talaat and Enver, who proceeded to deport and massacre in coldest blood 1,500,000 Armenians.

Kemal Ataturk arose and continued where his predecessors had left off. He put 300,000 Greeks and Armenians to death under the pretext tht he was fighting "imperialism;" and he decreed a "Westernized" state in which the nationalities and religions still continue to exist under the damoclean blade of genocide.

The awesome carnage of man and his cultures wrought by the Turks over a period alone extending from 1822 to 1922 is best reflected by the fact that over that period of 100 years, extending into our century, the Turks consigned to genocide more than 2,500,000 Greeks, Nestorians, Maronites, Syrians, Bulgarians, Yezidis, Jacobites and Armenians. This figure does not include 500,000 Kurds murdered, deported or displaced.[4]

The royalty of Ivan, Peter and Catharine was followed by the "proletarianism" of Lenin and Stalin, but little else was changed. The great purges and induced famines of the Bolsheviks wiped out millions of Ukrainians, and others, or else banished into oblivion such nations as the Chechens, the Inguish, the Kalmucks, the Karachians, the Balkarians, the Volga Germans as "necessities of war" and "traitors to the fatherland."

-131-

The policy of the Soviet Russian leadership today continues to be that of the formation of a "one nation, one culture, one fatherland" Russian state which will result in the successful "Russification" of its non-Russian peoples. In its consequent destruction of the political, economic and cultural identities of the nationalities--the contemptible "inorodtsy"--Soviet Russian goals are genocidal in nature.[5]

In noting that those who had committed genocide had gotten away scot free, Adolf Hitler was encouraged to embark on his mad career.

Addressing his Commanders-in-chief, gathered November 23, 1945 at Obersalzburg, a few days before the Nazi invasion of Poland, Hitler said:

> "I have decided to go with Stalin...Within a few weeks I shall shake hands with him on the German-Russian frontier and undertake with him a new distribution of the world. Our strength is in our quickness and our brutality. Ghengis Khan had millions of women killed by his own will and with a gay heart. History sees him only a great statebuilder. For the time being I have sent to the east only my Death's Heads units, with the order to kill without pity or mercy all men, women and children of the Polish race or language. Who still talks nowadays of the extermination of the Armenians?"[6]

Before he was brought to his end, Hitler slaughtered 6,000,000 European Jews, among whom were an estimated 800,000 children under twelve years of age-shades of the Khans, Hamid and Talaat!

The Convention on the Prevention and Punishment of the Crime of Genocide: a Discussion

The story of genocide is indeed an appalling story; and precisely because the charge of genocide can be levelled at many nations flourishing in our day, the United Nations, the newly-founded consortium of those and other nations, finds itself faced with a doubly complex and perplexing problem in its effort to devise the means and the methods of preventing and punishing genocide.

Because of its context of States both guilty and innocent of the crime of genocide, the society of nations in effect has cast itself in the role of both judge and defendant; and while most members of the United Nations are displaying a generally honest passion to outlaw genocide, each nation is anxious to keep its ugly genie tightly capped and out of sight in its own bottle.

Despite these and other difficulties, there are some hopeful signs on the horizon that man is genuinely stirring to eradicate mass annihilation.

The first of these was the parallel military tribunals held following World War II which tried, indicted, imprisoned or executed the Nazi and Japanese war criminals responsible for the fearful carnage of peoples before and during that war. The proceedings of the International Military Tribunal at Nuremberg and of the International Military Tribunal for the Far East constituted in nature a condemnation of genocide in toto, and set significant precedents in international morality.

The second of these was the passage of legislation against genocide by the United Nations.

In 1921, a Polish law student, Raphael Lemkin, who was later to teach at Duke, Yale and Rutgers, was "profoundly upset" by reports that a young Armenian, Soghomon Tehlirian, had found himself called upon to assassinate Talaat, a prime author of the Turkish genocide of the Armenians, in lieu of international default of responsibility. Discovering that international law bore no provisions for the trial and the punishment of those accused of mass murder and prodded later by the scene of the Nazi pogroms, Lemkin waged a life-long career to outlaw the crime, which he called "genocide."

With the organization of the United Nations, Lemkin took his proposals to that body of nations and following intensive debate on December 11, 1946 the General Assembly passed unanimously an agreement which was later to be introduced into the formal Convention as Article I:

> The Contracting Parties confirm that genocide, whether committed in time of peace or in time of war, is a crime under international law which they undertake to prevent and to punish.

In the same year, the General Assembly requested the Economic and Social Council to undertake studies with a view to drawing up a draft Convention on Genocide. In 1947 the Secretary General, at the direction of the Council, prepared that first draft and, in 1948, an ad hoc committee submitted a revised draft.

On August 26, 1948 the finalized draft was presented to the General Assembly, which adopted it in its present basic form on December 9, 1948, with a vote of 55-0. The Convention on the Prevention and Punishment of the Crime of Genocide went into force on January 21, 1951 ninety days after the twenty States had ratified or acceded to it.

Business pertaining to the Convention on Genocide is the immediate responsibility of the UN's Economic and Social Council, which in turn has delegated responsibility to its Commission on Human Rights. Of late, Convention affairs have been handled by the Commission's Sub-Commission on the Prevention of Discrimination and Protection of Minorities.

Article II provides the Convention's definition of genocide :

> In the present Convention, genocide means any of the following acts committed with intent to destroy, in whole or in part, a national ethnical, racial or religious group as such:
>
> (a) Killing members of that group;
>
> (b) Causing serious bodily or mental harm to members of the group;
>
> (c) Deliberately inflicting on the group conditions of life calculated to bring about its physical destruction in whole or in part;
>
> (d) Imposing measures intended to prevent births within the group;
>
> (e) Forcibly transferring children of the group to another group.

Article III enumerates five punishable acts, and Articles IV and V prescribe punishment for "responsible rulers, public officials and private individuals" guilty of the crime of genocide through legislation "to give effect to the provisions of the present Convention," while Article VI, which we shall discuss later, calls for those charged with the crime of genocide to be "tried by a competent tribunal of the state in the territory of which the act was committed, or by [an] international penal tribunal..."

Article VII pledges the Contracting Parties "to grant extradition in accordance with their laws and treaties in force." Other articles not referred to in this paper are administrative in nature and of little interest to our present purpose.

As of March, 1967 seventy member states had "acceded to or ratified" the Convention. Data in this regard is interesting. First to accede was Ethiopia (July 1, 1949) fresh out of its experience with Italy. Australia, almost blameless of the taint of genocide, acceded July 8, 1949 and Norway, the victim of Nazi excesses in World War II, followed just two weeks later.

Two of the prime predators in the United Nations, Turkey and the Soviet Union, have acceded under interesting circumstances. Turkey acceded and ratified on July 31, 1950 but its instrument of signature has not been received, which is a sort of exercise in closing a door but keeping the latch unfastened for a quick exit.[7]

The Soviet Union has both acceded and ratified (May 3, 1954), and signed (December 16, 1949), but has recorded two reservations.

The first of these is aimed at Article IX of the Convention which directs that disputes on the subject of the Convention "shall be submitted to the International Court of Justice at the request of any of the parties to the dispute." This simply means that the USSR is anxious to enjoy the privilege of prolonging and ultimately thus killing disputes arising on the Convention in which it itself is a participant by simply preventing a dispute from going to a competent party for adjudication. The importance with which the Soviet Union regards its reservation is manifested in that of the ten reservations cast by UN members against Article IX, nine emanate from nations of the Soviet bloc.

The Soviet's second reservation is homed in on Article XII, which gives the right to any Contracting Party (i.e. member of the United Nations subscribing to the Convention) to "extend the application of the present Convention to all or any of the territories for the conduct of whose foreign relations that Contracting Party is responsible."

The Soviet's concern in this matter is quite transparent and portentous. It neither wishes to be put in a position of defending itself against the charge that it is undesirous as an example of extending to Armenia, the conduct of the foreign affairs of which sovietized republic is the concern alone of Moscow, the right to ask United Nations action under the provisions of the Convention, nor does the Soviet want Soviet Armenia to enjoy such a privilege, which may turn out to be a two edged sword directed against Turkey, which the Soviet is presently wooing, and against the Soviet itself.[8]

The United States of America, on the other hand, is one among six United Nations States which have not ratified or acceded, although its signature endorsing the Convention was filed December 11, 1948.

There has been widespread interpretation of the failure of the United States to ratify the Genocide Convention as bearing with America's "sense of guilt" of its Negro problem, but a careful study of the subject reveals that Washington's concern is not directed unilaterally at the genocide agreement, but generally at the delicate matter of the conflict between the many United Nations Human Rights decisions and the traditional American concept of non-interference in the internal affairs of a constituted nation.

As an example of the problem faced by the United States Government on the subject of the genocide convention itself:

On August 14, 1946 then President Harry Truman affixed his signature to a document formalizing "Acceptance by the United States of the Compulsory Jurisdiction of the International Court of Justice,"[9] the United Nations agency referred to in Article IX of the Convention as the final arbitrator of all disputes between member States.

This _Acceptance_ however was tempered by the provision that the declaration "shall not apply to (b) disputes with regard to matters which are essential within the domestic jurisdiction of the United States of America as determined by the United States of America," which graphically reveals the questions facing the United States in its approach to United Nations work in a number of areas.

In March, 1967 the Senate of the United States postponed once again, this time for a period of a year, a proposal that the Genocide Convention be ratified. Apparently the knotty question of United States--vs. United Nations jurisdiction still remains unresolved in Washington. It can be said for the United States, however, that it has acted with exemplary honesty in this issue. By joining the other members of the United Nations in the unanimous adoption of Article I of the Convention (December 11, 1946), the United States accepted genocide as a crime legally and in principle; but rather than subscribing to the Convention with reservations, as others have done, which would make its accession technically meaningless, it has foregone a decision on the matter pending efforts to compensate its views on jurisdiction with those of the various United Nations instruments. Predictably, because of the mood of America favorable as it is to effecting further progress in the field of civil and human rights, and most especially because United Nations human rights documents simply echo provisions long found in the United States Constitution, American acceptance of the Genocide Convention will follow in the near future.

If that Convention was composed to formularize a principle and a theory, and nothing else, that is, as an exercise in expressing man's new-found morality, it is a beautiful, expressive and effective piece of prosology--a homily--and we suppose valuable for it. But the Convention was meant to be more than that; and because it has been proved that the document lacks the teeth to put into the bite, it is not more than that.

Recurring debates on the Convention, most recently in the Sub-Commission for the Prevention of Discrimination and Protection of Minorities, have brought to surface the following flaws:

(a) The Commission on Human Rights under the jurisdiction of which the Convention rests, is still without an administrative fountainhead. Late in March, 1967 the Commission endorsed establishment of the posi-

tion of a High Commissioner for Human Rights without
which the work of the Commission, including efforts in
the genocide field, would remain adminstratively
unmoored. The subject of such a Commissioner has long
been debated in the United Nations and a meeting of the
United Nations Economic and Social Council in May of
1967 was to entertain the proposal made by the Commission and adopted by it 20 to 7. It is significant to
note that the USSR, and other members of the Soviet
block, voted against the proposal to create the Commissioner's post. The United States voted favorably.

(b) Since the membership of the United Nations, on
the basis of its unanimous acceptance of Article I of
the Genocide Convention, has accepted genocide as an
international crime, it is important that legal machinery be established and perfected for the punishment of
that crime.

The authors of the Convention of course were well
aware of this need, and Article VI of the present
Convention, as shown, specifies trial of those accused
of genocide "by a competent tribunal of the State in
the territory of which the crime is committed, or by
such international tribunal as may have jurisdiction."
In other words, the Convention calls for the formation
of an international tribunal to try cases of genocide--
but this has not been done.

The first difficulty arising from Article VI is
that its proposition that a tribunal selected by a
State to try those guilty of genocidal acts within the
territory of that State is at best a naive proposition
simply because of the circumstances which surround a
genocidal act. Waiting for Poland, as an example, to
try the Soviet officials responsible for the Katyn
massacres would be a futile wait indeed, as would be
Turkey's readiness and competence to try the Turkish
authors of the Armenian massacres.

On the other hand, the allied proposition, the
establishment of an international tribunal, has been
severely contested by various nations. As an example,
early in the debates on the Convention, the USSR
opposed provisions for an international tribunal, argu-
ing that such a body would "weaken national responsibility". The Soviet Union also said that "the establishment of international jurisdiction was...unaccept-
able in principle because it violated sovereignty."[10]
The entire Soviet-bloc is in tune with Moscow in this
regard.

Briefly, then, everyone says that there is an international crime to be punished, but important United Nations forces do not desire the establishment of a competent tribunal to try those accused of that crime. The Convention thus will remain ineffective until such an international body is formed to put purpose into the law.

(c) Consideration of Article VI has been rendered difficult by the inability of the United Nations to agree on a definition of what constitutes "aggression". Since the connotation of <u>genocide</u> predicts the existence of an aggressor--that is, the genocidist--and of a victim, it is important that there be a clear understanding of what is aggression. The debate apparently colors a nmber of considerations before the United Naitons, and has been long and futily debated. Reports a United Nations document:

> ...the General Assembly, in resolution 1187 (XII), adopted at its 72th plenary meeting on December 11, 1957, decided to defer consideration of the question of an internal criminal jurisdiction until such time as it takes up again the question of defining aggression and the question of a draft Code of Offenses Against the Peace and Security of Mankind.[11]

Briefly, again, the institution of an international tribunal specifically in terms of the crime of genocide seems now to have bowed to the broader question of the establishment of an "international criminal jurisdiction" which would try not only the genocidist, but other crimes "against peace and security of mankind." This of course compounds the problem of establishing a tribunal meant solely to try case of genocide. The Convention meanwhile remains without its vitally needed enforcement agency.

An April 1967 meeting of the United Nations was to discuss the problem of "aggression" once again. Sources close to the United Nations continued to point out that unless a definition of aggression were accepted, the international juridical committee could not make a study of the creation of a tribunal on genocide. Again, the problem of aggression is an onerous problem because of the records of many of those who are called upon to render a consensus meaning of the term.

Still another weakness of the Convention is found in the compacted nature of the United Nations itself.

The Charter of that body excludes the right of a nation which is not a member of the United Nations to present a case for consideration either before the Assembly or before its allied organs.

Thus, a nation such as the Armenians, whose ancient patrimony today suffers the sovereignty of Turkey and of the Soviet Union, a nation victimized by a classic example of the act of genocide which the Convention seeks to punish and prevent, cannot appeal as a nation to the United Nations for redress! Unless a majority of the United Nations member States petition for a hearing before the UN on the Armenian Case, the Armenians have no right to have their Case heard!

This is an arrogation of privilege by the standing nations of the world. It means that a nation decimated by genocide, its lands preempted by larger nations, its sovereign government destroyed by the act of genocide, cannot accuse the malefactor before the United Nations, where sits the criminal himself in the full protection of the law of United Nations, which he himself helped establish!

The very character of genocide means that a nation subjected to genocide will more than likely be so weakened by the experience as to be unable to preserve its character of effective nationhood and thus be eligible for United Nations membership, where it can demand attention to its problem.

The United Nations has provisions for the participation of "non-governmental organization" in advisory capacities with the social and cultural agencies of the United Nations, but these societies cannot propose consideration of "political" matters.

To be effective, the Charter and the Genocide Convention must be altered to allow any "national, ethnical, racial or religious group" harboring a complaint of genocide freely to approach the United Nations--and at least be heard.

The Convention and the Armenian Problem

The case of the Armenians indeed represents the acid test of the efficacy of the Genocide Convention and of the honest intentions of the United Nations to punish that crime and to do away with it.

While the Jews had their Nuremberg and the Asiatic
nations had their Tokyo, where is the international
tribunal that will hear, at long last, the Armenian
complaint against Turkey for the "mother" genocide of
1915-1921?

The Turkish genocide of the Armenians qualifies in
every instance for United Nations action under the
definition of genocide as found in the Convention.

(Article I): Turkey's pretext that the deportations and massacres of the Armenians in 1915 were a
"wartime" measure becomes meaningless in face of the
Genocide Convention's assertion that genocide "whether
committed in time of peace or in time of war is a crime
under international law." Article I clearly states it
doesn't matter when or why genocide was committed; it
is still a crime for it.[12]

(Article II): The Turkish Genocide was in fact a
composite of "acts committed with intent to destroy, in
whole or in part, a national, ethnical, racial or religious group." The Armenians are a nation; they are
part of a distinct ethnical body; most are members of a
National Church and all are Christians by religion;
they are a branch of the Caucasian race.

(Article II, Section a): Since genocide has been
accepted to mean "Killing members of the group," then
Armenians were certainly murdered--1,500,000 of them;
(Article II, section b); If genocide comprehends "causing serious bodily or mental harm to members of the
group" then certainly such harm was done the Armenians
--and the evidence is still at hand in the shattered
families, the maimed bodies and troubled minds of the
survivors; (Article II, Section c): If genocide con-
notes "deliberately inflicting on the group conditions
of life calculated to bring about its physical destruction in whole or in part," one has but to read the
enormous literature on the subject to see just how
calculated was the Turkish effort physically to destroy
the Armenian nation; (Article II, Section 6): If "imposing measures intended to prevent births within the
group" constitutes an act of genocide, then the Armenians were subjected to that practice. Older or less
comely women were deported and murdered, others were
forcibly introduced to Turkish households, where they
begat not the children of their murdered Armenian
husbands, but of Turks. At the same time, the able
manhood of the nation were arrested as a prelude to the

grim events, marched off from their homes, and executed, thus rendering births impossible; (Article II, Section e): If "forcibly transferring children of one group to another group" is genocide, then what of the hundreds of thousands of Armenian children 5 to 13 years of age orphaned by the Turks and made parts of Turkish families, where they lost their sense of national or cultural identity or, if below the age of 5, on governmental orders, murdered?

Although faced with the above evidence, although a participant of the Genocide Convention as a member of the United Nations, the Turk rather than asking the United Nations to activate the Convention in terms of its crime against the Armenians, has simply used the United Nations as a forum of denials that an "Armenian massacre" ever took place.[13]

When confronted by Turkish disavowals of genocidal events in Armenia in 1915-21, members of the United Nations ought to ask the Turkish delegation:

At a moderate estimate, there were 2,500,000 Armenians in Turkey on the eve of World War I. At the most, there are now in Turkey as estimated 85,000 of those people. What happened to the 2,415,000 souls unaccounted for? How come there are today in the Armenian provinces of Turkey only about 15,000 Armenians?

History in fact shows that anti-Armenianism in Turkey became a national political concept, a philosophical entity and, as such, predicted the Nazi German "weltanschaung." It is a "compleat" state policy of genocide, arising from a suffusing animal instinct to eliminate a proprietor nation in order to ensure retention of that nation.

The continuing debate in the United Nations on the Genocide Convention has placed further emphasis on the virtue of the Armenian Case. For instance, there has been through the years a good deal of support for inclusion in the Convention of a clause recognizing genocide to mean also "cultural annihilation," the deliberate destruction of the language and broadly the culture of any national, racial or religious group.

In these terms, it is known that the Turkish Government of 1915 summoned its "holy war" on the Armenians on the knowledge that the Turkish people would support the geopolitical bases of the genocide by participating in a national effort to extirpate the language, religion and culture of the Armenian nation, kicking those glories into the grave being dug for the corpse of the dooomed nations--a complete entombment of man and his civilization!

In Turkey, Armenian cultural monuments have been torn down or else adopted by the Turks as symbols of "Turkic" culture. The great early church edifices of a nation, first to recognize Christianity as a State religion, have either been razed, defaced, or converted into military warehouses or governmental office housing. Armenian schools and libraries in the interior have been all but erased, vestiges of the patrimonial civilizaton have been systematically obliterated in the Armenian districts, for the unchallenged possession of which the Turks massacred the Armenians in the first place.

Although the concept of "cultural genocide" has been recognized as generic to the act of genocide, most members of the United Nations have felt that the pro-tection of a nation's right to retain its own unique cultural heritage was better the province directly of the Commission on Human Rights.[14] "Cultural genocide" remains however inherently implied in the Convention.

Because they have been the first modern victims of the crime of genocide, because the crime practiced against them has been defined minutely by the Convention on genocide, and because they yet have been stymied in their desire to place their case at the disposal of the United Nations as expounded in the present paper, Armenians were led to take the following vicarious measures:

--On March 16, 1966 representatives of the Delegation of the Armenian Republic (1918-1920) deposited with the Secretariat of the United Nations a "memorandum on the Armenian Cause" asking that the consort of nations study the Armenian Case and take action thereon.

--On January 5, 1967 in connection with sessions of the Sub-Commission on the Prevention of Discrimination and Protection of Minorities called to examine the proposal to set up an international tribunal on cases of genocide, the Delegation distributed among members of that sub-body a missive asserting the support of the far-flung Armenian nation in the effort to establish an international tribunal as called for under Article VI of the Convention.[15]

   --On January 16, 1967 the Delegation again approached members of the Sub-Commission with a second Memorandum. Citing the Turkish genocide of the Armenians and the consequent destruction of lives and property, the dispersal of the nation, the obliteration of the culture of the nation by Turkey, this instrument called vigorously for quick and universal acceptance of the need to establish a machinery of trial and punishment of those found guilty of genocide. It also urged all nations to ratify, accede to and sign the Genocide Convention.[16]

   --During Sub-Commission sessions of January 18-21, 1967 a demonstration of Armenians before the United Nations facility asked for passage by the United Nations of provisions to establish the needed tribunal.

   --On April 8, 1967 consonant with the sessions of the sub-commission to define aggression, a second Armenian demonstration took place before the United Nations urging immediate action on the definition of "aggression" as a step towards the establishment of an international penal tribunal as called for by Article VI of the Convention.

   Armenian insistence that it is not enough simply to talk about the need to eradicate the crime of genocide and to compose and to pass basic statements which recognize the act of physical, cultural and spiritual murder as an international malefaction will continue until the United Nations takes action to bring before the bar of justice those who have been in our time guilty of the crime of genocide, just as was done at Nuremberg and Tokyo, in order that by these examples the tragic folly of genocide, "the destruction in whole or in part of a national, ethnical, racial or religious group," will be discouraged and finally expunged from man's mind.

   Until those who have been victimized by the violence of genocide are given the fullest redress for the wrongs done them in exact conformity with the purposes and consideration which led the genocidist to his unconscionable crime against mankind, the Convention on the Prevention and Punishment of the Act of Genocide will remain an ineffective document, and millions more will face the threat of extinction.

Footnotes

1. The definition is that found in Article II of the United Nations' Convention on the Prevention and Punishment of Genocide. All quotations or references to the Convention are based on the text of that document as found in the release of the United Nations Economic and Social Council, Commission on Human Rights, Sub-Commission on Prevention of Discrimination and Protection of Minorities: E-CN.4-Sub.2-259-Rev.1; 14 Feb. 1966. The relatively contemporary nature of man's understanding of genocide and of his desire to place the apocalyptic forces under restraint is illustrated by a war-time remark attributed to Winston Churchill as he was told of the Nazi-made starvation which took the lives of 30,000 Greeks: "We are in the presence of a crime without a name." (See Robert Merrill Bartlett: They Stand Alone. New York: Crowell, 1959; p. 100).

2. The Crime of Genocide, a United Nations Convention. United Nations, N.Y. 1956; p. 1.

3. Ibid. On Prof. Raphael Lemkin, see later in this work.

4. For a discussion of Turkey and genocide, see: James H. Tashjian: Turkey, Author of Genocide--the Centenary Record of Turkey 1822-1922. A Publication of the Commemorative Committee on the 50th Anniversary of the Turkish Massacres of the Armenians, 212 Stuart Street, Boston, Mass. 02116. (Copies on request.)

5. Richard Pipes, Associate Prof. of History and Associate Director of the Russian Research Center, Harvard University, has traced the course of Soviet Russian policy in terms of the nationalities of the Soviet Union. The new Communist programme, he says, "leaves no doubt that the Stalinist nationality policy will be continued and carried to its logical conclusion..." which he interprets as "the indispensible minimum of lip service...to the rights of the national minorities." See his paper, "Nationalism and Nationality," in Leonard Shapiro (ed.) The USSR and the Future. Praeger Paperbacks, New York-London. 1962. The Pipes quotations are found on page 81 of the latter work.

For further discussion of the problem, see: The Soviet Empire: Prison House of Nations and Races, a Study in Genocide, Discrimination, and Abuse of Power. Internal Security Subcommittee (U.S. Senate). 85th Congress, 2d Session. Washington. (U.S. Government Printing Office). 1958; Doc. 122.

6. London Times, Nov. 24, 1945; p. 4. The November 23, 1945 proceedings of the Nuremberg tribunal also records this quotation.

7. Information in this section is based on material found in the text of the Convention on Genocide and allied papers as of footnote one, above. Normally, a nation first signs an international Convention, after which its Government, either through act of parliament, presidential decree or other constitutional action, ratifies the Convention. Following this, the nation's ratification will be acceded, as in this case, to the United Nations' legal department.

8. The reader is cautioned against succumbing to a grave typographical mishap in The Crime of Genocide (op. cit.), page 9, where the Soviet's second reservation is carried as Article XIII. Article XII is intended. As in the case of Article IX, every other nation in the Soviet bloc has joined the Soviet in reservation.

9. See text in Ruhl J. Bartlett (ed.): The Record of American Diplomacy. New York: Knopf; 1947; pp. 698699.

10. The Crime of Genocide (op. cit.); pp. 6-7.

11. See UN publication cited in footnote one, above; p. 3.

12. Deportation falls within the connotation of "genocide." See an able discussion in Bela Varga (Forwardist): Genocide by Deportation, Publication of the Hungarian National Council. New York. 1951. It may be noted that the 1895 massacres of the Armenians took place in a time of peace.

13. As an example, on Jan. 26, 1965 in a speech before the UN General Assembly, Turkish representative Eralp, in referring to the Armenian massacres,

spoke of "certain massacres alleged to have been committed by the Turks in the past."

14. <u>The Crime of Genocide</u> (op. cit.); p. 7.

15. The text of this Memorandum may be consulted in <u>The Armenian Review</u>, Boston, Mass., Vol. XIX, No. 3-75 (Autumn, 1966); pp. 3-16.

16. Ibid., Vol. XX, No. 1-77 (Spring, 1967); p. 41-43.

III. THE GYPSIES

III. THE GYPSIES

The Gypsies too have been victims of an "unremembered genocide," even more so than the the Armenians,
but less so than homosexuals during the Third Reich.

Gypsies, or Rom as they wish to be called, have a
rich oral folklore but few written documents, and there
are few Rom intellectuals and writers who have documented their destruction. However, in the past two
decades, the Gypsies have become better organized, both
locally and internationally, and have begun the long
overdue documentation of the past. Happily,
non-Gypsies have long taken an interest in the Rom, and
some scholarly journals on Gypsy life and customs are
nearly a century old.

Over half a million Gypsies perished in the Nazi
extermination programs. Philip Friedman, Jerzy Ficowski, Dora Yates, and Gabrielle Tyrnauer describe
aspects of these actions. The Rom were the second
largest ethnic group targeted for destruction by the
Germans and their collaborators. Their crime was not
simply racial but because they were seen as
"asocial"--unassimilable into German society--misfits,
lazy bums, and for these reasons they were executed.

THE EXTERMINATION OF THE GYPSIES

Philip Friedman

The original home of the Gypsies was in Northern India, the cradle of the so-called Indo-Germanic or Aryan race. Many scientists believe that the Gypsies are the most direct and least adulterated descendants of this prehistoric race. For reasons unknown to us the Gypsies left their ancient home about two thousand years ago and became nomads. This form of life evidently suited their taste for they displayed no inclination either to return to their native land or to become a sedentary people in the lands of their wandering.

The Gypsy migration to the west proceeded slowly. In the third century of the Christian era they were in Persia. By the year one thousand they reached Europe via the Balkan peninsula. By the beginning of the fifteenth century they made their appearance in Germany, Austria, Italy and other central European countries. At this stage they no longer constituted a homogenous people and broke up into tribes, each of which had its own king, dialect and beliefs. Some adopted the Christian religion. Others were converted to Mohammedanism.

Medieval Europe was suspicious of the Gypsies. They were accused of all sorts of crimes: idolatry, witchcraft, kidnaping. As a matter of fact they led a life of poverty and depended for their sustenance on handouts, fortune telling, music, primitive handicrafts and the repair of old utensils. Under these circumstances it was to be expected that they might, from time to time, resort to stealing animals or even to kidnaping. Consequently they were always shunned. Some countries forbade their entry or limited their residence to specific localities. Others prohibited their participation in specified trades. On many occasions they were subjected to bloody pogroms and expulsion from the country. As a general rule the Gypsies were deprived of all rights; only in the Balkan lands did they enjoy a measure of tolerance.

As time passed the anti-Gypsy laws were abrogated. Toward the end of the eighteenth century they were freed from nearly all restrictions throughout most of Europe. Germany and Austria were the exceptions to

this rule. These two countries, always marked by intolerance and rigid bureaucracy, retained on their books
numerous petty and vicious regulations against the
Gypsies.

The Gypsies were not in a position to take full
advantage of the rights conferred upon them during the
nineteenth century. By and large they remained nomadic
and it was not until after World War I that they began
to adapt themselves to modern forms of life. Gypsy
cultural centers containing schools, theaters, orchestras and a native class of intellectuals arose in
Czechoslovakia, Yugoslavia and elsewhere. But despite
this transformation, the bulk of the people still
retained their nomadic ways to such an extent that it
was impossible to determine their exact number on the
eve of World War II. Some Gypsy authors make exaggerated claims of a population exceeding five million in
Europe alone. Other students of Gypsy life gave more
reliable estimates. Thus Rabbi Moshe Gaster of London
estimated their number in Europe at 885,000 with perhaps another 350,000 on other continents. The Swedish
scholar Arthur Thesleff, an authority on Gypsy problems, computed the total number of Gypsies at the
beginning of the twentieth century as 1,422,000.

The Nazi treatment of the Gypsies was an indication of the degree of the seriousness with which the
Hitlerists took their own racial theories. By general
consensus the Gypsies are the purest of Aryans. But
Hitler was ashamed of these poor relations of aristo-
cratic descent. To get rid of them was a simple
matter. He commanded his "scientists" to declare the
Gypsies "non-Aryans," and the Nazi professors obedient-
ly accepted this assignment.

It was not an easy assignment. The accumulated
data on ethnography and anthropology had to be turned
upside down to prove the point. Some of the Nazi professors failed to perform the trick and were promptly
punished for their failure. It remained for the high
priest of Nazi "race science" to deliver the goods, and
he did not fail. In his book Rassenkunde Europas, the
Bible of Nazi anthropology, Professor Hans F. K.
Guenther wrote: "The Gypsies indeed retained some elements from their Nordic home, but they are descended
from the lowest classes of the population in that
region. In the course of their migrations they have
absorbed the blood of the surrounding peoples and have
thus become an Oriental, Western-Asiatic racial mix-

ture, with an addition of Indian, Mid-Asiatic, European strains. Their nomadic mode of living is a result of this mixture. The Gypsies will generally affect Europe as aliens."

Thus were the Gypsies expelled from the "Aryan" family. Nor was this a purely academic formulation. To be declared alien in the Nazi empire meant condemnation to death. Having received the opinion of their expert, the Nazi leaders energetically applied themselves to the "final solution of the Gypsy problem."

Up to date there has been little study of the tragedy of the Gypsies under Nazi rule. The Journal of the Gypsy Lore Society of London contains some records concerning this. A valuable article on this subject by Dora E. Yates appeared in Commentary in the United States. Compared with the extensive literature on the extermination of the Jews and the tribulations of other peoples under the Nazi yoke, the literature on the Gypsies is meager and full of gaps. It has not even been established clearly when the Nazi extermination of the Gypsies actually began.

Some light is shed on this last question by a document recently published. This is in the form of a memorandum from Portschy, the Nazi Gauleiter of Steiermark, to Reichsminister Dr. Heinz Lammers. This memorandum is dated January 9, 1938, but refers to previous communications to Lammers on the same subject. In it Portschy says, among other things, that the Gypsies constitute a threat to public health (How well European Jews understand the meaning of this statement!), are "parasites on the body of our people," a danger "to the racial purity of our peasants" and in general "confirmed criminals." Portschy suggested a Nazi solution to the problem: sterilization of the Gypsies and their mobilization for slave labor.

These suggestions were made in peacetime. After World War II broke out the Nazis became more severe toward "alien elements." A conference in Berlin held on January 30, 1940, decided to expel 30,000 Gypsies from Germany into the General Gouvernement in Poland. Many Jews and Poles were also included in this decree. At that time Goebbels also issued a directive to his propaganda offices that Jews, Poles and Gypsies should be treated as equals in their "educational work." Some of the occupied countries promugated laws which placed the Gypsies in the same category as Jews. On May 30,

1941, the German military commander in Serbia ordered the confiscation of all property of Jews and Gypsies. Attempts were make in Poland to confine Gypsies to Jewish ghettos, and when the mass extermination of the Jews commenced, the German propaganda in the press, literature and radio included attacks on the Gypsies as well. Toward the end of 1942 the Lemberger Zeitung and the Krakower Zeitung broke out with a rash of articles whose burden it was that it was intolerable to permit an entire nation of parasites to go on eating while the "New Europe" was suffering hunger as a result of the Allied blockade.

As a final step in their campaign the Nazis resorted to a blood accusation against the Gypsies. A big trial of an entire Gypsy tribe was staged in Slovakia. They were accused of cannibalism. The entire Nazi press seized on the hateful accusation and demanded that the "cannibals" be severely punished.

The fate of the Gypsies was sealed.

Late in 1941 Mordecai Hayim Rumkowski, "chief of the Jews in the ghetto of Lodz," was ordered by the Germans to clear the area on Brzezinska Street extending from number 70 to number 100. Jews living there had to vacate the premises at once and the area was blocked off with a triple fence of barbed wire and a wide moat.

The establishment of this special area was preceded by extensive correspondence among the Germans. In the fall of 1941, Hans Biebow, the notorious hangman of the Jews of Lodz, received an order to prepare the ghetto of Lodz for the admission of another 20,000 Jews and 5,000 Gypsies. He objected to the order on the grounds that it would tend to disorganize the production of war materials in the ghetto. He particularly objected to the introduction of Gypsies into his domain. But his protests were disregarded and between October 16 and November 4, 1941, twenty transports of Jews from Germany and a number of transports of Gypsies arrived. The Jews were distributed throughout the ghetto. The Gypsies were quartered in the area blocked off for them. The ghetto thus acquired a "colony" for whose support it was responsible though it had no say in its administration.

As soon as the Gypsies were installed in their special area within the ghetto, terrible screams and cries could be heard from there. Every evening Jews of the ghetto saw cars crammed with drunken Germans going into the Gypsy camp. All windows had been smashed there--this at the peak of the winter frosts.

Two weeks after the Gypsies were brought to Lodz a typhus epidemic broke out among them. The Germans gave no medical assistance. But after the German chief of criminal police died of typhus, the Jews were ordered to provide doctors. Two doctors volunteered and one of them, Dr. Glasser, died in service. Each day vans loaded with the dead left the Gypsy compound. Alongside those who died of typhus lay the mutilated bodies of those who had been murdered by the Germans.

The number of Gypsies in the Lodz ghetto rapidly melted away. In March and April of 1942 the Germans moved the few survivors to the extermination camp at Chelmno. A leather goods shop and a factory for straw shoes were set up in the vacated quarters.

The Jews of Lodz--excepting the two volunteer doctors--did not know who the inmates of the compound were. For some time rumors circulated in the ghetto that the place was occupied by Jews from Hungary. Other rumors maintained that they were Yugoslav partisans. The Polish underground movement believed that they were Yugoslav partisans. Only after the war ended was the true identity of the inmates established. It is possible that the Germans intentionallly planted the false rumors.

A similar procedure was used by the Germans in other ghettos. Thus, the Polish underground announced on June 23, 1942, shortly before the great extermination of the Jews commenced, that there were more than one hundred thousand Gypsies in the Warsaw ghetto. A Jewish survivor from Siedlce testified that of the three blocks of houses in the ghetto of his native city, one was occupied by Gypsies.

Fortunately for the Gypsies the Germans did not apply their extermination tactics to them with the same single-minded consistency that they employed toward the Jews. The directives issued concerning them were of the same severity as those applying to the Jews but were not always carried out with the same ruthlessness. The Einsazgruppen established on the eve of the war against the Soviet Union were ordered to destroy Jews, Gypsies, Communists, "undesirable elements," partisans

and the mentally ill. But in 1942, when the work of
extermination was intensified, Minister of Justice
Thierack wrote to Martin Bormann that the job of liquidating the above-mentioned groups was not under the
jurisdiction of the Ministry of Justice. The fate of
the doomed groups thus remained in the hands of the
local administrators, the police and the SS, who had
the power to postpone the decreed fate, at least for a
while.

Within Germany itself Himmler forbade the free
movement of the Gypsies and ordered their incarceration
in concentration camps, but his order was not always
carried out. The Vichy French government also tried to
end the roaming of the Gypsies and sent some of them to
camps where they perished. In Eastern Europe there was
a great confusion in the matter of the treatment of the
Gypsies. In some localities the Germans even tried to
draft them into the Army--such was the case in Latvia.
Curiously enough, in the midst of the extermination,
the Gypsy student Vanya Kochanowski was asked to write
a paper to prove the Aryan origin of his people. At
the very time when the Gypsies of central Poland were
being herded into extermination camps, those of Eastern
Galicia were treated liberally. As late as 1944 the
Gypsies in Lemberg were allowed to go about freely and
to engage in their traditional trades. I know the case
of a Jewish boy who tried to save his life by pretend-
ing to be a Gypsy, and for a time he traveled freely
throughout Germany.

But despite such exceptional instances few Gypsies
survived the Nazi regime. Of more than 16,275 Gypsies
in Germany only 12 per cent survived. The vast majority of those in Latvia perished. The 3,000 Gypsies of
White Russia and the Crimea perished together with the
Jews. In Croatia only one per cent survived. Similar
low percentages of survival were recorded in other
countries. It is impossible to obtain exact figures
because the statistics concerning the pre-war Gypsy
population are unreliable. Gypsy spokesmen estimate
the number of those who perished at five hundred thous-
and, fully one-third of all the Gypsies in the world.

The surviving Gypsies who returned in 1945 were
quartered in the same barracks at Lierenfeld where
their suffering had begun. Isolated from the "Aryan"
Germans they wait for justice and are growing ever more
skeptical of finding it. Justice in Germany is not
known for its swiftness and the Gypsies are no excep-

tion to this rule when they seek compensation for their losses (though it may well be asked whether one can speak of compensation for losses of the kind they suffered). The attitude of the German officialdom toward the Gypsy claims has been clearly stated in a circular letter of the Wuertemberg Ministry of the Interior published in 1950. In a fit of frankness this letter states that in all cases of Gypsy claims for restitution it should be borne in mind that the Gypsies had been persecuted by the Nazis not for any racial reasons but because of their "asocial and criminal record."

This weird official statement aroused the protest of some democratic German papers. One such newspaper in Duesseldorf wrote: "Hitler went down; race hatred has remained. Those who do not believe this are invited to be seen in the company of a Gypsy. They will have to run a gauntlet of insults and contempt..." And the trustee of the Gypsies, Herr Sippel, summed up the situation in the following words: "In Western Germany there are again in force unwritten laws like those of the Third Reich."

HITLER AND THE GYPSIES

THE FATE OF EUROPE'S OLDEST ARYANS

Dora E. Yates

It is more than time that civilized men and women were aware of the Nazi crime against the Gypsies, as well as the Jews. Both bear witness to the fantastic dynamic of the 20th-century racial fanaticism. For these two peoples shared the horror of martyrdom at the hands of the Nazis for no other reason than that they were--they <u>existed</u>.

The Gypsies, like the Jews, stand alone in the history of the world as an isolated race; both are, seemingly, miraculous survivals. Each of them has handed down its customs and traditions from generation to generation, as well as an ancient mother-tongue unknown to other peoples: the Jews, Hebrew, and the Gypsies, Romani. Throughout the ages both these peoples have been persecuted unmercifully: the Jews ostensibly because of the steadfastness with which they clung to their faith and because of their economic successes, and the Gypsies for exactly opposite reasons: because of their supposed want of religion and their aloofness and poverty.

In the Dark Ages both groups were subjected to the rack and wheel for preserving their own traditions and refusing to intermarry with the Gentiles. Anti-Gypsy legislation existed from about 1500 to 1800 CE in several countries of Europe (except Hungary and the Southeast), but in Spain and France it became a dead letter, and in England and Italy was seldom enforced. In point of severity there is little to choose between these laws, though those promulgated in Germany were more numerous than in other countries and perhaps somewhat more barbarous. By the 18th century, however, we are told (<u>Journal of the Gypsy Lore Society</u>, Third Series), "even the German conscience began to prick German writers: one was at great pains to justify inhumanity, another could not think without shuddering about 'the old, helpless, perhaps quite innocent Gypsy woman who was buried alive;' and a third asks, 'What judge would without judgment and right send a man to be hung who was guilty of no particular crime, but simply because he belonged to a particular race?'"

Before the close of the 18th century, such specific anti-Gypsy legislation had come to an end. The Romanis in Europe were left, more or less, to pursue their normal nomadic life, unharassed by any restrictions except the vagrancy laws and frontier regulations. Throughout the 19th and the first three decades of the 20th centuries, they earned their living by their own traditional occupations and handicrafts. In Bulgaria Gypsy men plied the trades of tinkers, comb-makers, iron-workers, gimlet-makers, spoon-makers, sieve-makers, and carpet-weavers, or reared the buffaloes by which their traveling carts were drawn. In Serbia smithcraft was considered the noblest occupation for the Romani; while in Turkey Turkish Gypsies sank so low in the social scale that they accepted employment as common hangmen. Many sedentary Gypsies in Albanian towns were occupied as porters, donkey-drivers, brick- and tile-makers and scavengers, and their women-folk found employment as charwomen. In other countries Gypsy fiddlers played at village weddings and dances; Gypsy horse-dealers and blacksmiths carried on a prosperous trade; old Gypsy women put their extensive medical knowledge and herbal lore at the service of the country folk among whom they dwelt; young Gypsy girls sold flowers in the streets of Bucharest and thereby gave to that capital much of its color and gaiety; and everywhere Gypsy fortune-tellers advised all and sundry as to their future fate.

After the First World War some of the more progressive countries of Eastern Europe tried out various cultural experiments to fit the Gypsies into modern life. At Uzhorod in Czechoslovakia, for instance, a special open-air school was started for Gypsy children, surrounded by a playground enclosed with trees, and the curriculum included drawing, handicrafts, and violin instruction--with the result that this institution became a general cultural center for the entire Gypsy colony and was able to produce a Gypsy theatrical company which was invited to tour the whole of Southern Czechoslovakia. Long before 1939 Gypsies had their own Romani newspapers in Rumania, Yugoslavia, and Soviet Russia, and already there were Gypsy doctors, lawyers, teachers, engineers, priests, and authors of considerable ability.

No exact statistics are obtainable on the distribution of the Gypsies in Europe before the two world wars--their ceaseless migrations from one country to another within Europe itself, and from Europe to

Australia and North and South America, make an accurate estimate impossible. But at the beginning of the 20th century Arthur Thesleff and other investigators gave the rough total of 1,422,000. For the present we have no accurate information as to how many have survived Hitler's New Order; but we do know that their losses were extremely heavy.

Hitler revived and exceeded the savagery of the old 17th and 18th century laws against the "Ziguener." He decreed the wholesale massacre of Gypsies in Central, Eastern, and Southern Europe, for the sole reason that they were Gypsies, a race of free men and women. In Germany, before he came into power, tribes of Sinti, Ungri, and Gelderari had wandered peacefully from one village to another, peddling their small wares, mending the kettles and pots and pans of the villagers, and providing the music at their festivities.

The precise date at which Hitler decided on the extermination of Gypsies is unknown to us, but it is obvious that the men and women of this dark-skinned, black-eyed race were not "Nordics." At first Hitler tried to persuade the German professors of ethnography and anthropology to declare that the Gypsies were non-Aryans, and many men of learning were interned for refusing to deny the Indo-Aryan origin of the Romani people and their language. So Hitler and his gangsters then chose to classify the whole race as "asocial"-- i.e., a nomadic people who did not fit into his New Order, and a proper object for genocide.

Of the hideous deeds of barbarity towards the Gypsies in Germany itself, we possess no written testimony. But from trustworthy interviews with "Ziguener" whose relatives were liquidated at the Belsen and other concentration camps, it has been estimated that of the five thousand nomadic Gypsies who roamed the roads of the Reich in 1939, less than seven hundred are alive today.

Reliable data on what actually happened in Nazi-occupied countries during the war are naturally difficult to secure. But from the evidence supplied by survivors I will quote two typical examples given by literate Gypsies from Latvia and Czechoslovakia respectively. The first of these is an account written by the Lettish Gypsy, Vanya Kochanowski, a university student who managed eventually to escape into France, "a living skeleton, with no flesh on my bones, but with feet swollen to the size of an elephant's paws."

"Before 1940," he writes, "life in Latvia was very wonderful. We Gypsies enjoyed absolute freedom and we could live and study as we wished. Anyone who wanted to work could earn a good livelihood, but work was not compulsory. Everyone carried on his own life according to his wishes. Then in 1940 our 'liberators' appeared from the East. Free discussion came to an end...but the Soviet government treated us Gypsies well, and although we were obliged to work hard and to attend school or university the Tziganes were satisfied with their regime...But that stage did not last long. The new 'liberators'--the Nazis--were a hundred times worse than any medieval oppressors, and deportations and tortures become the order of the day. All Jews were herded into ghettos and soon the forests near Riga became a veritable charnel-house..."

In Eastern Latvia all the Gypsies were assembled in three towns, Rezekne, Ludza, and Vilane. At Ludza they were locked up in a large synagogue where they died, in hundreds, of hunger and disease. When Kochanowski succeeded in telephoning to Ludza, the only reply he received was: "The Gypsies have already been reported to the forests"--the Nazi code phraseology for "murdered." The bitter protest he then lodged with official Nazi headquarters was met with the retort: "If you cannot prove to me that an adequate number of Gypsies are decent, hard-working folk, you will every one of you be exterminated."

So, with the collaboration of the chief of the Latvian Gypsies, Janis Lejamanis, this young student set to work to compile a register of "Tziganes honnetes." Then, in accordance with the ironic cruelty of the Nazi authorities, who thought the boy had had no education, he was ordered to write a dissertation proving that the Gypsies were Aryans. This, however, he accomplished satisfactorily and in scholarly fashion, giving as his source Miklosich's Mundarten der Ziguener in Europa. At last there came a decree that the Gypsies were not to be liquidated. But the "order of release" was diabolically delayed until it was too late: it arrived at 2 a.m., exactly two hours after fifteen to twenty-five hundred Gypsies had been massacred. Kochanowski himself, then a youth of strong physique, was spared, and in 1943 with other Lettish students sent to work for the Nazis, often for thirty-six hours on end under deadly fire from Russian troops, outside Leningrad. He was later imprisoned in a gruesome underground cell at Kaunas (Kovno), from the effects of which experience he still suffers in a sanitorium in France.

The second piece of evidence was contained in a letter written by Antonin Daniel to S.E. Mann of the British Ministry of Information, who before the war was lecturer in English at the Masaryk University in Brno and knew this Gypsy student well. In Czechoslovakia, in pre-war days, there was at Oslavany a flourishing colony of some one hundred and fifty Gypsy men, women, and children who contentedly followed their own trades and had made themselves acceptable to the country folk in that district by their skill as basket-makers, their exceptional knowledge of horses, and above all by the magic of their music. After the war Mr. Daniel wrote to Mr. Mann: "The whole Oslavany colony was taken a few years ago by the Nazis to Oswiecim, where they were done to death. There were only five survivors, among them myself, my sister, and my mother."

The Belgian review Message of November 13, 1942, reported a crime in Serbia more horrible than any in the three centuries of anti-Gypsy legislation: "One of the most recent crimes of the Germans seems to us to surpass by far all the others, because in addition to the suffering it gave rise to, it destroyed gentleness and beauty: all the Gypsies of Serbia have been massacred!...These merchants of poetry, prognostications, lies, and songs were hunted down on the roads over which they fled, mounted on their galloping scarecrows of horses, their rolling caravans full of cries, color, and mystery."

At that date it was impossible to get any confirmation of this tale of terror, but since then the following authentic evidence has been collected by the Gyspy Lore Society (of England) from eyewitnesses, Gypsies and others, who had survived these holocausts. From Sarajevo Professor Rade Uhlik, whose carefully corroborated evidence is indisputable, writes:

"Before the war no Gypsy settlements had ever been more propsperous and self-supporting: today they are utterly derelict, and the Gypsy survivors have fled to Northeast Bosnia...In so-called 'Independent' Croatia some twenty-eight thousand Gypsies were mercilessly butchered, and this computation, if not strictly reliable, is certainly underestimated. For the few children of fortune who did manage to escape from the hell of concentration camps and crematoria relate with horror that it was among a hundred thousand or so candidates for death that they witnessed the most awful and heart-rending scenes, when these barbarians tore Gypsy children from their mothers and fathers and hurled them into the crematory ovens...The whole of Gypsydom in Croatia between the rivers Sava and Drava have been exterminated. They were massacred chiefly as 'Non-Aryans'--what a terribly ironic fate for the oldest Indo-Aryan race in existence!--being so designated on racial-political grounds, but also because they professed the Greek Orthodox faith...I have to report with deep distress that their splendid, unique dialect of Romani has now become extinct. Only a few adult men, who at the outbreak of hostilities happened to be in prison, have survived the wholesale massacre. And since this remnant (perhaps one per cent of the whole number of Gypsies), having become nervous wrecks, are also useless from the biological point of view, owing to the total extermination of the women and children, there can be no Gypsy posterity for them--or for the world."

M. Frederic Max, of the French Embassy, early in 1946 sent us a first-hand account of the treatment of the Gypsies in Nazi concentration camps. Though himself never at Auschwitz "where thousands of Gypsies were interned and where whole tribes were sent to the gas chamber," he received faithful reports from a convoy of surviving Gypsies who came to Buchenwald in May 1944, which reports he confirmed by information from non-Gypsies, chiefly Jews, who had the rare good luck to return from that camp of death.

At Buchenwald the Gypsies from Germany, Bohemia, and Poland, he says, were lodged together in a block of "Blacks," so called because the inmates of this part of the camp were branded on the chest with a black triangle, to distinguish them as "asocials" from political prisoners, German law-breakers, and religious adversaries, who bore respectively a red, green, or violet stigma.

At Birkenau camp, the antechamber to Auschwitz itself, the Gypsies from Slovakia and the South of Poland were subjected to unspeakable tortures before being consigned to the gas chambers. "Many Gypsy women were selected for the 'experimental pavilion,' where

German doctors experimented with artifical impregnation followed by abortion." In January 1945, before the approach of the Russian Army, the Auschwitz camp was evacuated, and the prisoners were driven westward by long forced marches without food, so that many of them died of cold and hunger or exhaustion or were suffocated in the barns into which they were crowded at night. Others were beaten to death by the SS or murdered in the forests by the Volkssturm. Very few survived.

In Dr. Bendell's evidence, given in the Belsen trial at Luneberg (as reported in the London Daily Telegraph of October 2, 1945), the information supplied by M. Max is confirmed by the statement that "of 11,000 Gypsies in a special camp at Auschwitz all were killed except 1,500 selected for working parties," i.e., slave labor. But no further corroboration of this cold-blooded mass murder is needed beyond the callous sworn testimony of the Nazi commandant of Auschwitz himself, Rudolf Franz Ferdinand Hoess, as published by William S. Shirer in End of a Berlin Diary.

Throughout the war young Gypsies who regained their freedom, together with hundreds of others who had never come under the Nazi heel, devoted their liberty to helping the Maquis and other resistance groups in their fight against Hitler, and more than one escaped prisoner-of-war has had reason to thank his Gypsy hosts who passed him from camp to camp till a neutral country was reached. No wonder that a young Gypsy writer recently suggested that "the United Nations institute an enquiry into the source of those monstrous Nazi orders to exterminate our race..so that the Gypsy martyrs at Auschwitz be avenged, like those of France or Poland, not by the fury of barbarism but by the hand of Justice."

It would be proper, also, for the nations to see that the Gypsy survivors who may find a refuge among them are treated with decency and respect, and allowed to lead their own lives in their own way, unharassed by the authorities. Since peace came to the world, many hidebound government officials seem to regard the Gypsies as an "anachronism." There are protection societies for wild birds, wild flowers, and other rarities--but there is no protection, even in America, for wild Gypsies.

"What we Gypsy survivors desire," declared Mateo Maximoff, a talented Romani author now with his people

in Montreuil-sous-Bois, in France, "is complete liber-
ty--that is the right to travel freely in the pursuit
of our various trades, which would mean that facilities
to cross frontiers should be extended to all Gypsies...
Just as no one could prevent the flower from budding or
the bird from making his nest in the spring, so no one
should stop the Gypsy from wandering over the face of
the globe. For our race is a part of nature. We bring
joy and gaiety to the villages through which we pass,
because wherever we go we carry with us that element of
mystery that intrigues the whole world."

    History has proved again and again that the well-
meaning but misguided attempts of philanthropists and
missionaries to cure the Gypsies of their nomadism will
never succeed. Though they may settle down contentedly
in their winter quarters and send their children to
school regularly during six months of the year, as soon
as spring returns, "wanderlust" will attack them and
the urge to take to the road prove irresistible. If
Gypsies are freed from public interference, they will
find their own way of fitting into the modern world and
contributing their own unique value to their fellowmen.

THE FATE OF POLISH GYPSIES

Jerzy Ficowski

Translated by Jozef Rotblat

Poland was the main area of Nazi atrocities; it was there that the numerous extermination camps were situated in which many Gypsies perished together with numerous other victims. The Gypsies were also exterminated elsewhere: many of them died in Germany in the notorious camps of Matthausen, Ravenbruck and Buchenwald, but Poland was the main centre of extermination, since most of them were killed in Oswiecim (Auschwitz), Chelmno, and Treblinka.

It would, however, be erroneous to think that the destruction of the Gypsies was limited to murdering them in concentration and in extermination camps ('Vernichtungslager'). Gypsies used to be shot in the forests during almost the whole period of German occupation; large groups of them were often assembled in one place, then driven into wooden sheds and burnt alive. In comparison with the mass murders of the Gypsies in Auschwitz, those were relatively minor executions, but they were so numerous that they caused the tragic deaths of thousands of Gypsies outside the camps. In some regions these individual crimes assumed enormous proportions. For instance, in the Wolyn province (Eastern Poland before the War, at present included in the Ukrainian Republic of the Soviet Union) about 3,000-4,000 Gypsies were killed in the atrocious massacres committed by German and Ukrainian Fascists. Only adults were shot, the children were usually murdered by seizing them by the legs and smashing their heads against trunks of trees.

The losses of the Polish Gypsies during the German occupation were thus caused to a great extent by murders on a smaller scale that those in concentration camps. On the basis of rescued documents it is possible to establish fairly accurately the number of Gypsies killed in the Chelmno and Auschwitz camps. In the former, 5,008 Gypsies were murdered. How many perished in Auschwitz is not known for certain, but there are exact figures concerning the number of Gypsies registered in that camp. Members of the Underground Movement, organized by the prisoners at Auschwitz, managed to get hold of and hide the registration books containing personal data of all the Gypsies who passed through the camp. These books were unearthed in January 1949 and preseved. They contain the names of 10,097 men and 10,849 women, i.e., a total of 20,946 Gypsies. Of that number only a very small fraction survived, mainly those who were transferred from Auschwitz-Birkenau to Auschwitz I, and from there to Buchenwald, 'Dora' and Ravensbruck. The remainder-- that is, nineteen to twenty thousand--perished in Auschwitz. The large-scale extermination of the Polish Gypsies ended on 1st Aug. 1944, although minor incidents still occurred in the territories not yet occupied by the Red Army. In the concentration camps in Germany proper the murder of Gypsies still continued.

The situation of the Polish Gypsies during the whole of the German occupation was exceptionally bad, due to several factors. Unlike the nationals of all other German-occupied countries, the "Zigeuner" were persecuted with particular severity, hunted and murdered. They happened to live in a region which was the centre of annihilation, in the very midst of extermination camps, close to the terrible machines of the Nazi death factories.

Those of the Polish Gypsies who managed to survive the German occupation and found themselves in the territories lying east of the Vistula were already out of danger in 1943 or 1944 when the Germans were driven out from these districts. These Gypsies escaped the Germans in various ways: by fleeing into forests, joining the guerillas or by finding hide-outs in suburbs of large towns. Some of them managed to escape from prisons or transit camps.

Gypsies of the name Sokolowski, who originated from the neighbourhood of Baranowicze in North Eastern Poland (at present incorporated into the White Russian Soviet Republic) and who are now in the Bialystok province, near Warsaw, managed to survive, thanks to the protection of a Pole, who employed them in an ammunition works where he held a managerial position.

Gypsies from Wolyn, bearing the surname Wais, took to the forest in 1943, where they found protection among the Russian guerillas and thus escaped the German and Ukrainian massacres. Later they moved on to the Western part of Poland, where they are now wandering from town to town as a band of musicians. They are the last surviving group of Polish Gypsy virtuosi who play

-167-

the harp and cymbalom. Nearly three hundred years ago their forefather was a harpist at the court of Queen Marysienka, the wife of the Polish King Jan III Sobieski (1674-1696).

The Warsaw Gypsies lived during the occupation in the suburbs of Warsaw or in villages near the capital. The fact that some of them managed to escape is to a certain extent due to German carelessness and lack of consistency in their extermination action against the Gypsies. Gypsies used to be rounded up at random on the streets of Warsaw, or district, and placed within the walls of the Jewish Ghetto. There were numerous cases of Gypsies escaping at night by climbing the walls of the Ghetto, but those who were recaptured were usually sent to the Jewish prison. From the Warsaw Ghetto the Gypsies were dispatched to the death camp of Treblinka together with wagon-loads of Jews. In 1942 a group of Gypsies locked up in the Jewish prison in Warsaw mutinied and, after disabling the guards, managed to get away. Some Gypsies escaped the Germans, although they were living all the time in the suburbs of Warsaw without hiding.

In the Lublin province many Gypsies escaped death by joining the guerillas in the forests. There were also cases of individual rescues, thanks to the protection given to them by Poles--as, for example, in the case of a beautiful young Gypsy, in Milosna, near Warsaw. Her long black hair was cut short, bleached and waved. She was the only survivor of her entire family.

Immediately after the cessation of hostilities the Gypsies who survived in the German camps began to return. Emaciated figures from Buchenwald, 'Dora' and Ravensbruck, they wandered back to Poland by various routes. On their arms they bore tattooed marks, usually a number and the letter Z (Ziguener 'Gypsy'). Those who could not trace their families joined other Gypsies. Orphans were adopted by surviving families. Gypsies also returned from the regions now included in the Soviet Union, but a small number of them from the former province of Polesie, who managed to survive, remained there.

One might have thought that the six years of dreadful annihilation, of living in a state of continuous horror, would have left a stigma, an indelible mark on the minds of these Gypsies. After the loss of their beloved, after their bitter experiences, the Roma might have changed and become even more distrustful and cautious. It would only be natural if their women gave up wearing the broad pleated skirts or colourful blouses which make them so easily recognizable. One might have expected that as a result of these tragic years Gypsies would break down spiritually and draw practical conclusions from the tortures experienced.

None of this, however, has eventuated. With the exception of two songs from Auschwitz, sung very rarely, I have not noticed any trace of the war years in the present life of the Polish Gypsies. They rarely mention their martyrdom and do not like to dwell on that subject. Their cheerfulness has not abated. They seem to have completely dismissed from their minds the period of the war years. Their way of life has not changed at all. The ovens of the extermination camps have been forgotten. Their fertility is very great and the natural increase of population very high. The vitality of the Gypsies has conquered death. When one sees how little the poisonous memories of the recent years have affected the surviving Gypsies, one might think that Auschwitz, Treblinka, Belzec and Chelmno never existed.

According to not very accurate and rather hypothetical calculations, there were in pre-war Poland about 18,000 to 20,000 Gypsies; now only about 5,000-6,000 remain. In 1946 the 'President' of the Gypsies, Rudolf Kweik, made a kind of census of the Gypsy population in Poland, from which it appeared that about 4,500 Gypsies were then living there. This figure is probably underestimated, since by no means all the Gypsies attended this meeting. Somewhat earlier that year 'elections' were held at Bydgoszcz of a King of the Polish Gypsies and Rudolf Kweik was elected.

From the year 1946 Rudolf Kweik lived in Warsaw, where he worked as a coppersmith. In 1949 he moved to Swider, near Warsaw, where he still resides. He is a member of the Kwiek dynasty from which, after the first World War, descended the Kings of the Polish Gypsies, whose signet is a crow holding a ring in its beak. The following Kweiks 'reigned' successively: Michael I, Rudolf, Basil, Michael II, Matthew and the present 'President' Rudolf. The Kweiks came to Poland from Rumania fairly recently, and for this reason are considered by the Roma who have lived in Poland for centuries as not Polish but Rumanian Gypsies.

Although in private life Kwiek calls himself
'King' officially he relinquished that title and declared himself 'President' of the Gypsies of all Europe
(sic!) and also Chairman of the World Council of the
Gypsies. He procured for himself a round seal with the
inscription 'World Council of the Gypsies--Chairman'
(with an orthographical error!). I am not sure what
the activity of that 'World Council' is. The only
information I have was obtained from Rudolk Kwiek
himself, and this, of course, should not be accepted at
its face value. It must, however, contain some grain
of truth since I saw an arms licence issued to Rudolf
Kwiek by the Regional Office of Public Security which,
under the heading 'occupation,' states that he is
Chairman of the World Council of the Gypsies. Kwiek is
reluctant to give any explanations on this subject. He
maintains that meetings and conferences of the Gypsies'
World Council are being held under his chairmanship in
Katowice, Poland. He claims to be constantly in touch
with his 'subjects,' the Gypsies of Hungary, Rumania,
Czechoslovakia, France, and Portugal. He says that
they write to him and that the leaders of the Gypsies
from many countries visit him and pay homage, as to
their head. How much of this is true and how much imagination is difficult to estimate. Polish Gypsies whom
I interviewed about this World Council were not able to
tell me anything about it, and maintained that they
knew nothing about the existence of such an organization.

Later, in 1946 a Russo-Rumanian Gypsy, Mikhail
Wassilij, arrived from Moscow with a group of about a
hundred Gypsies and took up residence at the small town
of Wawer, near Warsaw. He claims to be the Chief of
all Polish Gypsies. Of course, neither Kweik, 'elected' by other Gypsies, nor the impostor Wassilij, are
acknowledged by the Polish Gypsies, who speak of them
most antipathetically. The numerous abuses of the
Kwieks against their subjects, their method of collecting taxes, etc., brought about an unpopularity and a
lack of sympathy for these "monarchs" which dates from
the First World War.

The group of 'Moldavian' Gypsies, as the Gypsies
who arrived from Soviet Russia, and who live now at
Wawer, call themselves, is making a living as traders
and organizers of concerts of songs and dances. None
of their women tell fortunes, and they are offended
when asked to do this. If any of his Gypsies is
arrested for any offence their leader, Mikhail

Wassilij, intervenes personally, often successfully, arriving at the Police Station in his own car. He takes good care of his own Gypsies, but is ill-disposed towards the Polish ones. No wonder that the latter do not like this Xaladitko Rom. Personal antagonisms between Gypsies is a very common phenomenon.

Polish Gypsies have various ways of classifying their fellow tribesmen residing in Poland. Two principal groups are distinguished according to their mode of life, as the Foritka Roma, the town Gypsies, and the Vesitka Roma, the forest Gypsies. To the first group belong many of the Warsaw Gypsies who, though vagrant in the summer, usually camp near Warsaw or other large towns, or their suburbs, in the winter.

Others classify the Gypsies according to their descent, but this grouping is more subject to individual views. For instance, some Gypsies who consider themselves as Polish are called by others, who have lived in Poland many more years, Russian or Rumanian. Sasitka Roma is the name given to German Gypsies (or those of German origin). Xaladitka Roma are Russian Gypsies (or those of Russian stock). Polska Roma are Polish Gypsies. Among the latter there is also a distinct group called Raikanitka Roma, the name given to the Gypsy aristocracy (literally meaning Gypsy gentlemen). Apart from these classifications there are many smaller divisions defining more accurately the place of abode of a particular group. There exists some kind of antagonism between these different groups of Gypsies which, however, is overruled by a supreme tribal solidarity.

Almost all the surviving groups of Gypsies, who, before and during the War, lived in the Eastern part of Poland, which now belongs to Soviet Russia, have either completely or partially moved into the present borders of Poland. I say almost all, since, for instance, Gypsies of the marshy province of Polesie, the so-called Mukans, mostly blacksmiths and coppersmiths, who usually travel in boats over the extensive waters of that province and are held in contempt by other Polish Gypsies, have remained beyond the borders of Poland. I think that in the course of time the dialectical differences between the Polish Gypsies will disappear and change, since, although individual groups at present keep to their own form of speech, the constant change of abode and contact with other Gypsies cannot remain without influence.

Whilst the Gypsy "Kings" in Poland were never popular with their subjects, the spiritual leader of the Polish Gypsies is regarded with great respect and reverence. He is the judge of the Gypsies, who passes judgment in matters of custom and religion. The official title of the Gypsy spiritual leader is <u>Baro Sero</u>: Great Head. The present <u>Baro Sero</u>, a white-haired man of about eighty, is named <u>Zoga</u>. He survived the War in one of the suburbs of Warsaw, Sluzewiec, together with a related group of Warsaw Gypsies, who fortunately escaped annihilation. In 1948 <u>Baro Sero</u> was staying at Legnica (Silesia) and at present he is at Koszalin (German: Koslin), a town in the Western part of Pomerania. His authority (somewhat analogous to the authority of the Jewish rabbis) is granted to him under elections which take place at Gypsy Congresses.

Many Polish Gypsies, though not all of them, acknowledge the wisdom and authority of the Great Head and call on him to give judgment in difficult cases arising from offences against the unwritten law of <u>mageripen</u>. Sometimes local elders pronounce certain Gypsies to be <u>magerdo</u> (defiled), without referring to the <u>Baro Sero</u>. In more serious cases they have recourse to Zoga. An external expression of the great respect for their spiritual leader is the habit of kissing the hand of <u>Baro Sero</u> when greeting him or taking leave of him.

There exists a certain analogy between the <u>Mageripen</u> code and the Jewish law of "Kosher," but the Gypsy law is even more rigorous and contains more restrictive taboos. Thus, for instance, it is prohibited to have any contact with an "unclean" woman, i.e., during child-birth or during the two weeks after; to strike a Gypsy with anything made of iron; to allow the hem of a skirt to touch a dish containing food (which would render the food <u>magerdo</u> "unclean"), or for a woman to strike a man with her slipper (which would make the man <u>magerdo</u> "defiled"). All such breaches of the rules of ceremonial purity are offences against the <u>Mageripen</u> code and must be judged by a special Gypsy court or tribunal. The penalty most frequently inflicted for that kind of offence consists in the temporary exclusion of the guilty person from the family communion: he must eat his meals alone, from a separate dish, while the rest of the family have their meals together, eating from a large common bowl. The <u>Baro Sero</u>, however, is entitled to abrogate the punishment of the

penitent outcast. Passing judgment in questions concerning property and debtors is probably also included
in the functions of the Polish Baro Sero, as with the
"Chiefs" of Rumanian and other Gypsy tribes.

It seems to me that the excessive suspiciousness
and distrust of the Polish Gypsies in relation to
non-Gypsies (gadzie) has increased after the last War,
as a result of their experiences. When a Gypsy woman
from Warsaw found out that I was writing a book about
the martyrdom of the Gypsies during the 1939-45 years,
I completely lost her confidence previously gained with
great difficulty. Looking at me with mistrust she said
uneasily: "Kon isi mulo, ius na dzidzol...Soske tu
lester dre gazeta chines?" (Who is dead does not live
any more...Why do you write about him in the papers?)

The largest concentrations of Gypsies in Poland
are in Lower Silesia, in the neighbourhood of Wroclaw,
in Lodz, and district, near Warsaw, Lomza, Lublin and
in Podkarpacie. In summer the Vesitka Roma wander
about the country and even cross the borders of Poland
for a time. Thus, for instance, the above-mentioned
family, Wais, was in 1948 at Frankfurt, whence they
returned to the neighbourhood of Wroclaw. A small
group of Polish Gypsies from the neighbourhood of
Boryslaw (Poland before the War, at present in the
U.S.S.R.) arrived in Poland in May 1949, staying for a
few days in Warsaw.

At present the number of Gypsy coppersmiths in
Poland is relatively small. Most of the surviving
Gypsies are musicians and fortune-tellers; among the
latter are women who indisputably have some physical
abilities, since drap te del 'to tell the future,'
'bewitching,' 'deceiving,' 'cheating,' is one of their
amazing gifts. I know of cases of Gypsy women who
managed in some unexplained way to coax considerable
amounts of money, gold, jewellery, etc., from 'be-
witched' persons who gave it without opposition. I
know that before the War there existed secret Gypsy
schools of magic (analogous to schools of theft). One
of these schools was at Lubcz on the river Niemen, near
Nowogrodek (at present U.S.S.R.). Old Gypsy women used
to teach the young ones, who arrived there for instruction from many places. Usually, however, the arts of
magic were handed down by mothers to their daughters.
There are two definite groups of magic: magic for tribal use, inherent in the beliefs of the Gypsies, and
another kind akin to trickery, the purpose of which is

to cheat the stupid 'non-Gypsy,' in which the Gypsies themselves do not believe, but consider it as a way of increasing their living or of making money.

Petty delinquency among the Gypsies is very rife, particularly among the women. The authorities have not yet begun any cultural activity among them (almost 100 per cent of the Gypsies are illiterate) nor have they as yet, as in England, initiated any plans for turning the Gypsies to productive jobs. The Gypsy problem in Poland is still neglected, but it is to be hoped that, in connection with the general action to combat illiteracy, some experiments, based on the experience of Soviet Russia, will be made in the not too distant future. It is quite possible that the Gypsy leader Mikhail Wassilij may, together with his subordinates, take an active part in such activities. So far nothing has been done in this social sphere.

Two Gypsy Songs from Oswiecim (Auschwitz)

The songs, the text of which is given below, were recorded from Gypsies in the concentration camp at Auschwitz, in the part of the camp known as Birkenau (Brzezinka). They were sung for me by a young Gypsy man and a Gypsy girl from Warsaw, who had not been in Auschwitz themselves.

The first song, 'Dri Osviecim' was sung for me by Stacho, a seventeen-year-old Warsaw Gypsy, in August 1948, in a camp consisting of five tents which his family pitched in Szczesliwice, near Warsaw. He learnt it from his aunt who was in Auschwitz and who survived, thanks to a transfer to Ravensbruck. I do not know this old Gypsy woman and I cannot ascertain whether the version which I heard from her nephew was adulterated or changed at a later stage. Stacho's aunt told him that, during the roll-calls at the Auschwitz camp, the Germans did not allow the Gypsies to talk to one another, but they allowed them to sing. Therefore the Gypsies communicated with each other by means of songs improvised on the spot. In this way--according to the not too reliable report of Stacho--there came into existence numerous songs and among them 'Dri Osveicim'.

The second song was sung for me in September 1948 by a Warsaw Gypsy girl in the Ujazdowski Park of Warsaw. Her name is Seweryna Majewska and her family call her Phabui (apple). She is eighteen years old and, in contrast to Stacho, who has light eyes and not very dark hair, she is much more of the Gypsy type, with her dark eyes and black hair and swarthy complexion. She, too, was not in Auschwitz herself and she could not name the source of this song. I suppose that the song (Ai Romale, Romale) is much longer and that what Phabui sung was only a fraction of it.

Dri Osviecim

Dri Oswiecim	At Auschwitz
Kher si baro	There is a large house,
Te iov menge	Which is there for us only
Bibaxtalo:	To bring misfortune:
Okec, Okec!	Heigh ho!
Dri Oswiecim	In Auschwitz
Isi mandir	I have
Cirikloro,	A bird
Te ligires	To carry
Do liloro	A letter
Ki mre dai,	To my mother
Ki mro dadoro.	To my daddy.
Nuno mange	I feel sick
Pharo mange.	(And) heavy-hearted.
Andre Ausfic	At Auschwitz
Kher si baro.	There is a large house.
Devel dela	May God grant
Kai wydzava!	That I escape from there!
I mre dasa	And with my mother
Me dikhava:	Meet again:
Mre semenca	With my family
Na obdikhav.	(Whom) I do not see.
Mre semencasa	With my family
Bravinta piava.	I will drink vodka.
Andre Oswiecim	At Auschwitz
To one men maren,	They beat us up,
One menge	They to us (bring)
Bibaxtale.	Misfortune.

Ai Romale, Romale! - (fragment only)

Ai, Romale, Romale!	Oh! Gypsies! Gypsies!
Ke buti men traden;	To work they drive us;
Te xal maro na den,	They do not give us bread to eat,
A ke buti traden.	And to work they drive us.
So Devel dela	May God grant
So Saso n'avela!	That the German will cease to be!
So do Saso n'avela,	When the German be no longer here,
Fededir menge vela.	It will be better for us.
So Saso iavela	Should the German be there
Gosedir menge vela...	It will be worse...

Anthem of the World Romani Congress

Composed by Jarko Jovanovic to a traditional melody

Opre Roma

Gelem, gelem, lungone dromensa
Maladilem baktale Romensa
A Romale katar tumen aven
E tsarensa baktale dromensa
A Romale, a chavale

Vi man sas vari familija
Mudardas la e kali legija
Aven mansa sa lumniake Roma
Kai putaile e Romane droma
Ake viama, ushti Rom akana
Amen hutasa mishto kai akana
A Romale, a chavale

Rom Arise

I've travelled, travelled long roads
And stopped with happy Rom
Romanies, from where have you come
With tents set on fortune's road
Romanies, o fellow Rom

Once I had a great family
The Black Legion murdered them
Now come, all the world's Rom
For the Romani road has opened
The time's arrived to arise
We shall stand up as one
Romanies, o fellow Rom

Romani Population in Europe 1970

Based on available census figures and previous estimates, and including in some cases associated nomadic
groups:

Jugoslavia	650,000
Romania	540,000
Spain	500,000
Hungary	480,000
U.S.S.R.	414,000
Bulgaria	363,000
Czechoslovakia	300,000
France	190,000
Italy	80,000
West Germany	70,000
Poland	52,000
Albania	50,000
Britain	50,000
Greece	45,000
Portugal	40,000
Netherlands	30,000
Belguim	14,000
Ireland	10,000
Switzerland	10,000
Austria	9,000
Sweden	8,000
Finland	6,000
Norway	4,000
Denmark	3,000
TOTAL:	3,198,000

"MASTERING THE PAST": GERMANS AND GYPSIES

Gabrielle Tyrnauer

In the vast body of Holocaust literature, the story of the Gypsy extermination has become an almost forgotten footnote to the history of Nazi genocide. Under Hitler's rule, approximately half a million European Gypsies were systematically slaughtered. Yet there was no Gypsy witness at the Nurenberg trials and no one was accused of the crime. Neither the scholars who provided the data, nor the officials who formulated the "final solution to the Gypsy problem," nor the bureaucrats and military men who executed it were ever called to account. The Gypsies became the forgotten victims of the Holocaust.

But all this is changing in the Federal Republic of Germany. Thirty-four years after the end of World War II, the victims have at last broken their long silence. In a dramatic reversal, German ministers of state were summoned to the former death camps for negotiations with one-time inmates and their children. A Gypsy civil rights movement had sprung, phoenix-like, out of the ashes of the Holocaust to demand an accounting for the past and to call attention to continued discrimination against Gypsies in Germany. A new chapter in the historic process of Vergangenheits-bewaltigung (mastery of the past) is under way.

The Legacy of Persecution

Centuries of prejudice and persecution in Germany and elsewhere prepared the ground in which the seeds of genocide were planted. Since the Gypsies' first appearance in Europe in the early 14th century, they were regarded with a blend of fear and fascination by the sedentary peoples among whom they moved. Their language and their appearance were strange. They were not farmers or laborers, their women told fortunes and they all seemed to have a special relationship with the supernatural. They were treated as vagrants, criminals and spies by the secular powers, often as witches, heretics, and pagans by the Church, even when they were nominally Catholic. A 16th century Bishop's edict in Sweden, for example, forbade the priests to administer the sacraments to the Gypsies.[1]

Gypsies were imprisoned, expelled and enslaved by the princes through whose territories they passed. There were also some early attempts to forcibly settle them. The best known of these was that of the 18th century Austro-Hungarian empress, Maria Theresia, who wanted them to become God-fearing peasants and proceeded to forbid them nomadism, the use of their language and most of their traditional occupations. They were given land and called "New Hungarians," while their children were taken away from them to be raised by more "civilized" foster parents.[2]

At the same time, Gypsies became an important part of the European cultural scene. Individual dancers, musicians and circus performers acquired legendary reputations among the gaje or non-Gypsies. With the advent of the Romantic movement, their unfettered life style became attractive to a restless young generation. There were elements of envy as well as contempt in the composite stereotype. It led to a curious ambivalence in the attitudes of the settled peoples towards the colorful nomads in their midst.[3]

It was in the Nazi concentration camps that this ambivalence assumed its most bizarre forms. The Commandant of Auschwitz, Rudolf Hoss, expressed his fondness for the Gypsies in his charge. They were his "best-loved prisoners," "trusting as children." He ordered special rations of salami for them en route to the gas chambers and built a playground for their children a month before their final liquidation.[4] Dr. Mengele never failed to bring the Gypsy children candy before taking them from their parents to perform his deadly experiments. SS officers organized Gypsy orchestras in Auschwitz and other concentration camps.[5] Academic researchers whose work provides the foundation for the system, immersed themselves, like good anthropologists, in the language and culture of the people they helped to destroy.

The real Zigeunerfrage (Gypsy Question) was only formulated, according to one German historian, about the time of German unification in the late 19th century. Since then, successive German governments have worked diligently at its solution. Under the monarchy, data collection on the Gypsies began, first with the establishment in 1899 of a "Gypsy Information Service" (Zigeunernachrichtendienst). In 1905 the government of Bavaria started a "Gypsy Book" (Zigeunerbuch) in which acts and edicts related to Gypsies in the years 1816-

1903 are compiled as guidelines for the continuing battle against the "Gypsy Plague" (Zigeunerplage). Matters did not improve for Gypsies under the Weimar Republic, when a variety of legislation aimed at "Zigeuner, Landfahrer und Arbeitsscheue" (Gypsies, Travellers, and Malingerers) was passed. In 1926, a "Gypsy Conference" was held in Munich to bring some uniformity to the legislation of the different provinces (Lander). In fact, laws against Gypsies were so harsh during this period, that the Nazis continued to use them for their own purposes.[6]

The Third Reich and the "Final Solution"

While the Weimar laws sufficed for the first few years of National Socialist rule, soon new legislation, consistent with Nazi racial ideology, was sought. At the Party's 1935 convention in Nurnberg, the new racial laws were announced. These made Gypsies as well as Jews "artfremd", "alien to the German species." It followed that both could be deprived of their German citizenship.

There began a period of unprecedented government support for research intended to provide the "scientific" underpinnings for future policy. The Rassenhygienische und Bevolkerungsbiologische Forschungsstelle was founded in 1936 as a part of the Ministry of Health. By 1942, Dr. Robert Ritter had collected over 30,000 geneologies by means of which he classified almost all the Gypsies of the Reich as either of "pure" or "mixed" race. He designated the "mixed race" Gypsies as "asozial" and recommended their sterilization, as did his student, Eva Justin. For those of "pure blood" who--to the embarrassment of Nazi ideology --were closer to the "Aryans" than any other people of Europe, these two scholars recommended a kind of "reservation."[7]

By 1942, Gypsies had been removed from the "normal" criminal procedures and delivered wholly to the jurisdiction of Himmler's SS. The distinctions among them were abandoned as orders were issued for mass deportation to the concentration camps of the "eastern territories." According to a record book hidden by an inmate of the Gypsy camp in Auschwitz, 20,967 Gypsies from all over Europe were transported to the Nazis' most notorious death factory. The first contingents arrived in several cattle cars attached to Jewish transports in February, 1943.[8] A year and a half later, about 4,000 remained and these were, on Himmler's orders, exterminated in a single night. Commandant Hoss describes the matter routinely in his prison autobiography:

> There remained until August, 1944 ca. 4,000 Gypsies, who must still go to the gas chambers. Up to this time they did not know what awaited them. They only noticed it when they were taken barrack by barrack to Crematorium V. It was not easy to get them into the gas chambers.[9]

The next morning, there were no Gypsies left in Auschwitz.

The Past Becomes Present

On October 27, 1979 a group of Germman Gypsies, or Sinti, as they call themselves, gathered at the former concentration camp of Bergen Belsen to honor their Holocaust victims and call attention to the continuing discrimination against them in the Federal Republic. The event was organized by three groups: the Verband Deutscher Sinti (Federation of German Sinti), a national organization, the Romani Union, an international organization recognized by the United Nations in 1979, and a non-Gypsy support group, Die Gesellschaft fur Bedrohte Volker (The Society for Threatened Peoples). Roma (as the Gypsies are now known internationally) representatives from France, England, Switzerland, the Scandinavian countries, Belgium and the Netherlands, Yugoslavia, Greece and Italy were there. For the first time German government officials paid homage to the other victims of the "Final Solution." The guest of honor was the president of the Council of Europe, Simone Veil, herself a survivor of Bergen-Belsen, who declared her personal solidarity as well as the support of the Council of Europe.[11] The wreath was laid by the charismatic young Sinti Romani Rose, who has taken over the leadership of the Verband Deutscher Sinti from his uncle, Vinzenz Rose. Thirteen members of Rose's immediate family died in the concentration camps of Hitler's Germany.

The next and still more powerful expression of the Sinti's rendezvous with history was a hunger strike at Dachau--the first concentration camp--on April 4, 1980.

In the presence of more than 100 German and foreign journalists and several television crews, fourteen hunger-strikers including one German social worker (the only non-Sinti) began their fast on Good Friday, following an ecumenical service in the chapel. Their objectives included official recognition of the Nazi crimes against the Roma and Sinti, appropriate restitutions,[12] an end to legal discrimination and police harassment, and the establishment of a Sinti cultural center at Dachau. The strike continued for eight days until satisfactory negotiations were initiated with government officials. Members of all three major political parties represented in the Bundestag and representatives of church groups also took part in the negotiations. While Rose proclaimed a "victory" for the Sinti, in fact their demands were met more with supportive rhetoric than real concessions. The city of Dachau vigorously opposed the establishment of the cultural center, expressing the fear that the "unjust" prejudices against the Sinti would be transferred to the city of Dachau if such an institution existed, adding to the burden it already carries through its past association with the concentration camp.[13]

Between these two powerfully symbolic events, Sinti, or as they are still more widely known, Zigeuner (Gypsies), burst into the German consciousness with the force of a 35-year time bomb. Within the next year, there was an unprecedented media boom and half a dozen German universities were conducting research on some aspect of past and present Sinti problems.[14] An event which really triggered the explosion, according to many German observers, was the telecasting of the American TV dramatization entitled "Holocaust." For a generation, particularly which had little or no knowledge from home or schools of the Nazi period, it became a powerful catalyst to questioning and probing of what remains little more than a common cliche "die unbewaltigte Vergangenheit," the "unmastered" past. It was estimated by newspaper surveys that 48% of the German population over the age of fourteen saw it. Although it contained only fleeting references to the fate of Gypsies, it created an atmosphere in which the Nazi past in all its facets could be reexamined by a new generation. For many Sinti it meant "coming out of the closet" to publicly acknowledge their ethnic identity, past persecution, and hopes for the future. Many could for the first time share their remembered sufferings and individual terrors with members of their own community and outsiders.

In the course of the next two years in almost every city with a concentration of Sinti, an organization came to life. The largest of these are The Verband Deutscher Sinti and The Sinti Union. In Hamburg there is a unique association of Sinti and Roma, the Gypsies from eastern Europe who play a prominent role in the international organization. Many of the Roma have only recently come to Germany with the waves of immigrant workers or "Gastarbeiter." They are culturally and linguistically distinct from the Sinti who have been mostly sedentary and partly assimilated to German culture for centuries. The Sinti attitude towards the Roma ranges from indifference to outright hostility, particularly when their sporadic encounters with the police carry over in the popular mind to Sinti.[15]   So a joint association, like that in Hamburg, is unusual.

The best known product of this association is the "Duo-Z," two young Gypsy musicians, who have developed a repertoire of bitter satirical songs and a national reputation.[16] The duo was among the hunger strikers at Dachau for the first few days, but it was generally decided that their media work was of greater importance to the movement and that their concerts should not be cancelled.

Several Gypsy jazz groups in the tradition of the late Django Reinhardt have been popular for years and are increasingly becoming openly engaged in the Sinti, as well as the international Roma, movement.[17] They are much in demand at universities, festivals, and concerts throughout Germany. They can reach a wider audience than can the political leaders, and on a number of musical occasions during the past two years have effectively carried the political message.[18]

The Underlying Factors

The rediscovery of the Holocaust is a historic event for both Germans and Gypsies, which has been made possible by the conjunction of a number of factors. Some of the most important of them are as follows:

1. A post-war generation of Sinti who have grown up in an increasingly, though unintentionally, pluralistic society as waves of foreign workers transformed Germany during the past two decades into an immigrant society.[19]   Better educated and more militant than

their elders, they are no longer content to choose between assimilation and dissimilation but are proclaiming
their ethnic identities and persuading many of their
elders to follow suit. These elders, as Romani Rose
remarked in explaining his own leadership position, are
often broken in spirit as well as in body from their
experiences in the Third Reich. "We cannot expect them
to carry the burden."[20]

In addition to the social milieu in which the
post-war Sinti have grown up, there is a psychological
dimension, which has recently acquired a name in the
studies of the second generation Jewish Holocaust
survivors. Dr. William B. Niederland, a psychiatrist,
claims to have coined the term "survivors' syndrome"
after extensive study of Holocaust survivors. The survivors live constantly with their memories and their
fears which are conveyed to their children, who in
reaction often exhibit strong tendencies to seek positive action or resistance to compensate for their
parents' passivity.[21]

2. Continuing popular prejudice and official
discrimination, recently accentuated by the ever-
increasing number of immigrants and an economic recess-
ion which often makes them competitors for scarce
resources. The discrimination, of course, reinforces
the Sinti consciousness of minority status and minority
rights. This has deepened their historical consciousness (which is conspicuously absent in the culture of
most Gypsy groups in other countries) so that they
quickly relate present discrimination to past persecution climaxing in the Holocaust. It also makes them
more sensitive than most members of the population
(with the exception of Jews) to any stirrings of neo--
Nazism. Reactions have ranged from street demon-
strations against SS reunions,[22] civil disobedience
against exclusion from camping places[23] to the dramatic
hunger-strike at Dachau which demanded remembrance of
the past, just restitution for its victims and the
dismantling institutions, such as special police offices for "Travellers," as well as destruction of data
collected by Nazi officials and researchers. They
maintain (and their claims can be substantiated), that
the new wave of xenophobia has led to stricter enforcement of existing laws applying to foreigners, especially to "migrants" or "travellers." Some of these laws
dating back to the Nazi period or still earlier, were
largely ignored (though in many cases, never abolished)
in the post-war years. Also, deadlines and legal tech-

nicalities related to applications for restitution (Wiedergutmachung) and citizenship have been enforced more rigidly, so that there are cases of Sinti whose grandparents were German citizens but who must themselves carry a foreigner's identification (Fremdenpass), with restrictions on work and residence.[24] This has led to increasing resentment and fears that "the Nazis are coming back" or, in some cases, never left. One dramatic instance of this is the case of an Auschwitz survivor who drove into a camping place with his trailer and family. When the local official in charge saw the concentration camp number still tatooed on his arm, he said to him, "This place is not for you."[25] Another, even more shocking incident was that of a woman, also an Auschwitz survivor who was sterilized under Nazi law and when she applied for restitution in the city which had always been her home, found herself, at the required physical examination, face-to-face with the physician who had performed the sterilization operation.[26] The Sinti's new eagerness to speak publicly about the Nazi past and their experiences in it grow out of their escalating fears of its repetition, perhaps in altered form.[27]

3. The support of key non-Gypsy groups has been an important factor in the whole difficult process--particularly so for a people still largely illiterate and powerless--of remembering the past and organizing for the future. These groups can be divided into religious organizations, ad hoc citizens' groups, social workers and secular leftists groups some of which have grown out of the student movement of the late 1960s. There have also been committed unaffiliated individuals in the press and at various universities, some of whom have come together for more effective action. These groups have given moral, financial, and technical support. They have sponsored and helped to organize congresses and issued publications, in almost all of which the Holocaust figures as the central historical experience of Gypsies in Germany.[28]

4. The existence of an international Gypsy organization known as the Romani Union and admitted to membership of the Economic and Social Council of the United Nations as a non-Governmental organization. The fact that the most recent Congress (the third since the organization's founding in 1971) was held on German soil (in Gottingen, May, 1981) and that Romani Rose, the German Sinti leader, was elected vice-president of the organization suggests the importance of this international connection for German Sinti.

5. Continuing war crimes trials and the controversy over the statute of limitations. The five and a half year Maidanek trial, in which one of the defendants was a naturalized American citizen (the only one sentenced to life imprisonment) who was extradited for the trial, was to recent German history what the Eichmann and the Auschwitz trials were to the generation coming to maturity in the early and middle sixties. It was well covered by the German media and remained a constant reminder that the past was not yet "mastered." While it created guilt feelings in some young people who had no personal experience of that past, it raised a wall of anger and hostility in many of the older people who wanted to hear no more about it. In either case, it kep the past in the foreground of the news.

6. A similar polarized effect resulted from the showing on German television of the American Holocaust dramatization, as mentioned previously. The videotape and the instructional materials which accompanied it were used extensively in the schools, sometimes by teachers who had not wanted or had not dared teach their pupils the history of the Third Reich. It also stimulated spontaneous and organized group discussions throughout Germany. The impact on the Sinti, who are avid television watchers, was powerful. Now, they felt, their story too could be told.

Conclusion

All these elements combined to create, in the late 1970s an awareness and a movement that had been gestating for more than three decades. The elders broke their long silence and spoke publicly about things that had only been whispered in the presence of close family members since the end of World War II. One elder Sinti whose entire family was murdered in Auschwitz, whose wife was sterilized by Dr. Mengele, while her family too was killed, makes a pilgrimage to Auschwitz annually, sometimes twice a year. When asked why, his wife replied simply, "Because my whole family is there. I go there to pray." Her husband has, during the past two years, lectured at clubs, schools and churches.

Thus, in the twilight of the twentieth century, a new generation of Germans and Gypsies are coming together to wrestle with their still "unmastered" past, trying to assure that the forgotten victims of the Holocaust will be remembered and that their children

can live as full and equal citizens of the Federal
Republic.

Footnotes

1. Donald Kenrick and Grattan Puxon, <u>Sinti und Roma,</u> <u>Die Vernichtung eines Volkes im NS-Staat.</u>, Gottingen: Die Gesellschaft fur Bedrohte Volker, 1981, p. 24. The first edition of this book was in English; <u>The Destiny of Europe's Gypsies</u>, London: Chatto-Heinemann-Sussex, 1972.

2. Ibid., pg. 45.

3. The traditional ambivalence springing from the conflict between the Romantic cult of individual freedom and the Protestant ethic of hard work and postponed gratification was reflected in much of the literature which appeared in Europe during the 19th century. A recent survey of such literature in relation to Gypsies was called "Burgerfluch und Burgersehnsucht: Zigeuner in Vorstellungsbild, the Imagination of the Literary Intelligentsia) in Hohmann, Schop and others, <u>Ziegeunerleben</u>, Darmstadt, 1979.

4. Jerzy Ficowski, "Die Vernichtung" in Tilch, op. cit., (pp. 91-112), p. 109.

5. Two particularly shocking stories among the many survivors' accounts of the SS staff's "music appreciation" are recounted by Kenrick and Streck. The first concerns the Auschwitz Gypsy Orchestra organized by SS Officer Broad. On the 25th of May, 1943 a concert was given for the SS. It was however, interrupted in the middle, the musicians sent back to the barracks while on special orders a thousand prisoners were gassed. (Donald Kenrick, "Das Schicksal der Zigeuner im NS-Staat" in Donald Kenrick Grattan Puxon, Tilman Zulch (eds.) <u>Die Zigeuner</u>, <u>Verkannt--Verachtet--Verfolgt</u> Hannover: Niedersachsischen Landeszentrale fur politische Bildung, 1980, pp. 37-74, pp. 68-69. The second story comes from a death camp in Bosnia, Jasenovac, and was first related by a Franciscan priest who served as chaplain in the German Wehrmacht. "Each 12 man Gypsy ensemble played one month, from the first day until the last. A month with 31 days was luck, a gift for the 12 Gypsies. One day more, 24 hours. They played until noon, they played in the evening and on the last day until morning... After dinner the

electric light was switched off and only candles were lit... now each of the 12 Gypsies prayed that the Kommandant would not become sleepy. When the Kommandant began to grow tired and the night began to glide away, he would point to one of the Gypsy musicians. He would have to lay down his instrument and would walk through the candlelit room to the door of the Casino where his escort already waited to take him into the forest. When the shot from the forest came--one could hear it even while the music played in the room--the next one prepared himself. But he continued to play until the Kommandant pointed to him. (Bernhard Streck, "Das Ende der Musik: Zigeuner hinterm Stacheldraht" in Georgia A. Raklemann, _Zigeuner_, Materialien fur Unterricht und Bildungsarbeit, Gesellschaft fur entwicklungspolitische Bildung: 1980). A grim photograph shows prisoners being led to the gallows accompanied by musicians. The prescribed song for the occasion was "All the little birds are here." (Ibid)

6. Bernhard Streck, "Die Bekampfung des Zigeunerwesens". Ein Stuck moderner Rechtsgeschichte in Tilman Zulch (ed.) _In Auschwitz Vergast, bis Heute Verfolgt_. Hamburg: Rowohlt Taschenbuch Verlag, 1979, pp. 64-87.

7. Alwin Meyer, "Holocaust der Zigeuner" in _Zeichen_ (Mitteilungen der Aktion Suhnezeichen/Friedensdienste), No. 3, Sept. 1979, p. 6.

8. Ibid.

9. Ibid.

10. Karl-Klaus Rabe, "Zigeunerische Personen sind Asozial" in _Zeichen_, no. 3, September 1979, p. 16.

11. Her speech is reproduced in a special publication documenting the occasion, _Sinti und Roma im ehemaligen KZ Bergen Belsen am 27. Oktober 1979_, Gottingen, 1981, pp. 49-57.

12. There has been a long history of controversy over the subject of "Wiedergutmachung" for European Gypsies who survived the Holocaust. In the postwar period, the continued fear of official persecution and the lack of required documentation resulted in a situation where few Gypsies exer-

cised their rights and official deadlines for applications passed. Many applications were rejected after a statement by the Minister of the Interior of Baden-Wurttenberg in 1950, circulated to judges who were concerned with such applications, reminding them that Gypsies were, in the early years of the war, not persecuted on "racial" grounds (which was the legal basis of Wiedergutmachung, but on the basis of an "asocial and criminal past" and a security threat. After 1959, when the first Wiedergutmachung law expired, and was renewed, the situation improved somewhat. Today individual Gypsies can receive DM 5 per day they spent in a concentration camp and some additional money for damage to health. Sterilization was not classified as such a damage. (Grattan Puxon, "Verschleppte Wiedergutmachung, in In Auschwitz Vergast, Bis Heute Verfolgt, pp. 149-157, Documents, ibid, pp. 168-171.

13. Dachauer Neueste Nachrichten, May 7, 1980.

14. Academics, for the most part, approached the subect with extreme caution because of the unhappy past involvement of German scholars with the "Gypsy Question." With the exception of an older scholar, Hermann Arnold, who has become the subject of a storm of controversy, most of the present "Tsiganologues" are young and politically committed and engaging in "action research."

15. A recent example of this was a well-reported incident involving a group of Roma alleged to have been involved in a large number of burglaries. The police rounded them up in their trailers and broadcast an appeal for witnesses. The Nurnberger Nachrichten reported that the police rounded up a "100 head Sinti clan" (July 1, 1981).

16. The name of the duo was chosen ironically. "Z"-- for "Zigeuner" was the symbol Gypsies had stamped on their papers by the Nazi officials. Their theme song is a grim parody of a traditional German folk-song called "Lustig ist das Zigeuner-lebel" (Merry is the Gypsy Life) which describes the Gypsies' life in Auschwitz and Buchenwald. The son of a Sinti leader in the Nurnberg area who wanted to perform it for a school festival was prohibited from singing it by his teacher, who explained that it was "too sharp."

17. The names are confusing and reflect the schisms normal among culturally diverse groups attempting to unite politically. Even in the framework of an international congress of the "Romani Union" the Sinti have insisted on retaining their name. The outgoing president of the Union, Czech emigree Dr. Jan Cibula, now living in Switzerland, urged all Gypsies to adopt the term "Rom" as a generic title. But the Sinti were not persuaded and all posters at the Congress in Gottingen (May, 1981) referred to "Roma and Sinti." Thus, today the term Roma may designate either a particular ethnic group of mainly Balkan Gypsies or, as used by Romani nationalists, it may refer to all Gypsies.

18. Hans'che Weiss, for example, one of the best known of the Gypsy jazz musicians, has popularized a Romanes song entitled "Let us demand our Rights." The program notes for a Gypsy music festival in Darmstadt in 1979, were in fact, essays on the past genocide and present persecution of the Gypsy people written by some of the politically engaged young "Tsiganologues" from Giessen University.

19. Friedrich Heckmann, "Socio-Structural Analysis of Immigrant Worker Minorities: the Case of West Germany," Mid-American Review of Sociology, 1980, vol. V, no. 2: 13-20.

20. Interview, May 29, 1981.

21. "Das Uberlebendensyndrom der Opfer und ihre Kinder," Zeichen, 3, p. 14.

22. As an example of this might be cited the demonstration in Wurzburg on September 18, 1976 a meeting of former SS men, which escalated into a fight resulting in some minor injuries and prosecution of seven demonstrators, six of whom were Gypsies.

23. Inge Britt, "Zigeunern ist die Benutzung des Campingplatzes untersagt," Zeichen, 3, pp. 18-20.

24. The Nazis stripped Gypsies, like Jews, of their German citizenship. Some Sinti even served in the armed forces until the order came in 1942 that all Gypsies must be sent to Auschwitz. (e.g. Julius Hodost, "Wir werden Euch vertilgen wie die Katzen" Zeichen, no. 3, p. 7). After the war, many of

these stateless Gypsies did not have the necessary documentation to regain their citizenship.

25. Personal communication, July 5, 1981 Erlangen Folk Festival.

26. Personal communication, May 29, Frankfurt.

27. This feared continuity under a changed name is illustrated by a recent cartoon which shows a police official speaking to his two subordinates who are rifling through mountains of disorderly fils. "Have you found something on 'Landfahrer' yet? he asks. "No," one of them replies, "Only on Zigeuner, Herr Minister."

28. Some of the most important of the religious groups are the Catholic Caritas, the Evangelischer (Lutheran) Aktion Suhnezeichen, Innere Mission, Diakonisches Werk, Jewish organizations such as the Berlin Jewish congregation, its leader, Heinz Galinski, and the well-known Jewish Nazi hunter Simon Wiesenthal; in the last 2 years, probably the most active group, the liberal secular Gesellschaft fur bedrohte Volker; der Verband der Verfolgten des Nazi regimes, individuals and groups close to the Social Democratic Party, journalists such as Anita Geigges and Bernard Wette, social workers associated with the Deutsche Verein fur offentliche und private Fursorge, etc. Information about the work of a few of these groups can be found in C. Freese, M. Murko, G. Wurzbacher, Hilfen fur Zigeuner und Landfahrer, Stuttgart. Kohlhammer, 1980.

IV. POST WORLD WAR II GENOCIDES

IV.   POST WORLD WAR II GENOCIDES

The period after World War II has seen at least
half-a-dozen genocides, most of them in isolated areas
of the globe, usually in Africa, Asia, or South America.   Often, like extinct animals, unknown tribes
vanish.   Only State Department specialists or stamp
collectors have even heard of some of these
nations--Rwanda, Burundi, Timor, and the Ache of
Paraguay.

Other genocides, like those in Tibet, Cambodia
(Kampuchea), and Bangladesh are more well known, but
still remain vague entities in the Western consciousness.

The tragic conclusion one draws from this litany
of death and cultural destruction is that little can be
done to stop it.   By the time the United Nations gets
around to even discussing the matter, the damage is
done.   In fact in only one case--Pakistan--has the U.N.
labeled and condemned an act as genocide. Nongovernmental groups like Clergy and Laity Concerned, the
International Commission of Jurists, and various
missionary and human rights organizations have investigated acts of genocide and have attempted to alert
the world with only minimal success.

Furthermore some will not even recognize these
instances as acts of genocide (for example, Timor and
Cambodia), thus making it even more difficult for the
United Nations Genocide Convention to intervene.

THE HUTU-TUTSI CONFLICT IN BURUNDI

Rene Lemarchand

There are few parallels to the human holocaust that took place in Burundi in 1972 in the wake of a tortuous competitive struggle between the country's two major ethnic groups, the Hutu and the Tutsi. Scarcely noticed (let alone understood) by public opinion anywhere, the killings are conservatively estimated to have caused between 80,000 and 100,000 deaths. Approximately 3.5 per cent of the country's total population (3.5 million) were physically wiped out in a period of a few weeks. In comparative terms this is as if England had suffered a loss of 2 million or the United States about 8 million people. To speak of "selective genocide" to describe the outcome of such large-scale political violence seems scarcely an exaggeration.

The Setting: The Country and Its People

Situated in the Central African rift valley, in the very heart of the continent, Burundi is roughly the size of Belgium (11,000 square miles). Along with Rwanda, its neighbor to the north, it has one of Africa's highest population densities (185 per square mile in 1955). The growing pressure of overpopulation on the land, together with the general scarcity of natural resources, lie at the root of the country's economic and social problems. What mineral resources exist, aside from small deposits of cassiterite, have yet to be exploited, and much of the economy consists of subsistence agriculture. With the recent discovery of substantial nickel deposits in the southeast the economic picture may change drastically in years ahead; so far, however, no concrete steps have been taken to tap this otherwise promising industrial potential. Coffee is the main cash crop, generating approximately 80 percent of the country's foreign exchange (the equivalent of about $14 million annually), to which must be added such marginal crops as tea, cotton, and rice. Agricultural output is as yet incapable of meeting the demands of Burundi's fast-growing population, let alone of yielding the surplus production required for rapid economic growth.

Economic scarcity is of course as much of a reality today as it was in precolonial and colonial times, when Burundi was just one of several traditional kingdoms spread through the interlake zone. Today, however, perceptions of economic scarcity are increasingly filtered through the prism of regionalism and ethnicity, thus adding a radically different dimension to the political environment. To appreciate the significance of this transformation, at least passing reference must be made to Burundi's traditional system of social stratification, one of the most complex and least understood in the whole of Africa.

The standard image of Burundi society conveyed by much of the colonial literature is that of an ethnic pyramid in which the cattle-herding Tutsi, representing 14 percent of the population, held the commanding heights of power and influence; next in rank came the Hutu agriculturalists, forming the bulk of the population (85 percent); at the bottom of the heap stood the pygmoid Twa, a group of relatively little significance numerically (1 percent) and otherwise. Presumably reinforcing this hierarchy of rank and privilege were the physical characteristics commonly attributed to each group: Proverbially tall and wiry, the Tutsi have been said to "possess the same graceful indolence in gait which is peculiar to Oriental people;" the Hutu, on the other hand, were seen as "a medium-sized type of people, whose ungainly figures betoken hard toil, and who patiently bow themselves in abject bondage to the later arrived yet ruling race, the Tutsi."

However satisfying to most European observers, such simplicities can only convey a highly distorted view of Burundi's traditional social system. Not only do they conceal the existence of major differences within each group, but they also tend to exaggerate the depth of cultural discontinuities among them. These distortions are closely connected. Neglect of intra-ethnic cleavages is liable to obscure the basis for cross-ethnic links among each group at the same time that it reduces their respective physical and cultural characteristics to a parody of reality.

Attention must be drawn, first, to the existence of two separate categories of Tutsi--the lower-caste Tutsi-Hima group, and the higher caste Tutsi-Banyaruguru, literally, "those who came from the north." Note, however, that the term ruguru has other connotations, meaning "from above," and hence from regions of high altitude or, figuratively, from high-ranking status, that is, "close to the Court." Outside obser-

vers have unduly emphasized the geographical derivation
of the term, to the point of equating all Banyaruguru
with northern Tutsi, which is far from being the case;
the Banyaruguru are found in both northern and southern
provinces, and this is also true of the Hima. The
governor of the Ruyigi province is a defrocked Anglican
deacon named John Wilson Makokwe, a Hima from Buhiga, a
northern locality. To assume that the Hima are inevitably from the south and the Banyaruguru from the north,
as many observers have been prone to do, would be a
gross exaggeration. The former are said to have
migrated into the country from the eastern borderlands
in the seventeenth or eighteenth century, about two or
three centuries later than the Banyaruguru, who generally hold them in deep contempt, supposedly because of
their upstart attitudes and innate resourcefulness.
Nevertheless it is the lower-caste Tutsi-Hima from the
south who are politically dominant. "The Himas," writes
Father Rodegem, "seem gifted for leadership and direct
action," a statement wholly consonant with the emergent
pattern of leadership in contemporary Burundi: a substantial number of civilian and military elites are
recruited from the Hima stratum, and the president of
the republic (Michel Micombero) is himself of Hima
origins. The Banyaruguru, by contrast, though represented in the government are virtually powerless.

Cutting across this and other cleavages are different social rankings attached to the various patrilineages (imiryango) within each group, Tutsi, Hutu,
and Twa. The usual distinctions are between the very
good families, the good families, those that are
neither good nor bad, and bad. No less than forty-
three different patrilineages thus enter into the
Tutsi-Banyaruguru segment, each in turn falling into a
specific ranking of social prestige. In this fashion
lineage affiliations could substantially rectify the
formal rank-ordering established through ethnic
divisions. The degrees of social distance within the
Tutsi stratum, for example, were at times far more per-
ceptible and socially significant than ethnic differences between Hutu and Tutsi. This multiplicity of
reference-group identifications within the same broad
ethnic stratum has created the basis for potential
conflicts among clans, families, and lineages; yet the
sheer fluidity of such identifications is also the
source of considerable ambiguity as to how one ought to
be defined in terms of clan or family affiliations.
This very ambiguity in turn may help to mitigate
intragroup conflict. A case in point is the socalled
Basapfu clan.

Whether the Basapfu are actually of Hima origin, as claimed, is open to doubt. The historical evidence suggests that they may have been of Banyaruguru origin. The significant point is that today the Basapfu identify themselves, and are often identified by others, as being neither Hima nor Banyaruguru. They are just referred to as Basapfu, as if they formed yet another reference group within the Tutsi stratum. This, and the fact that they are more or less evenly spread throughout the country, is what later enabled some of their representatives to act as the arbiters of regional conflict, and indeed of Hima-Banyaruguru conflict. For if the incumbent elites are largely drawn from the Bururi-based Hima-led faction, within this faction some Basapfu hold key positions within the government and the army.

Neither Hutu nor Tutsi hold traditional claims to authority. The real holders of power in the traditional society were the princes of the blood, or ganwa. Because of the special eminence conferred upon them by the accidents of history, they become identified as a separate ethnic group, whose power and prestige ranked far above that of ordinary Tutsi. They formed the core of the political elites and as such held most of the chiefly positions available under the monarchy. Despite or because of this, they never stood as a very cohesive group. Intra-ganwa rivalries are indeed a recurrent theme of Burundi's precolonial history. Out of the competing claims of rival dynasties bitter feuds periodically broke out among the representatives of different Houses culminating in the middle of the nineteenth century in a major struggle between the sons of Mwami (King) Mwezi Kisabo (1852-1908) and the descendants of the previous incumbent, Mwami Ntare Rugaamba (1795-1852). Temporarily held in check but by no means dissipated by the spread of the colonial pax, the late fifties saw a sudden resurgence of these antagonisms. Even at this late date political conflict did not express itself in ethnic terms, but in the form of factionalism between representatives of opposed unilineal descent groups.

What gave a measure of unity and cohesiveness to this otherwise highly fragmented social order is that below the ganwa stratum no single line of cleavage could be said to govern the allocation of social status, wealth, or power. Ethnic divisions were largely irrelevant to the distribution of social prestige, and of only marginal significance with regard to wealth.

And although power was in theory the monopoly of the princes, the record shows that subchiefs and palace officials were sometimes recruited from among Hutu and Tutsi. What is more, the competitive relationships that developed among the princes made it imperative for them to seek the support of both Hutu and Tutsi, hence substantiating Simmel's observation that "conflict may also bring persons and groups together which otherwise have nothing to do with each other." In this case, however, Hutu and Tutsi were not nearly as compartmentalized as the foregoing might suggest. Through the institution of clientship (bugabire), Hutu and Tutsi were caught in a web of interlocking relationships extending from the very top of the social pyramid to its lowest echelons, with the Mwami acting as the supreme Patron--which in turn underscores the unifying role of the monarchy, both as a symbol and an institution. Through the use of specific symbols, ceremonies, and rituals the monarchy imposed itself as a major focus for popular loyalties. No other source of legitimacy was as compelling as the Royal Drum (Karyenda) in holding society together.

Although the traditional society contained a great many potential sources of conflict, in practice conflict was seldom if ever activated along ethnic lines. To view the recent holocaust as "an extreme case of the old African problem of tribalism" is indeed difficult to square with the realities of traditional Burundi society. If the term tribalism has any meaning in this context it is a very recent phenomenon, traceable to the social transformations introduced under the aegis of the colonial state and the consequent disintegration of those very structures and mechanisms that once gave cohesiveness to society as a whole.

Dimensions of Conflict

In its most acute and devastating manifestations the Hutu-Tutsi conflict was the last in a series that spread over a period of at least twelve years, covering almost as wide a range of potential oppositions as the traditional society had to offer. Grafted onto this were the tensions arising from the introduction of new forms of political self-expression, that is, parties, trade unions, and parliamentary institutions. Out of this combination of traditional and modern types of opposition developed an extraordinary hybrid and complex polity.

The introduction of the vote in 1956, six years before independence, initiated a process of political mobilization that gradually reached every sector of society, activating one group after another, pitting princes against princes, monarchists against republicans, army men against civilians, north against south, Hutu against Tutsi. At first, traditional cleavages tended to act as so many breakwaters, allowing the political mobilization of one group at a time. In contrast to what happened in Rwanda, where the mobilization of the Hutu masses was greatly facilitated and accelerated by the existence of a sharp, vertical split between the Tutsi aristocracy and the Hutu masses, in Burundi the mobilization of the population along ethnic lines was significantly delayed by the complexity of the traditional social system, and by the fact that the monarch was relatively free from ethnic bias. Even when ethnic loyalties were stirred into action, this did not eliminate the play of narrower loyalties. One of the most striking aspects of the country's recent political evolution is the extent to which ethnic self-perceptions have tended to coexist with, and at times to become subordinate to, residual attachments to the region or to the clan. As environmental threats shifted from the ethnic to the regional or clanic level, corresponding shifts of identification occurred among political actors.

It is only fair to recognize that the seeds of ethnic conflict were planted long before the occurrence of violence. Tempting though it may be to emphasize the traditional dimensions of the recent slaughter, the evidence on this score is very scanty. Meyer's statement that "as long as the Batussi [sic] are masters in the country, spiritual and cultural progress is impossible for the Burundi people, for it is only the present low position of the Bahutu, kept in seclusion for centuries, that ensures the Batutsi their dominance" does not seem too convincing as an argument, confusing as it does political and social (or economic) dominance while failing to distinguish between a potential basis for ethnic conflict, it never experienced such conflict on a scale even remotely approaching what happened after independence.

Of far greater relevance is the process of social transformation set in motion during and after the colonial interlude. The external dimensions of this phenomenon are especially important to bear in mind, in at least two senses. The Rwanda revolution, for one thing, had a decisive psychological impact on ethnic self-perceptions in Burundi. The coming to power of Hutu politicians in Rwanda led many of their kinsmen in Burundi to share their political objectives, in turn intensifying fears of ethnic domination among the Tutsi of Burundi. Thus by giving the Burundi situation a false definition to begin with, a definition patterned on the Rwanda situation, Hutu politicans evoked a new behavior both among themselves and the Tutsi that made their originally false imputations true. Ethnic conflict thus took on the quality of a self-fulfilling prophecy.

In some respects the Burundi situation had already been defined by the Belgian colonizer as one approximating to Rwanda, with the result that something of a caste structure had already begun to emerge during the colonial period. Long before aspiring Hutu politicians sought to emulate the goals and strategies of their ethnic brothers across the border, Belgian policies in Rwanda served as a model for colonial administrators in Burundi. It was both simpler and more efficient to view Burundi as consisting of a Tutsi aristocracy and a Hutu peasantry and pursue a policy of indirect rule that would maintain the dominance of one over the other. Few efforts were made during the colonial period to extend educational facilities to the Hutu masses, or for that matter to provide them with what few opportunities were available for a political apprenticeship. Student enrollment at the Ecole des Freres de la Charite (better known as the Groupe Scolaire of Astrida) between 1946 and 1954 shows a clear predominance of Tutsi over Hutu--a disproportion that becomes even more striking of course in the case of Rwanda.

The result is that on the eve of independence relatively few Hutu could claim the status of a modern elite, and those who did were all the more anxious to translate their egalitarian commitments into reality. Yet precisely because of the nature of their commitments, their access to positions of authority could only be viewed with the greatest suspicion by the Tutsi minority. Extension of the vote, on a per capita basis, evoked similar apprehensions. Just as social equality spelled the end of Tutsi supremacy, majority rule for many Tutsi was seen as synonymous with Hutu rule. Even in its most restrictive sense (implying equal representation of ethnic interests in key governmental and bureaucratic posts) equality never became a reality of postindependence politics. A mere glance at the ethnic distribution of top civil-service positions in 1965 shows the extent of Tutsi predominance in the political system.

The years that followed in independence (1962) saw a widening of the gap between the level of aspiration of Hutu elites and their actual share of political responsibilities. Their sense of frustration stemmed from being denied the share of power to which they considered themselves entitled, and from their perception of a vast disproportion between their numerical importance as a group and their very limited access to material rewards. But it also expressed their repeated failures to tip the scales of power to their advantage and the severe penalties they suffered as a consequence of their abortive efforts. As long as the policies of the Crown aimed at excluding both Hutu and Tutsi from the decisions of the Court (as happened to be the case in the years immediately following independence) Hutu grievances could be kept within manageable bounds. What brought their grievances to the point of exasperation were the repressive measures to which they exposed themselves time and again in their efforts to alter the staus quo, and their ultimate realization that through their own political ineptitude, they unwittingly played into the hands of their opponents.

The Anatomy of Violence

The attacks began between 8:00 and 9:00 P.M. on April 29, 1972, and were carried out nearly simultaneously in Bujumbura and in the southern provinces of Rumonge, Nyanza-Lac, and Bururi. In these provinces the assailants consisted of Hutu and Mulelists operating in small bands of 10 to 30 people. In Bururi alone the so-called Mulelists numbered between 1,000 and 1,500. Approximately 25,000 Zairian refugees, most of them Babembe, lived in southern Burundi at the time of the initial risings; though culturally distinct from the local Hutu populations, they nonetheless shared many of their grievances against the Bururi group and were therefore highly receptive to the incitements of the rebel leadership. The hard core of the rebel forces, however, reportedly came from bases located in Tanzania near the Burundi border. Armed with small automatic weapons, machetes, and spears they proceeded to kill and mutilate every Tutsi in sight, including women and children as well as those few Hutu who refused to join them. All in all it is estimated that about 10,000 rebels, both Hutu and Mulelists, took part in the initial risings. They quickly overran the provincial capitals of Nyanza-Lac and Rumonge. According to official reports they even organized a people's republic in the Bururi region, and held on to the liberated enclave for two weeks before being routed out. Among the victims of the slaughter in Bururi were Micombero's brother-in-law, the provincial governor, and some 40 provincial administrators. In Bujumbura, meanwhile, some 100 rebels launched coordinated attacks against the radio station and the military camp, but were almost immediately repulsed. In its initial stage the rebellion is said to have cost at least 2,000 lives, with Bururi claiming by far the heaviest losses.

The early pattern of violence bore striking similarities with what was observed in Zaire during the 1964 rebellion. In Burundi as in Zaire rebel tactics showed a heavy reliance on the use of drugs and magic; in each case the attacks were conducted in the most indiscriminate fashion, and were accompanied by senseless cruelties; and in each case violence took place within a very rudimentary organizational framework. Like the simbas in Zaire, many of the Burundi rebels sought sustenance in hemp smoking, and invulnerability to bullets through resort to magic. Some were identified as "wearing white saucepans stained with blood as helmets, their bodies tattooed with magic signs as immunity against attacks." If we are to believe Micombero's testimony "witch doctors played an important role. Mulelist trainers would shoot blank bullets at a man to show his immunity and then shoot a dog or cat with real bullets to show that the animal had died because it did not cry out the words that conferred protection." Here again the parallel with the Zairian rebellion is striking, as were the deliberate cruelties inflicted on the victims. In each case the rebellion owed its initial success to the receptivity of the milieu within which it developed rather than to the solidity of its organizational apparatus.

By contrast the pattern of counterviolence initiated by the government and the army was more systematic and hence more efficient in terms of human destructiveness. The counterattacks began on April 30. On that day the army and the jeunesses began to coordinate their efforts to exterminate all individuals suspected to have taken part in the rebellion. Martial law was proclaimed throughout the country, and a dawn-to-dusk

curfew enforced. Meanwhile Micombero approached the
Zairian authorities with a view to securing troop rein-
forcements and air support, both of which arrived on
May 3. With Zairian paratroopers in charge of defending the airport the Burundi army moved in force into
the countryside. What followed was not so much a
repression as a hideous slaughter of Hutu populations.
According to Martin Howe of the New York Times, "the
revolutionary youth brigades (JRR) took the lead in
what is widely described as arbitrary arrests and
killings. These were aggravated by personal acts of
revenge, with people being denounced as plotters
because of disputes over land or a cow." In Bururi the
army attacked all Hutu more or less indiscriminately.
In Bujumbura, Gitega dn Ngozi all cadres of Hutu
origins--including not only local administrators but
chauffeurs, clerks, and skilled workers--were systematically rounded up, taken to jail, and either shot or
beaten to death with rifle butts or clubs. In Bujumbura alone an estimated 4,000 Hutu were loaded up on
trucks and taken to their graves. According to one
Tutsi witness "they picked up almost all the Hutu
intellectuals above the secondary level," and many
more, one might add, below that level.

Some of the most gruesome scenes took place on the
premises of the Universite Officielle in Bujumbura, and
in secondary and technical schools. Scores of Hutu
students were physically assaulted by their Tutsi con-
freres; many were beaten to death. Meanwhile groups of
soldiers and jeunesses/youths would suddenly appear in
classrooms, call the Hutu students by name and take
them away. Few ever returned. At the Universite
Officielle about one-third (120) disappeared in these
circumstances. The Ecole Normale of Ngagara, near
Bujumbura, lost more than 100 students out of a total
of 314; of the 415 students enrolled at the Ecole
Technique de Kamenge-Bujumbura, 60 are believed to have
been killed, while another 110 fled; out of 700 students enrolled at the Athenee (secondary school) of
Bujumbura, at least 300 have since disappeared, some
killed and others fleeing to avoid being killed; at the
Athenee of Gitega some 40 students were killed, raising
the total of missing students to 148; at the Institut
Technique Agricole, also in Gitega, 40 students out of
a total of 79 are currently missing, of whom 26 are
said to have been executed. The Ecole Normale Super-
ieure and the Ecole Nationale d'Administration also
suffered heavy losses. The list also extends to con-
fessional schools, both Catholic and Protestant. Not

only the Hutu elites but nearly all potential elites were thus physically liquidated.

Nor was the Church spared. According to Martin Howe, "12 Hutu priests are said to have been killed, and thousands of Protestant pastors, school directors and teachers. In the Bujumbura hospital six doctors and eight nurses were arrested and are believed to be dead." No sector of society was left untouched. The repression took on the qualities of a selective genocide directed at all the educated or semieducated strata of Hutu society.

What kind of explanation can one give for such massive violence? Before turning to this question several preliminary observations must be made. Attention has already been drawn to the prominent role played by Mulelists in the early stages of the rebellion, and to the remarkable similarity between their tactics and those employed by the Zairian rebels in 1964. Just as the instigators of the attacks in the south were of mixed origins, so were the victims of the repression. But what needs to be emphasized here is that the victims were not only Hutu and Mulelists but Tutsi as well. Moreover, it is not unreasonable to assume that among the Tutsi killed during the reprisals some were refugees from Rwanda. We shall retun to this point in a moment. Suffice to note that about 100 Tutsi were executed in the provincial capital of Gitega on May 6. On that day, according to Jeremy Greenland, "war councils met in the provincial centers and the guilty were executed the same evening. A Congolese driver, working in Burundi for an Italian firm was ordered out that night to excavate two large holes outside Gitega. He dumped 100 fresh corpses in them and swears that the victims were mainly Tutsi." This, adds Greenland, "is unique evidence of Tutsi being killed in the repression."

Yet another element to bear in mind has to do with the circumstances surrounding the return of ex-king Ntare to Burundi, in March 1972, and his subsequent execution in Gitega, on April 29. The return of the ex-king Ntare to Burundi was negotiated between President Idi Amin of Uganda and Micombero shortly after his arrival in Kampala on March 21. On the strength of the verbal and written guarantees of safe conduct given by Micombero, Amin allowed Ntare (who was now once again known as Charles Ndizeye) to return to Bujumbura on March 30. "Just like you" wrote Micombero in this

letter of March 28 to Amin, "I deeply believe in God...
Your Excellency can be assured that as soon as Mr.
Charles Ndizeye returns back to my country he will be
considered as an ordinary citizen and that as such his
life and security will be assured." No sooner had the
ex-king landed in Bujumbura, however, than he was
immediately taken to Gitega under military escort and
placed under house arrest. The news of his death
reached Bujumbura via an official radio broadcast
announcing that the ex-king had been killed in the
course of rebel attacks against his residence. Later,
however, Micombero admitted that he had been tried for
plotting against the government and executed on the
night of the attacks, on April 29. Official allegations were that Ntare tried to invade the country with
the aid of foreign mercenaries.

The official position of the Burundi authorities
is that two different sets of actors were plotting
against the government. On the one hand there was ex-
king Ntare, who, according to Micombero, "tried to trap
him," presumably with the complicity of foreign mercenaries; on the other hand there was a Hutu plot, involving top-ranking personalities in the army and government. The first plot was quickly nipped in the bud,
and turned out to be of relatively little consequence,
except of course for Ntare himself. The Hutu plot,
however, was a much more serious one. Indeed the
entire rebellion is officially described as the outcome
of a gigantic conspiracy aiming at the physical liquidation of all Tutsi.

Phrased in these terms neither explanation is
entirely satisfactory. Can one imagine for a moment
that Ntare could single-handedly prepare the ground for
an invasion of foreign mercenaries, or indeed that he
himself thought he could do so? Or can one really
believe that on the strength of his own limited char-
isma he could spontaneously rally the Hutu masses
around himself and promote peasant uprisings throughout
the land--all this in the name of a monarchy that had
long ceased to exist?

The notion of a master plot concocted by Hutu
officials, though far more plausible, also leaves a
number of questions unanswered. If it is true that--
according to the official version given by the Burundi
authorities--a number of Hutu officials had given
financial aid to the rebels, that thousands of machetes
were discovered at the home of the Hutu minister of

public works, that a map showing areas of Tutsi concentration had been found at the home of the Hutu minister
of post and telecommunications, why has no evidence
been produced to substantiate these charges? If there
is any truth to the allegations that two million Burundi francs, along with quantities of arms and ammunition, were seized at the home of Second Lieutenant
Ndayahoze, and that Ndayahoze himself was intended to
become president of a Hutu republic, where is the
evidence? Again, where is the proof that lists of Hutu
conspirators were found in possession of some rebels?
What is the explanation for the abrupt dismissal of the
cabinet by Micombero on April 29? Moreover, since the
Hutu leadership had been reduced to a skeleton of its
former self as a result of previous purges, can one
really believe that a mere handful of Hutu officials
would be bold enough to organize a major rebellion
against an army largely dominated by Tutsi officers?
It is not impossible to imagine that a few Hutu
officers and noncommissioned officers were in fact
plotting against the government; what is impossible to
imagine is that the plot involved as many individuals
in the government and the army as was subsequently
claimed by the Burundi authorities.

Two other alternatives need to be considered:
either the rebellion was the result of a deliberate
provocation by the Bururi lobby, intended to provide a
final solution to the Hutu problem--and a provisional
one to the Banyaruguru problem; or else it was the outcome of a tactical alliance between the Banyaruguru and
Hutu elements. The first of these alternatives seems
rather implausible, if only because of the enormous
risks it entailed. Moreover, one is led to wonder
whether the few hours that elapsed between the dismissal of Micombero's cabinet and the outbreak of the
rebellion were sufficient to allow some of the dismissed cabinet members to organize such a rebellion.
One must also note that the area most hard hit by the
rebellion, and where the initial uprisings were most
devastating, was in fact the stronghold of the Bururi
lobby. That some of the dismissed cabinet members
should have deliberately instigated a rebellion in the
area where their position was most vulnerable is difficult to conceive. A more reasonable interpretation,
suggested by Jeremy Greenland, is that Micombero must
have had some advance knowledge of a Hutu plot, and
that he dismissed his ministers in order to have a free
hand to deal with the uprising when it came. The
strongest evidence in support of this explanation,

which also shows how little awareness Micombero and his advisers had of exactly when or how the blow might fall, is that on April 29 the whole Tutsi administration of the Bururi province accepted an invitation to a party at Rumonge--only to discover that the invitation was in fact a ruse to assassinate them. All the guests were killed, except Shibura and Yanda.

If the idea of a plot has any plausibility in this context it did not involve a tactical alliance between Hutu and Banyaruguru as much as a precarious coalition of interests between Hutu and Mulelists on the one hand, and possibly between some Banyaruguru and Rwanda refugees on the other. What, exactly, relationships were between each group is difficult to ascertain. The Mulelists, as noted earlier, were heavily concentrated in the southern provinces; the Rwanda refugees, at least until 1965, were found primarily in the north, where the Banyaruguru were the most numerous. In spite of fundamental ethnic and cultural differences between them, each group of refugees shared somewhat similar experiences. They both fought side by side during the Zairian rebellion, in 1964-65; they both shared specific grievances against the Micombero regime, the Mulelists for being denied the support they needed to continue their struggle against the Zairian authorities, and the Rwandese for having been denied the opportunity to fight their way back into Rwanda. Of Tutsi origins for the most part, the Rwanda refugees (also known as inyenzi) made their way into Burundi from Zaire, in 1965, after fighting at the side of the Mulelists and being pushed back by the counteroffensive of the Zairian army. Although they came into the country at the request of certain Tutsi personalities in government as a guarantee against a possible Hutu uprising, they were subsequently disarmed by the joint efforts of the Burundi and Zairian armies. Yet no matter how real their grievances against the Micombero clique, their grievances against Hutu elements were greater still. In these conditions the idea of a tactical alliance of Mulelists and inyenzi seems far-fetched; even more far-fetched was the idea of a parallel alliance between Banyaruguru and Hutu. What sems to have developed is more in the nature of a temporary concurrence of interest between each group of refugees and those domestic factions with whom they had most in common culturally and politically, the Mulelists with the Hutu and the inyenzi with the Tutsi. Rather than each group of refugees working hand in hand with the other, each group become a tributary to its domestic ally. In view

of the ethnic context within which the initial uprisings occurred, one can see why at first neither the
inyenzi nor the Banyaruguru had any inclination to jump
into the fray, preferring for the time being to let the
Banyaruguru and the Hutu (and Muleists) destroy each
other. That these were included among the motives
attributed to the Banyaruguru by the Bururi authorities
finds partial confirmation in the killings of Tutsi
elements in Gitega on May 6, 1972. This, as Greenland
noted, was unique evidence of Tutsi killing Tutsi.

It may be that in the minds of some Banyaruguru,
the Hutu uprisings would in time be deflected from
their original target through the propitious intervention of Ntare--with the rebellion then transforming
itself into a carrier movement destined to restore both
the monarchy and Banyaruguru hegemony. In the absence
of solid evidence, however, this can only be presented
as a very hypothetical proposition.

Regardless of who the plotters were, involvement
in violence clearly stemmed from very different motives. For the Mulelists the rebellion expressed more
than just an accumulation of grievances against the
Bururi lobby; it also expressed a displacement of
aggression from one target (the Zairian authorities) to
another (the Tutsi authorities)--their victims in
effect serving as a substitute target for their Zairian
enemies. Not only culturally and ethnically but in
terms of their behavior and motivations the Mulelists
formed a radically different group from the locally
recruited Hutu insurgents. Among the latter some
joined the rebellion out of fear, others out of opportunism, others still because of their genuine hatred of
all Tutsi regardless of clan or region. Between the
rural activists and the Bujumbura plotters the contrast
is equally striking. Assuming that something in the
nature of a plot was hatched by Hutu officials in the
army and the government, their modus operandi and ultimate goals had relatively little in common with those
of the local insurgents, Hutu and Mulelists. The aim
of the rebellion in Bujumbura was not to kill every
Tutsi in sight but to gain control of the radio station
and military camp as a preliminary step toward a formal
seizure of power. Again, assuming that the Banyaruguru
had hoped to seal a tactical alliance with Ntare,
possibly to use him as a symbol of legitamacy to recu-
perate the rebellion, this was evidently for motives
quite different from those actuating Hutu insurgents in
Bujumbura and Bururi.

Behind the orgy of counterviolence triggered by the repression one can also detect a variety of motives. Fear of an impending slaughter of all Tutsi, men, women, and children--reminiscent of what happened in Rwanda in 1959-1962, and again in 1964--certainly played a crucial part in carrying the repression to the extremes noted earlier. Personal animosities, individual hatreds of local Hutu elites, and the anticipation of the material gains that might be derived from seizure of the victims' property (his cows, his land, his bicycle, his hut, or even his bank account, as the case may be) also fed into anti-Hutu violence. But none of these factors are sufficient to account for the systematic purges that followed the uprisings. Indeed the most astonishing feature of the repression is the rapidity with which it transformed itself into a genocidal-type operation aiming at the physical liquidation of nearly every educated or semieducated Hutu. This is how Jeremy Greenland described the logistics of the operation:

> Local Tutsi, sometimes soldiers, sometimes civil servants, arrived and motioned Hutu teachers, churchleaders, nurses, traders, civil servants into Landrovers with their guns. Bands of Tutsi combed the suburbs of Bujumbura and carted away Hutu by the lorry-load. Throughout May and half of June 1972, the excavators were busy every night in Gitega and Bujumbura burying the dead in mass graves. In secondary schools teachers stood helpless as many of their Hutu pupils were removed...Those arrested were usually dead the same night, stripped and practically clubbed to death in covered lorries on the way to prison, then finished off there with clubs at nightfall. Using bullets would have been wasteful.

Prophylactic violence thus became a major element in the strategy of counterinsurgency adopted by Tutsi authorities to deal with the Hutu problem. The aim was to decapitate not only the rebellion but Hutu society as well, and in the process lay the foundation of an entirely new social order.

From the drastic surgery performed during the repression, a new society has in fact emerged, in which only Tutsi elements are qualified to gain access to power, influence, and wealth; what is left of Hutu society is now systematically excluded from the army, the civil service, the university, and secondary schools. The four Hutu holding ministerial positions are virtually impotent, their sole function being to mask the fact of Tutsi domination. Tasks formerly performed by Hutu are now the privilege of the Tutsi, as are virtually all other positions in the modern economic sector. (The reimposition of school fees in September 1973 has had the effect of further reducing the number of fatherless and other Hutu children in primary and secondary schools; as one missionary put it, "having dealt with the 'elite' fathers, the potentially 'elite' children are now excluded from education." Hutu status has become synonymous with an inferior category of beings; only Tutsi are fit to rule, and among them none are presumably better qualified than the Banyabururi.

What Next?

The annihilation of the Hutu elites has effectively eliminated all potential threats to Tutsi hegemony from the Hutu, at least for the next generation; but it has by no means eliminated all sources of conflict. One of the unintended consequences of the slaughter has been to create the conditions for further conflict within the dominant stratum. Now that Hutu threats are no longer perceived as significant by the Tutsi minority, the focus of intergroup conflict is likely to move back once again to intra-Tutsi divisions, pitting north against south, Banyabururi against Banyaruguru, radicals against moderates. So far the Bururi lobby has proved remarkably adept at exploiting the Hutu-Tutsi conflict to its own advantage, using violence as a resource to consolidate its position vis-a-vis both Hutu and Banyaruguru; but the latter (unlike the Hutu living in Burundi) are unwilling to give up their claims to power. In these conditions the continued exclusion of Banyaruguru elements from positions of responsibility within the army and the government may well become a source of increasing tension in years ahead within the Tutsi stratum, possibly leading to new confrontations. Another source of tension lies in the mutual hatreds generated among Tutsi as a result of the excesses committed during the repression. Conscious as most Tutsi were of the threats posed to their collective interest, indeed to their survival, by an impending Hutu takeover, many have since come to realize the enormous disproportion between the nature of the threat on the one hand, and the scale and arbitrariness of the repression on the other. Many are the Tutsi who lost Hutu friends, domestic servants, and clients at the hands of the army and the youths, knowing full well they were innocent. This forceful and unnecessary severance of the few remaining bonds of personal friendship and loyalty between themselves and their Hutu neighbors is what a great many Tutsi in the rural areas are as yet unable to comprehend or forgive. Nor are they likely to forget the share of responsibility borne by the Bururi elites in this and other matters. Thus it would be grossly misleading to conceive of the dominant minority as being all one politically and otherwise. Beneath the monolithic surface of Tutsi hegemony one can discern a variety of potential sources of conflict—some rooted in cultural and regional antagonisms, others in basic disagreements over the scale of the brutalities committed during the repression, others still in the frustrations experienced by specific groups of individuals as a result of their differential access to the rewards of office.

Whether intra-Tutsi tensions can be effectively mitigated by their awareness of future Hutu threats to their security is difficult to say. Internally, the ruling elites have no reason to anticipate further challenges from the Hutu community: lacking all potential sources of leadership, decimated and deeply traumatized by the terrible vengeance visited upon them, the Hutu living in Burundi are neither willing nor able to instigate further revolts. Entirely different, however, is the attitude of the Hutu refugee community in exile. The slaughter of 1972 has generated a massive involuntary migration of Hutu populations into Rwanda, Zaire, and Tanzania (approximately 150,000) creating in each state a kind of privileged sanctuary for the launching of refugee-led guerilla operations against the Burundi government. This situation is made all the more explosive by the occasional spill-over of anti Hutu raids into neighboring territories—and the possibility that the raids might miss their intended targets, killing civilian populations. Judging by the extreme seriousness of the diplomatic incident triggered by the mistaken strafing of a Tanzanian village by helicopters of the Burundi National Army in the spring of 1973, one can see why these retaliatory moves might lead to unintended hostilities between Burundi and any of its neighbors. Yet another element of uncertainty concerns the attitude of the Rwanda government vis-a-vis both the Hutu refugees from Burundi and the Burundi government: can the Rwanda government exercise effective control over the refugees and prevent both guerilla attacks and retaliatory raids? Can it prevent a tactical alliance between the Hutu refugees from Burundi and the Hutu opposition--an alliance presumably designed to create border conflicts that each partner might then seek to exploit to its advantage, the refugees to fight their way back into Burundi, and the domestic Hutu opposition to recapture power? There are no precise answers to these questions. What does seem reasonably clear is that the capacity of the Bururi lobby to maintain itself in power will depend to a large extent on its ability to cope with the conditions of chronic instability arising from the spread of anti-regime (that is, Hutu) forces into neighboring political arenas.

Even more fundamental in the long run are the amounts and kinds of assistance that the Micombero regime can expect from foreign powers within and outside Africa. Burundi's strongest allies, for the time being, are Zaire and France, each for very different reasons. In the light of the ominous threats faced by the Zairian authorities during the 1964 rebellion, it is easy to see why the Mulelist component of the Hutu rebellion should have produced a quick and positive response from Kinshasa--in the form of military assistance. The rapprochement brought to light during the crisis is more than a conjunctural phenomenon. A crucial element militating in favor of continued close relationships between Kinshasa and Bujumbura is the presence of a substantial number of Tutsi elements (most of them refugees from Rwanda) in specific sectors of the Zairian civil service--primarily in agriculture and education--as well as in top decision-making positions. The second most powerful figure in Kinshasa is none other than a former Tutsi refugee from Rwanda. In a way ethnicity is part of the social cement that makes for potentially close relationships between the two states, above and beyond the convergence of short-term interests.

The case of France is more difficult to explain, involving as it does a mixture of ignorance and opportunism, and a fetishlike attachment to the presumed virtues of <u>francophonie</u>. That 100,000 francophones or potential francophones, happen to be massacred in the name of Tutsi supremacy makes little difference as long as France's brand of <u>francophonie</u>--meaning in effect the promotion of French, as distinct from Belgian,

-213-

cultural values--stands to profit. Nor does it matter
if in this case Tutsi supremacy should contradict the
fundamental principles of 1789. What matters ultimately is the expansion of France's sphere of influence
in black Africa, culturally and politically. And since
the Tutsi as a group are being viewed as having greater
nimbleness of mind and greater expressional skills than
the Hutu and on the whole more willing to do business
with the French, they are generally viewed as a better
investment by French diplomats. These considerations
are essential to an understanding of the supporting
role played by French military assistants during and
after the rebellion. As one knowledgeable observer put
it: "French military assistants flew and are still
flying the regime's helicopters. This airborne was
crucial in routing out the rebels in the south...
Frenchmen were holding the helicopters steady while
Burundi soldiers were machine-gunning Hutu rebels out
of the side windows, and Frenchmen were at the wheel of
the same helicopters in the incursions into Tanzania,
in the course of which numerous Tanzanians were
killed." Under the cover of a Societe de Transports
Aeriens du Burundi (whose initials, STAB, convey a more
realistic appraisal of its role) French pilots and
helicopters supply the Micombero regime with minimum
guarantees of security against further rebel attacks.

The prominence of the French presence in Burundi,
not only at the military level but in cultural, educational, and technical spheres, has meant a corresponding loss of influence for Belgium, thus removing all
credibility from the threats of economic sanctions
raised in Brussels during the 1972 events. While
Belgium was making a last-ditch effort to make sure
that the educational component of its aid program would
not be used for discriminatory purposes, the French
promptly offered to make up for whatever aid Belgium
might withdraw! Such being the case one wonders
whether there is any point in laying blame on the
United States for its failure to act in any decisive
way during the crisis. In a recent sponsored report by
the Carnegie Endowment the suggestion is made that
since the US buys approximately 80 percent of Burundi's
coffee (representing 60 percent of its foreign earn-
ings), the State Department possessed sufficient economic leverage to induce a basic change of attitude on
the part of the Tutsi authorities. This is extremely
dubious, however. When ethnic hatreds reached the
point where people slaughter each other by the thousands, how much do they really care about the long-range

-214-

implications of a reduction of coffee exports? Nor is it a foregone conclusion that this form of economic sanctions would in the long run produce the expected results. The Hutu masses would probably suffer just as much as the Tutsi elites from the consequences of this policy. But perhaps the basic flaw in the argument advanced by the authors of the Carnegie report is that it assumes that the United States enjoys a position of economic omnipotence in Burundi. It would be very surprising indeed if, in the event of an American decision to bar coffee imports from Burundi, alternative buyers did not materialize.

To bring effective pressure to bear upon the Burundi authorities would have required a concerted action on the part of all Western powers accredited in Bujumbura. Only in these conditions and through pressures involving not only moral persuasion but continued threats of economic sanctions, was there a chance of limiting the scale of the massacre, and perhaps initiating a more liberal trend in the sphere of Hutu-Tutsi relations. At the time of the crisis, however, there was little agreement among Western diplomats as to what should or could be done. In fact some of the key figures in the Western diplomatic corps were not even on speaking terms with each other. The rift was even more conspicuous in the case of Communist powers. Whereas North Korea and China were the only powers outside Africa to officially support the regime, the Soviets showed no compunctions about signing the Western note of protest, in part because differences of opinion among Western diplomats made the note sound platitudinous, if not downright hypocritical. With the exception of Belgium, the dominant impression one gains of Western diplomacy during the crisis is one of almost total indifference in the face of an unrelieved tragedy.

Just as astonishing is the silence of the UN and the OAU, and the total inability, or unwillingness, of either organization to register any kind of effective protest. In the case of the OAU this passivity is sometimes justified by the argument that since the Burundi crisis was a purely domestic matter (which it most emphatically was not), it was clearly outside the jurisdiction of the OAU. Perhaps a more realistic explanation is that most African states are, to a greater or lesser extent, potential Burundis. No African state wishes to establish a precedent that might prevent it from dealing with such crises by means of its own choosing. Even so, the wording of the resolution adopted at the OAU Summit in Rabat in late June 1972 strikes one as little short of astounding, amounting in effect to a message of support for Micombero: "The Council of Ministers is convinced that, thanks to your saving action, peace will be rapidly reestablished, national unity consolidated and territorial integrity preserved."

These considerations are equally relevant to an understanding of the striking indecision displayed by the UN. According to the Carnegie report, Washington had apparently banked on UN observers constituting what one official described as "a foreign presence that would be likely to halt the massive killings." But when the two missions (sent by the UN) were limited to only five persons, that expectation evaporated. "We had no illusions about what the UN could accomplish," admitted a high U.S. official later. The fact that emerges with striking clarity from the record of UN involvement, or noninvolvement, in Burundi is that the latter ranked far too low in the scale of international priorities to justify anything more than a pro forma intervention. To put the matter crudely: as long as the killings involved only Hutu and Tutsi the crisis could be regarded as lying essentially within the domestic jurisdiction of the state of Burundi; only inasmuch as Hutu and Tutsi could be identified as being respectively pro-Western and pro-Communist (which was no longer the case in 1972), could the matter conceivably be viewed as a threat to peace by Western powers. Only then could a rationale be established for intervention, and a criterion made available for discriminating between friend and foe. In the spring of 1972 the UN clearly lacked a rationale for intervention; yet, judging from the use made by the Burundi authorities of UNICEF trucks during the repression, the field agencies of the UN were by no means at a loss for identifying friends and foes. As Greenland tersely puts it, "the UN said little, even when their own vehicles were requisitioned and used to take Hutu to their deaths. It was ironic to see Landrovers marked UNICEF being used for this purpose..." This is perhaps the reason why, until his death in Geneva, the head of the UN Department Programme in Bujumbura, Marcel Latour, was one of the two most highly regarded Western officials in Bujumbura, the other being his long-time friend, war comrade, and compatriot, Henri Bernard, the French ambassador.

Reflecting on the appalling events of 1972 one journalist was prompted to ask: "does an international conscience exist?" The answer given by a Western diplomat sums up the dilemma: "Nobody wants to start up another fuss in a faraway country if personal interests are not involved." Insofar as it can be detected at all, what goes by the name of an international conscience is the expression of convergent national interests, not of a global commitment to moral values. How else is one to explain the blissful indifference of world opinion to what must be regarded as one of the most brutal massacres in the history of any single state? How can one otherwise explain the commotion produced in Africa and Europe (and particularly in England) by the alleged massacre of 400 Africans in Mozambique by Portuguese security forces, and the fact that the far larger killings in Burundi went almost unnoticed? The sad truth is that Burundi is too far away, too exotic, too small, in short too marginal in terms of the priorities set by international diplomacy to elicit concern or compassion among Westerners. Thus the death of scores of Africans at the hands of the Portuguese colonialists is viewed as an intolerable scandal by white liberals (as it should); the Burundi killings, by contrast, are seen as a mere statistic.

The crux of the dilemma concerning Burundi's future is whether further periodic massacres can be instituted without triggering conflicting moves on the part of its neighbors, Rwanda, Tanzania, and Zaire. The latter two in particular, by virture of their geographical position and political weight, have a vital role to play, not only in influencing President Micombero toward more moderate policies, but in preventing the occurrence of a client war in which Rwanda would side with Tanzania and Zaire with Burundi. The most one can hope for the time being is for the three states that once made up Belgian Africa to evolve a common framework of cooperative relations with a view to maximizing their chances of economic viability while at the same time reducing the risks of confrontation and hostility at the domestic and international levels. If neither the UN nor the OAU were able to influence the course of events in 1972, one would hope that they might at least try to mobilize world opinion in support of initiatives aiming at preventing the recurrence of these events in the foreseeable future.

THE ACHE OF PARAGUAY

Richard Arens

The Ache Indians of Paraguay, a peaceful and primitive tribe that has lived for centuries in the jungles
of South America, hunting and gathering food, is being
systematically exterminated. As a matter of official
policy, the Ache have been hunted like animals; the
survivors of these manhunts have been sold into slavery
or forced onto reservations. Today, their tribe numbers no more than 1,000, and as a result of the continuing genocidal policies of the government of Paraguay,
is in danger of extinction.

What have the Ache done to deserve this fate? In
recent years Paraguay has experienced something of an
economic boom. In 1965 and again in 1968, roads were
cut through the jungle, making it more accessible and
vastly increasing land values. Large lumber and cattle
interests began moving into the interior of Paraguay.
When this happened, as one observer has noted, the Ache
became "inconvenient." Quite simply, they became an
obstacle to economic development. And, as the corporations and their willing accomplice, the government of
Paraguay, saw it, the Indians had to be removed.

The official policy was to "sedentarize" the Ache
on reservations. Unofficially, the Paraguayan government set about to remove the Indians from the land by
any means necessary. It is well documented that the
man in charge of the "sedentarization" project, Manual
de Jesus Pereira, conducted manhunts against the Ache.
Bands of Ache were slaughtered by rifle and machete,
and the survivors were sent to reservations. Conditions on these reservations have been described as comparable to those in Nazi concentration camps.

These basic facts were first brought to the
world's attention in 1973 by the German anthropologist
Mark Munzel in a publication of the International Work
Group for Indigenous Affairs (IWGIA), an organization
based in Copenhagen. The International Commission of
Jurists and the Anti-Slavery Society of Great Britain
found his report persuasive, and the International
League for the Rights of Man, as well as the Roman
Catholic Church of Paraguay, denounced what they
labeled as a campaign of genocide against the Ache
Indians. Still, the atrocities continued, and the

Paraguayan government continued to deny their existence.

In 1976, Temple University Press published, under
my editorship, Genocide in Paraguay (reviewed in American Indian Journal, Vol. 3, No. 6) in which the Paraguayan government was charged with complicity in the
extermination of its Ache Indians. The genocidal practices perpetrated against the Ache included, but were
not limited to, the following:

> Ache were subjected to manhunts in which they
> were pursued like animals. Many were killed
> outright. The survivors were taken to reser-
> vations.

> Many of the Ache on the reservations were
> sold as slaves--the men as manual laborers,
> the women as prostitutes, and the children as
> domestic servants. Others were simply left
> to die. Reservation officials would induce
> periodic waves of starvation in which both
> food and medicine would be withheld.

> Indians on the reservation were denied the
> right to speak their language, sing their
> songs, practice their religious rites, and
> give their children Ache names. The purpose,
> and result, of these prohibitions was to
> create a feeling of helplessness and despair
> among the Ache and to destroy their cultural
> identity.

Genocide in Paraguay succeeded in attracting additional attention, including some expressions of concern
by congressmen, to the plight of the Ache. Not long
after its publication, the director of Indian affairs
of the Paraguayan Ministry of Defense invited me to
come to Paraguay, so that I could be convinced, he
said, on the basis of firsthand observation that the
life of the Ache--and of other Paraguayan Indian
tribes, as well--was not as bad as had been described
in the book. The U.S. ambassador to Paraguay, George
Landau, also telephoned my office several times to persuade me that my going to Paraguay would serve a useful
purpose and that, if I went, my safety would be guaranteed.

This was, in fact, no small concern. About the
time Genocide in Paraguay was published, the Paraguayan

government arrested the staff members of a project called Marandu, which had sought to provide the forest Indians with food and medical assistance and to inform them of their rights under Paraguayan and international law. The members of the Marandu project were drugged, beaten, submerged in excrement to the point of near drowning, and the women were subjected to grotesque forms of sexual abuse. In 1976, the Paraguayan government deported six Roman Catholic priests who had denounced the genocide of the Ache; it also arrested and tortured a seminarian. Six Protestant missionaries doing Indian relief work were arrested.

However, the representatives of both the Paraguayan and U.S. governments persisted, charging that by not accepting the invitation to go to Paraguay I would be acting perversely. They declared that as editor of Genocide in Paraguay, I bore a special responsibility at least to see for myself that the book was based on false information. Not to do so, they said, would prove that I was unwilling to test the argument of the book against the facts.

It appeared as if I had to go.

Funded by Survival International of Great Britain, I left for Paraguay on August 17, 1977, and arrived in Asuncion on August 18, 1977. I was met by Colonel Alberto Samaniego, the director of Indian affairs; a civilian member of the Asociacion de Parcialidades Indigenes (API), the successor to the defunct Marandu; and the third secretary of the U.S. embassy.

My arrival had been presaged by the arrest and detention (as usual withough charges) of Oscar Rodriguez, a member of the API staff. The U.S. embassy seemed confident on the day of my arrival that his release was imminent, but in January 1978 he was still a prisoner. (His current status is not known).

At 7:00 sharp the next morning, General Marcial Samaniego, the minister of defense, received me in the presence of a retinue of aides. There was much heel-clicking and I was photographed alongside a smiling minister. He assured me that a German anthropologist, whom he accused with some virulence of misconduct involving Indians, had concocted the lies about Indian suffering, and that now that I could see for myself, I should easily be able to tell fact from fiction. The fact was, and he put his right hand over his heart

(above a most impressive paunch) in a gesture suggest-
ive of the taking of an oath, that "we love our Indians." He added immediately thereafter that it was the
policy of Paraguay "to integrate them into our society"
--an expression I had come to understand as meaning
that the Indians had to be driven out of the forests
and rendered sedentary. As has often been noted, the
"sedentarization" of a free hunting community, without
decades of careful material and psychological preparation, inflicts suffering and, ultimately, death upon
those rendered "sedentary." When I tried to raise this
point, the minister shook my hand as though I had just
expressed a sentiment of appreciation. A question
about the imprisoned API staff member was left similarly unanswered. The minister assured me of the
willingness of the Paraguayan government to let me see
everything. I was not told that a northern part of the
Chaco region in western Paraguay was barred to all
unauthorized visitors, which included me. (I never was
permitted into that area.) I was informed that I would
be accompanied by a Ministry of Defense official who
would serve as my interpreter wherever I went to meet
Indians. After several days of surveillance, the young
man attached to me from that moment on admitted, over a
drink, that he was a member of the Intelligence Service
of the Paraguayan Army and was reporting on me at
required intervals.

Not until after an officer of the Ministry of
Defense had telephoned the Colonia Nacional Guayaki on
August 18 about an impending visit, was I finally permitted to proceed to the Colonia on August 20, 1977.
This was the major reservation for Ache Indians, located in the eastern part of Paraguay, which Mark Munzel
and others had described as a death camp. It took
approximately five hours to reach it by embassy limousine, starting on moderatly well paved highways and
continuing upon dirt tracks and rocky and untended
mountain trails.

The reservation was in a secluded area of the
jungle, much of which showed evidences of ravages by
the white man. Approximately 30 miles before reaching
the reservation, the jungle changed from lush and
wooden terrain to a lunar landscape, marked by ghostly
emptiness save for grotesquely charred protruding tree
stumps, mute relics of the Paraguayan deforestation
program that had dispossessed the Ache nation in this
area. Neatly constructed houses for officials of the
New Tribes Mission, which is in charge of the reserva-

tion, contrasted sharply with dilapidated hovels available for the Aches at a not insignificant distance from the missionaries.

The hovels reserved for the Indians consisted of a makeshift collection of logs haphazardly attached to the ground and maintaining a precarious balance as they swayed in the Paraguayan winter wind. Gaps left between the logs were often wide enough to admit a child or even an adult, to say nothing of the elements. Canvas and paper and odd pieces of aluminum would occasionally be used to plug such openings. Logs of comparable quality were used for the creation of a roof. Here, too, the logs were in no way suited to keep out the elements--although they might be reinforced by canvas, cardboard, or aluminum sheeting.

A glance at the interior of the hovels revealed an absence of any bedding materials, with the occasional exception of a piece of wood; in only one instance was the wooden slab raised from floor level. The hovels were strewn with offal, an occasional log for making a fire, rusty food utensils, and scraps of newspapers handed to the Indians by the missionaries as cover against the winter cold. No sanitary facilities were visible save for the outhouses of the administration.

An unmistakable odor of human excrement lingered over the Indian part of the reservation.

The Indian population we encountered consisted predominantly of elderly women and young children. A few elderly men were observed. There was a striking absence of young adult males.

Indian adults were squatting in positions of abject depression. No man or boy was seen wearing the traditional lip ornament known as the beta. All evidence of Indianness had been vigorously suppressed. Children disclaimed all knowledge of the Ache language. Indian women responded to inquiries about their native songs by saying that they had not sung them for a long time. When asked why, the women said they were weak and lacked energy. An Indian maintaining a conversation with me through an interpreter in a standing position would sit or lie down on the ground in what seemed total apathy or fatigue within minutes of the conversation. Yet the conversation was not cut off. It seemed that he lacked energy to stand for any protracted period of time.

The missionaries proudly announced that all Indians were Christians. I asked for the name of a four-year-old Indian boy, and one of the missionaries' wives replied, "It is Felipe, a civilized name." When I asked the boy what name he preferred, he unhesitatingly gave his Indian name.

Ache Indians lack a sense of time as it is understood in the industrialized West. But they knew that they had been in the Colonia Nacional Guyaki for what could pass for a lifetime. When asked who had brought them there, almost all of them said, "Pereira"--Manuel de Jesus Pereira, the first administrator of the reservation--and with a frenzy born of a recollection long stifled, began displaying the scars left on the bodies of those who had survived the machetes wielded by Manual de Jesus Pereira and his manhunters. And they remembered those who had been struck down, never to rise again. But then the frenzy died as suddenly as it had started, and men and women, prematurely old, sank back against the ground, as if in anticipation of final interment. Psychological death stared us in the face.

The appearance of the children, who at times appeared to play fitfully as though they lacked energy for more demanding games, was marked at first glance by excessive fat. A closer look revealed unevenly distributed fat deposits, an unhealthy chubbiness, in point of fact an appearance of bloating highlighted by distended abdomens, sometimes to the point of angularity. There was, moreover, not a child who did not suffer from festering sores, lesions, and blotches covering arms, legs, and scalp, which was often completely denuded of hair. All the children were coughing and had runny noses. Both the diet (the staple on this reservation is the sweet potato) and the physical appearance of the Indians--above all, the appearance of the Indian children--were consistent with the protein-deficiency disease known as kwashiorkor.

Outside one of the huts, seated near his mother, was an Indian boy, barely 18 years old. Though no sound passed his lips, tears were streaming down his cheeks as he looked into space, clearly avoiding eye contact with any person. The mother approached the interpreter of the API and explained that he had been like this for at least six weeks. She showed us a half-empty aspirin bottle that the missionaries had given her for his use. When I turned to the missionaries for an explanation, I was told that the boy was merely trying to attract my attention. While this explanation was being offered, the boy went into convulsions on the ground, and one of the women in the missionary group said: "Oh, just look at him. Isn't he a marvelous actor?" I replied that I did not think this was a matter of acting and that while I could not speak for the embassy, I could assure the reservation official that the fate of the boy would be watched with keen and sympathetic interest by such international human rights organizations as Survival International and the International League for Human Rights. The immediate response was surly, but the warning at least produced some action. We were permitted to take the boy in the embassy limousine to a doctor living some 50 miles up a rocky jungle path, though not to a hospital, because that would cost money. We were told, however, that if the doctor recommended it, hospitalization might then be considered.

Upon arriving at the doctor's office after a bumpy three-hour ride, the Indian boy, Santiago Duarte, was pronounced gravely ill and in need of instant hospital attention. At the end of another three-hour ride in the embassy limousine, the boy was received in an Asuncion hospital in a semiconscious state. Within days, the biopsy that was performed revealed a metastized malignancy. Doctors familiar with the case said that the boy's condition had been ignored by the reservation officials for at least 18 months and that the prognosis was grave. Within days of this development, representatives of the New Tribes Mission had removed the boy from the hospital, claiming that the boy was unhappy there and that the cost of hospitalization was prohibitive. Their claim was without foundation as they could not converse with Santiago in his Ache dialect. I had promised to hold myself personally responsible for the cost of the first few days of hospitalization, and API had assumed full responsibility for his treatment. I immediately informed Colonel Samaniego of the boy's removal from the hospital and urged him to take the necessary steps to see that treatment was in fact made available. Samaniego ordered the boy brought to a military hospital from which removal by the New Tribes Mission would be barred. Within days, the New Tribes Mission filed a letter of complaint against me with the U.S. embassy.

I visited the Father Livio Farina Mission of Puerto Casado on August 22, 1977. The mission is

located near a tannin factory, which is the industrial
mainstay of this part of the Chaco. It houses some 700
Indian residents, drawn on for unskilled labor for the
factory. Approximately 800 more Indians, occasionally
attracted by the factory, bivouac in the neighborhood
within a radius of 30 miles. They include the Angarte,
Sanapana, Cuana, Lengua, Toba, and Guarayos.

Upon entering the mission proper, one was immediately struck with the same stench of excrement noted
in the Colonia Nacional. Here, however, it appeared
more pervasive. The mission's Indian settlement was
conspicuously divided by a fence segregating "Christians" from "pagans." While the hovels in which Indians
lived were essentially indistinguishable on both sides
of the fence, the "Christian" area did have a sheltered
outhouse, while the "pagan" area lacked all sanitary
facilities. The ramshackle housing, incapable of
offering shelter against the elements, was again the
dominant characteristic of Indian living. The interi-
ors of the hovels in which Indians lived were, like
those of the Colonia Nacional, devoid of bedding but
contained charred logs and rusty eating utensils.
Elderly men and women, some near death, could be seen
squatting or lying in the debris. I asked a woman
whose eye had been gouged how she had sustained the
injury. She shrugged and said it was an accident.
When I asked whether she had asked for medical attention, she gestured with contempt and said that she did
not have the money and medical attention had to be paid
for. Another woman, clearly in pain and lying on the
ground of a hovel, was asked why she had not requested
medical attention. She replied that it was not made
available.

The adult males in this mission made their living
as unskilled laborers, working a 12-hour day in the
tannin factory. Looking clearly emaciated and resigned, they could be seen struggling with bags of produce on their backs.

When believed to be unobserved, an Indian would
occasionally display his back to a visitor to reveal
the abrasions and sores caused by the weights that he
carried, day in and day out in the factory. Festering
wounds were shown to have been left unattended.

Factory wages for Indians were not easily ascer-
tained, although it was clear from the general level of
undernourishment that they were below any reasonable

subsistence level. Occasionally, "wages" could be disbursed in rotgut whiskey. Numerous Indians could be seen lying drunk or comatose upon the ground. One Indian, his eyes glazed with alcohol, wandered past our group. His gait was steady and his speech only slightly slurred. He said he was happy. The alcohol had wiped out all recollection of his suffering and yet he could still enjoy the sun and the trees. Within minutes he had collapsed upon the ground.

During our stay at Puerto Casado, an Indian died within a few feet of me. When I asked if an autopsy would be conducted to determine the cause of his death, I was told that Indians did not rate autopsies. Besides, said the officials, the multitude of Indian deaths at work would render normal autopsy procedures financially and practically prohibitive.

The political and religious purity of the Indians was policed by nuns. They followed me to overhear each conversation I had with an Indian, "Christian" or "pagan." Asked whether the Church looked after such matters as Indian health, one nun replied that most Indians could not pay for it but that "serious" emergencies would be handled without cost to the patient. The impression that I gleaned was that the nuns were the liaison officers between the priest, the industry and the police.

The reservation was supervised by a priest of the Saliciano Order. He addressed several of his parishioners in my presence with such remarks as "Hello, you old liar," or "Buster, you're due for another warning from me." It was widely claimed that he had reported as Communists parishioners who appeared to be troublemakers at the plant. What appeared beyond dispute was that this mission--acting in defiance of habitual Catholic church policy in Paraguay--had prohibited Indian songs and dances and did not tolerate the open practice of Indian religious rites, even for the "pagans" segregated behind their ghetto fence.

I told the priest that I was shocked by the sanitary and health conditions of his mission--on both sides of the fence--and appalled by the practice of dispensing medicine, even for snakebite, on what seemed a cash-and-carry basis. The priest said that life was hard and medicine high and that we had to be patient. In the only outburst of anger I permitted myself in Paraguay, I replied that life was sacred and that patience with life-destroying conditions was intolerable. The priest nodded and said that it was all very sad. He seemed stooped and older than his years; some of the residents of his mission said that he was sick, and some that he drank to excess. He walked with difficulty toward his quarters, apparently resigned to realities beyond his strength.

A cesspool was located in the heart of the reservation on the "pagan" side. It was flanked by four hovels constructed in part of aluminum and timber, and with scraps of cardboard, newspapers and rags stuffed into the more prominent gaps. A photograph in my possession displays this particular scene with the further addition of a gnarled woman attempting to prepare some edibles outdoors. She is sitting outside her hovel, flanked by a tree and a number of branches, which have fallen into the cesspool. A vulture perched on one such branch is facing the woman, the hovel and its inhabitants.

On August 26 we arrived by military plane at Faro Moro in the Chaco. We taxied down a makeshift airfield located in what at first glance looked like a wild expanse of wilderness. Almost immediately upon arrival, our military aircraft was surrounded by approximately 100 Indians. They were Moros or Ayoreos. It seemed that more than the novelty of a flying machine in a primitive wilderness had attracted them, for they stroked it and clung to it until they finally turned compulsively to every one of the strangers who emerged. Each Indian had something to tell. I was unable to make immediate verbal contact with an Indian as I was temporarily separated from the Moro interpreter whom we had brought with us from the nearby settlement of Filadelfia.

In the interim, I found myself talking to the mission administrator--this was yet another reservation under the jurisdiction of the New Tribes Mission. The mission administrator informed me that he had about 200 Moro Indians on his premises, that he regarded their food as adequate, and that he saw no health problems among his flock, 90 percent whom he regarded as Christians. When asked whether the Indians were given freedom of religion and cultural expression, he replied in the affirmative, adding however, "but we forbid immoral and wicked chants."

Everywhere I looked, I found the overcrowded makeshift hovels, wide open to the elements and cluttered with charred wood and offal, yes, and an occasional snake. Nowhere I looked were there sanitary facilities for Indians, and the place reeked of excrement with a pungency which exceeded even that of the Father Livio Farina Mission.

Again, there seemed a strange absence of young adult males. Fewer than a handful could be seen.

Upon returning to our Moro interpreter, I was in direct and friendly contact with the Indians for the rest of our stay, and their story was the worst of all we had heard.

They had, so they said, insufficient and inedible food, no doctor and no medicines. They were faced, they continued, with a never ending and demeaning interference with their folkways. An Indian informed us that one Indian had died the day before our arrival; another, a few weeks before. Both were described as having lingered for weeks without medical attention. As I looked about one of the Indian hovels, I noted a mound of recently shoveled earth. I was told that this was a grave of a man buried within the last few weeks. Were there more than I had been told about? The Moro interpreter communicated my question and waited. I was met with silence as an unspoken fear transmitted itself to all present--the figure of the reservation adminis- trator, absent at the start of the interview, now loomed over the assembled Indians and their interview- ers. One thing, however, was clear: since the Indians traditionally buried their dead in the jungle, the graves suggested either a total psychological and cul- tural disorganization on the part of the Indians, or else a refusal by the New Tribes Mission administration to permit Indians to bury their dead according to their rites.

As I mingled with more and more of the Indians, I found myself engulfed by the collective gloom of a people who had given up on life. The administrator asked me how the Indians impressed me. I replied: "They are terribly depressed." "Repressed?" asked the administrator in a note of indignation. "No, depressed," I replied--and the administrator shrugged as if at something inconsequential. Yet, the people collectively bore the demeanor of a group of mourners at a funeral--and this is understatement, since the expression of mourning appeared mingled with despair.

I was about to enter another Indian hovel, but was stopped by an Indian woman, Kai Che Ke. She flung herself at me with a face contorted with grief, but without tears. She reported that four of her children had recently died on the reservation without medical attention. As I entered the hut, I encountered a Moro Indian, approximately 20 years old, struggling to support himself in a sitting position which, in the custom of his tribe, is the ceremonial position anticipatory of death. The mission administrator, who had previously told me that there was no health problem, stepped inside and said that this Indian was a terminal tuberculosis case, and that there was nothing that could be done for him. Several seriously emaciated Indian children hovered in the background. The immediate family of the dying Indian, whose name was Epajai (although the whites, against his wishes, called him Roberto), showed me a bottle of aspirin, the medication he was given for his illness. He was visibly convulsed by stomach spasms and coughs, and told me, through the interpreter, that he was no longer able to stand upright.

I asked the reservation administrator why Epajai could not be taken in our plane to a hospital. The administrator replied that he could not afford it. When told that he would not be responsible for the expenses, he replied that the Indian would be unhappy away from his family. "Nothing can be done for him, in any event," he concluded. The administrator then promptly contradicted himself by saying that the Indian had been working the fields only a few days ago--and then added, hastily, that he had been doing only light labor. Once again, he turned down a request to permit the Indian to be taken to a hospital. On leaving the hovel, we were surrounded by another group of Moro Indians. Once again, the striking fact was the absence of any normal proportion of adult males. Many cried and said that now that we were about to depart, they would soon die. A Moro woman, perhaps 50 years old but much older in appearance, took my arm and said she did not want to live. I held her hand and made the usual superficial remark about hope. She recoiled but replied without bitterness, "My husband died only a little while ago and so did the rest of my family. I want to follow them."

We had spent approximately two hours on this reservation. As we proceeded to the aircraft, we inspected some of the primitive cooking utensils utilized by the Indians. We found no food we would have regarded as edible, but we discovered foul-smelling animal skins, apparently intended for Indian consumption. The physical appearance of the adults tended toward the emaciated. Children varied--some showing the conventional signs of malnutrition, others the bloated appearance described at the Colonia Nacional.

As we entered the plane, Indians tried to delay our departure, as if life itself depended on our continued presence. Some of them held on to the plane as though to keep it in place. For a minute or two all of us, and particularly the pilot, sat immobile in response to their plea. Then as if accepting the verdict against them, the men and women who had surrounded the plane stepped aside. The pilot started the engine. The plane took off and the unhappy Moro Indians dissolved into the distance.

At 7:00 a.m. on September 2, 1977, I kept an appointment made for me by the U.S. embassy with Paraguayan Minister of Defense Marcial Samaniego. I was received by a number of uniformed aides and then left with the minister and the member of the Paraguayan Intelligence Service (my security escort) as the only interpreter. For almost two hours, I was forced to listen to a monologue maintained by the minister between sips of tea, which was handed to us in porcelain cups refilled with almost embarrassing regularity.

The tone of the monologue was an extraordinarily friendly one. Paraguay was the best friend that America had in the hemisphere. It tolerated no iron curtain embassies or missions and was a haven for American investment, which was not subject to the fluctuations of less carefully regulated markets like North America.

The minister moved his chair toward mine conspiratorially as he explained to me how I, or any American national, could make a modest investment multiply with almost lightning rapidity in Paraguay under proper guidance.

I barely had a chance to raise a question or two about the plight of the Indians, to which the minister replied that the situation was much worse in Brazil. At this point, heel-clicking men in uniform entered the room, headed by Air Force General Ranalfo Gonzalez. My interview with the minister was over.

A new stage of the proceedings was about to begin; I was escorted into yet another conference room adjoining the minister's, for yet another exposure to Paraguayan governmental procedure. The meeting was chaired by General Ranalfo Gonzalez.

A group of approximately eight people in civilian clothes had marched into the room from one of the other doors and had seated themselves at the conference table. They were led by General Bejarano, the president of the Asociacion Indigenista del Paraguay, the official government-sponsored group for Indian welfare. Yet another group of approximately six uniformed men had accompanied General Gonzalez alonside the director of Indian affairs, Colonel Alberto Samaniego, who was silent from beginning to end, and almost worshipful in the anxious glances that he cast toward his superior. There could be no doubt who was in charge of both the conference and the ultimate disposition of Indian affairs--Air Force General Ranalfo Gonzalez, one of whose more colorful "campaign" ribbons signified three years service as Paraguayan air attache in the political campaigns of the Washington cocktail party circuit.

General Gonzales, who had once told a senior official of the Inter-American Foundation who had come to see him from Washington to intercede for a political prisoner, "I don't recognize you as an American. You are just a Chicano," adopted an identical tone with me. His suggestion, by no means veiled, was that I go back where I came from, Eastern Europe, where the matter of human rights violations was more likely to be usefully explored than in Paraguay. This was followed by a crude attempt at testing my political purity when he inquired about my opinion of Solzhenitsyn and the failure of the White House to receive him. Hoping to salvage what I could from this conversation, I replied that Solzhenitsyn was one of the world's great writers, and that the general would appreciate that I had not been consulted as to whether he should be received by the White House, but that Secretary Kissinger doubtlessly had. "Kissinger," continued the general, "is not an American either. He is a Jew and a German." As for me, resumed the general, and his tone was now coldly prosecutorial, I was patently guilty of libeling his country and his government. The only reason that he could conceive for the lies I had peddled in Genocide in Paraguay was the desire to undermine the only stable anti-Communist government in South America, and only one conclusion could be drawn from that: I was a Communist.

-231-

Since the API had begged me to make every effort I could to plead for an Indian land grant, I found myself, however reluctantly, striking a conciliatory note. I told them that the picture I had seen of Indian life on my brief trip in Paraguay was not as bad as had been anticipated, although it would be a serious distortion for me not to point out that wherever I went I had found Indians suffering and dying. No, I had not seen any Indian manhunts--surely an improvement attributable to Paraguayan government policy--but I had seen repeated evidence of Indian slavery. The response to this statement was morose silence, followed by ad hominem attacks by generals and their aides, shifting from the contributors to the book to me.

General Gonzalez's assessment of me as at least a crypto-Communist was swiftly supported by General Bejarano. Pounding the table with his fist for emphasis, he shouted that the claim that there was genocide in Paraguay was "a lie, a Communist list, a diabolical lie." His colleagues in civilian clothes and military uniforms nodded and looked appropriately outraged. I had, moreover, continued General Bejarano, pointing to me, avoided every opportunity of meeting with him, notwithstanding the repeated requests that he had made to the U.S. embassy. He had been prepared from the start to explain to me the inferiority and savagery of the Indian. A recent example was an attack staged by an 11-year-old Indian savage on a white woman for whom the Indian boy has worked in Asuncion.

"I will at this stage," declared the general, "proceed with you to the headquarters of my organization, where you will be left in no doubt as to existing realities." General Bejarano rose at this point, accompanied by his cohort of civilian flunkies and assorted military aides. I remained seated and replied that I was going nowhere except to the U.S. embassy, where I was shortly expected, and then to the airport, at which I was to catch my flight back to the United States in the afternoon. "You have said," responded General Bejarano, "that Paraguayans are assassins." "No," I said, "I regard Paraguayans as some of the most charming people I have met." General Gonzalez spoke up: "Your apology comes too late. You, as a guest of the Paraguayan government, have soiled its honor." I replied that a Paraguayan government policy of concern for its Indian population could be readily expressed by terminating the slave trade. I reported specifically having met four Indians who had been slaves less than two weeks before I met them, and added: "Where was the prosecution of the slave traders?" But there was not even a ripple of interest in this theme, let alone a taking of notes, as I offered to provide the names of the slave traders to the military and civilian gentlemen determined to uphold their honor.

As I rose to leave, I was not sure that I would be leaving under my own power or with the help of an armed escort directing me to the Departamento de Investigaciones. But to my surprise there were perfunctory handshakes. I was told, in stern military tones, to inform the American public that the Paraguayan government loved its Indians and that was why it would persist in resettling them, and, further, that my report would be expected in Paraguay without fail and would be studied with care.

If the purpose of my trip to Paraguay was to persuade me that conditions of Indian life had improved under a Paraguayan government spurred, for whatever reasons, to a policy of greater benevolence toward Indians, it was not a success.

My view of Indian life in Paraguay was, in fact, significantly more pessimistic after I had come and seen for myself, and the fact that I was on a strictly conducted tour--with large areas of Paraguay barred to me--did not help.

Let me deal with my findings on the trip in the order of their seriousness.

The book had recounted the subjection of the Ache to manhunts. Did I see manhunts?

No. I did, however, see survivors of the manhunts, carried out, among others, by the notorious manhunter, murderer and slave trader, Manuel de Jesus Pereira. The survivors I saw were kept at the Colonia Nacional Guayaki. As previously described, they gave full and gory accounts of their capture and transportation by Pereira. They displayed the scars that had been inflicted upon them with machetes, and they spoke of those who had never risen after a manhunt and of those who had been taken far, far away on the trucks of the white man. These eyewitnesses have not been interviewed by Paraguayan officials with a view to securing their testimony in a court of law. They have been left to rot. So has their testimony. Eyewitnesses who made a concerted attempt to put the evidence of the massacres, and the identity of the perpetrators, before the Paraguayan authorities have been literally intimidated from going anywhere near the U.S. embassy to prevent such information from being transmitted to Washington. There is no indication that the State Department has intervened in this harassment of individuals seeking to communicate with our government. Statements by credible informants have asserted that "Peace Corps" volunteers have, at least in one recent instance, actually attempted to discourage a potential informant from trying to contact the U.S. embassy with such information.

It is true that the Pereira reign over the Colonia Nacional was formally terminated around 1973. Pereira, however, was allowed to settle on a plantation of his selection, serviced in all of his needs by Ache Indians. The estate is at present open to inspection to visitors like myself, although I chose not to see it. It is clear, however, that Pereira is aging in the comfort of the semiretirement and that the Paraguayan government is not proceeding against him on the basis of the evidence of mass murder, torture and slave trading, which is readily at hand. Rumors have him reporting to the minister of defense as a consultant in Indian affairs--even though General Gonzalez vigorously asserts that Pereira has fully severed all connections with the Paraguayan armed forces.

I interviewed an Ache Indian--outside of the reservations I visited--about manhunts. And he told me, with the culturally conditioned smile used to avoid distressing listeners, how he and a group of 30 Ache, singing around a fire they had built in a jungle forest, were set upon by white men (in a maneuver evidently planned with some care) and mowed down from all sides by rifles or shotguns. Almost all were killed, including the wife of my informant. They had heard of manhunts before, but had tried not to believe in them. That night, he and his band of Indians had suddenly found themselves surrounded by white men who shot them down. His voice consistently flat, his face consistently smiling, he explained how he had made his escape. He carried one of his children in his arms as he fled through the forest.

As he gave his account, the flatness of his voice at times gave way to what sounded like a giggle, at times to a prolonged hysterical-sounding laugh.

Throughout, however, his eyes reflected unremitting sadness and resignation, rarely lightened by the suggestions of a gleam of appeal to his listeners. Had he reported this massacre to the authorities? His answer to me carried the patience of an adult responding to the question of a child. But for the first time the flatness of his tone seemed controlled with some difficulty. "It would have been very dangerous," he replied through an interpreter.

Are the Indians of Paraguay held as slaves? I interviewed a member of the Paraguayan bureaucracy (who cannot be more directly identified) who reported that an American New Tribe missionary, known by the first name of Roberto, had acquired 300 Indian slaves in 1975. These slaves worked for him in a remote part of the northern Chaco. Yet another informant, an Indian told me that the owner of an estancia, Jose Dolorez Pereira, was widely believed to have participated in manhunts. He was now keeping an Indian girl slave and refused to return her to her family, in spite of all entreaties. He lived approximately nine kilometers from an Indian settlement in Laurel.

I interviewed three 15-year-old girls who had found refuge from slavery less than two weeks before meeting me. I found a 15-year-old boy who had also been a slave and had escaped only a few days ago. Each of them had been sold after a manhunt, one as recently as 1973. All spoke of other slaves whom they had known while acting as domestic servants or manual laborers, some of them in Asuncion. They provided the names of their slavemasters and, in one case, of their captors. The three girls had been used for domestic labor. All complained of overwork, malnutrition, and being kept in rags. Two of them displayed evidence of barbaric punishment. One showed large scars on her legs, which, she explained, had been the result of a beating; the other showed another scar on her leg resulting, she explained, from having boiling oil thrown at her by her slavemaster. An attending doctor confirmed that her scar was consistent with second-degree burns. She escaped when taken to a hospital in Asuncion for childbirth and informed that immediately after delivery her child would be sold to other Paraguayans. Mother and child escaped with the assistance of a nun.

The boy remembered being captured in the jungle by Pereira around 1973. Taken to the Colonia Nacional Guayaki, he was sold as well, but finally made his escape. One of the girls had been bartered in exchange for two dogs.

A summary of recent information on known episodes of slavery in Paraguay, submitted to the Inter-American Commission on Human Rights and left uncontroverted by the Paraguayan government, has pinpointed six specific areas of thriving Ache slavery. The number is almost certainly an underestimate.

The overall impression based upon these materials, as well as upon my interviews, is that Indian slavery, far from being inhibited by the Paraguayan authorities, has been permitted to flourish and strike deeper roots --at times, it seems, with the assistance of Paraguayan army units.

Genocide in Paraguay documented the pervasive existence of deculturation, the destruction of Indian-ness, and the intimate link of deculturation with the growing death rate of the Indians.

What I now found was that deculturation and its induced death rate, mainly from tuberculosis, influenza and diseases of malnutrition, yes, and even more subtle forms of "psychic death," had grown apace.

And this is a report on reservations that the Paraguayan government was willing to display. What about those to which access was barred? At least one New Tribes Mission in the northern Chaco, for example, is still out of bounds for ordinary travelers. Indians are suffering and dying at all but one of the reserva-tions I saw--the only exception being the reservation at the Mission of St. Augustin, which is financed by the Inter-American Foundation and staffed by the API.

The descriptions of the other reservations do not need restatement. Literally and figuratively they deserve to be called cesspools, calculated to induce disease and death. Given the further evidence of tub-erculosis, and the utter lack of medical care or con-cern for Indians on the reservations, it would be fool-hardy to assume that even 50 percent of the Indians seen by me in all but one of the reservations will not die within a year, if not in a matter of months.

Are we to assume that the horror of existing con-ditions of Indian life is the product of a nationwide state of impoverishment that affects white and Indians

alike? The short answer to that suggestion is that
Paraguayan whites, including the poor, whose death rate
is admittedly high, are not upon the threshold of extinction as a group. The Indians are. In a word, we
are witnessing the Paraguayan version of a "final
solution" directed against the forest Indians of the
land. Ache. Moro and all the remaining forest Indians
who, however indirectly, have blocked the economic
devlopment plans of the government of Paraguay.

THE PEOPLE OF EAST TIMOR

Mike Chamberlain

While the U.S. Government and the major media have given much attention to accounts of widespread killings and starvation in Cambodia, Indonesia's protracted invasions and massive violation of human rights in little-known East Timor has only begun to gain public notice. Why hasn't anyone heard about how Indonesia has illegally annexed, slaughtered and starved the people of East Timor? The U.S. Government is deeply involved in both the tragedy and the coverup.

The East Indies island of East Timor is located 350 miles off Australia. Portugal ruled the eastern half of the island for more than 400 years, while the Dutch ruled the western half of the island. After World War II, the Indonesian Republic was formed, made up of islands that has been the Netherlands East Indies. East Timor, however, remained a Portuguese colony. Largely due to centuries of isolation, East Timor is quite different, ethnically and linguistically, from the surrounding Indonesian islands. Independence for the territory only became a possibility in 1974, when the fifty year old dictatorship in Portugal was overthrown. But the 1975 Indonesian invasion has brutally denied East Timor the right to determine its own future.

Although the Indonesian government strenuously denies it, there are credible reports that 200,000 East Timorese have died since the 1975 invasion. Most of the survivors have been forced into "resettlement camps" where starvation was widespread until a few months ago; even now, deprivation is acute. In a land that once supported 690,000 people, another 20-25,000 have died of diseases brought on by advanced malnutrition, according to refugee relief specialists. During hearings last December before the House Subcommittee on Asian and Pacific Affairs, Bruce Cameron of the Americans for Democratic Action cited a leaked report prepared by U.S. officials after a September 1979 visit to East Timor. The report stated that it was rare not to see a child or an adult in "an advanced state of malnutrition." Thousands were suffering from marasmus, a wasting disease that results when the body begins to consume its own protein. The report also noted widespread malaria and tuberculosis.

The Indonesian regime, with crucial backing from the U.S. State Department, has tried to claim that current conditions are the result of a brief civil war that took place over four years ago, drought and other "geoclimatic factors;" the consequences of the Indonesian invasion are downplayed to the extent that one has to search for mention of this in U.S. Government testimony. However, there is compelling evidence that the tragedy is a direct result of the Indonesian army's policy of starving the East Timorese into submission.

The U.S. Connection

The United States has important oil interests and other important investments in Indonesia, an OPEC country. Indonesia is also an anti-communist, largely Muslim nation with the fifth largest population in the world. It commands sea lanes between the Pacific and Indian Oceans. After the U.S. withdrawal from Indochina in 1975, American policymakers assigned added importance to Indonesia's role in Southeast Asia.

Since General Suharto's military regime came to power in 1965, amidst a bloodbath that destroyed the powerful Indonesia Communist Party, the United States has given strong support to Indonesia. In spite of the longstanding and brutal violations of human rights, the United States has forcefully defended the Suharto regime. The State Department has had its own longstanding policy of being unwilling to annoy the Indonesia generals in any way when it comes to human rights questions. In this context, it is easy to understand why the U.S. has given its complete cooperation to Indonesia in the East Timor affair--militarily, diplomatically, and--a matter of key importance--in helping to orchestrate a coverup.

Under Congressional questioning, the State Department has admitted that "roughly 90%" of the arms available to the Indonesian military at the time of the invasion were U.S. supplied. U.S. officials also testified that Indonesia could not have carried out the Timor operation without U.S. equipment. And shortly after the invasion, the U.S. began to ship a squadron of Rockwell OV-10 "Bronco" counterinsurgency aircraft to Indonesia. A Portuguese Catholic priest who witnessed Indonesian operations said that the "broncos" were a key element in the scorched earth policy that led to widespread starvation. Shipments of those and other arms were made at crucial times, coinciding with planned Indonesian offensives. U.S. military sales to Indonesia jumped from $3.1 million in 1976 to $112 million in 1978.

The State Department claimed that the U.S. secretly stopped processing new weapons orders for Indonesia in the six-month period following the December 1975 invasion. This stoppage was so "secret," in fact, that the State Department admits that they never told the Indonesians about it. In early 1978, it was revealed that this policy never went into effect: four separate orders, mainly for OV-10 Bronco spare parts and maintenance, were processed during the 1975-76 period.

Recently, however, the State Department coverup over East Timor has been coming unravelled, as the dimensions of the Timor tragedy have received some attention in the U.S. press. At a December 1979 hearing, Rep. Tom Harkin (Dem.-Iowa), spoke out against the State Department position. And in early March 1979 other Members of Congress joined Harkin in cosponsoring a resolution that will soon go to the House floor. The resolution calls for increased humanitarian aid to East Timor and much more international monitoring to go with it; for free emigration from the territory (few people have been allowed to leave since the 1975 invasion); and, importantly, the resolution calls for an Indonesian withdrawal from the territory. It appears that pressure for a change in U.S. policy is continuing to grow, while the national media is showing more interest in the issue than ever before. What has been made obvious to Senators and Congresspeople is not only the horror of East Timor, but the level and character of U.S. involvement.

Violations of human rights by the Indonesian military regime are nothing new. More than half a million people were arrested during anti-communist programs in 1965-66. At least 30,000 political detainees were held for more than 12 years despite the fact that the government itself admitted that there was insufficient evidence to try them. Following a worldwide campaign on the Indonesian prisoners by Amnesty International in 1976 and 1977, and a series of U.S. Congressional hearings, largescale releases were carried out. This shows that concerted pressure can move the Indonesian government--and the U.S. State Department--to change its policies. While high U.S. officials have praised the Indonesian generals for carrying out the releases,

Washington has completely ignored the carnage in East Timor. But how did the tragedy come about?

Origins of the War

Following the April 1974 change in government in Lisbon, decolonization talks began between the Portuguese and several newly-formed political associations in East Timor. Independent observers noted that an overwhelming majority of the population favored independence; there was also a small group that wanted union with Indonesia. It has been reported that the Indonesian regime feared the possiblity of an independent East Timor because such a state would be weak and thus subject to big-power influence; in this view, it would also stimulate separatist movements in Indonesia. Some experts, however, see the Indonesian invasion as the product of a tiny group of dictatorial army generals who saw and seized an opportunity to extend their control. The generals are willing to tolerate the Portuguese presence and nothing else. Others have stated that if East Timor had become a successful small state it would be a dangerous example for nearby, poverty-stricken Indonesian islands--dangerous, that is, to the right-wing military regime in Jakarta, the Indonesian capital. Nonetheless, most experts believe that all these fears were groundless.

In late 1974, Indonesian military intelligence began to create tensions between Timorese groups by any means they could. By August 1975, the right-wing Timorese Democratic Union (UDT) staged an armed coup, with Indonesian backing. The coup was designed to eliminate many leaders of FRETILIN (Revolutionary Front for an independent East Timor), a popular, nationalist coalition that had instituted agricultural cooperatives, literacy and medical programs, and other important reforms and also felt pressure from the Indonesian military which was threatening to invade unless FRETILIN was neutralized. But the Timorese troops in the Portuguese colonial army supported FRETILIN and quickly defeated UDT. Although neutral observers have said that the FRETILIN adminstration that governed from September to early December 1975 was responsible and moderate, the stage was set for an Indonesian invasion. Portugal, in the middle of its own domestic crisis in late 1975, hastily abandoned the territory. Although Lisbon did not support an Indonesian invasion, it took no effective steps to prevent it--a source of much of the collective guilt that is evident in Portugal today whenever Timor is discussed.

Indonesia launched its full-scale invasion on December 7, 1975, the day after President Ford and Secretary of State Henry Kissinger visited the Indonesia capital, Jakarta. While there, Kissinger told the press that the "United States understands Indonesia's position on the question of East Timor."

The United Nations immediately called for the withdrawal of Indonesian troops, but instead of withdrawing, the Indonesian army intensified their attacks. The failure of the U.S. and other countries under U.S. influence to support U.S. initiatives gave Indonesia the green light to continue the invasion. FRETILIN, for its part, put up stiff resistance in the mountainous interior, on familiar terrain. Indonesia's hopes for a quick victory vanished. Still, President Suharto announced the annexation of East Timor in July 1976; the U.N.--but not the U.S.--still rejects Indonesia's claim to sovereignty over East Timor.

Since the war against FRETILIN had proved to be costly and difficult, the Indonesian forces turned to aerial bombardment as a strategy to force the population out of FRETILIN-held areas, and here, the OV-10 Broncos showed their usefulness. Villages were bombed, crops were destroyed, and people were herded into the so-called "resettlement centers." Once in the camps, people were prevented from farming their lands, making the situation worse. For people who managed to elude the Indonesians, the bombing made food production impossible, particularly in 1977 and 1978.

By September 1978, it became clear that the Indonesian military had never adequately supplied the people it had forced into the camps; strong evidence indicates that tens of thousands literally starved to death. The Indonesian military kept independent relief agencies out of the territory until 1979 in an effort to keep the situation quiet. Meanwhile, relief aid, food and medicine, were used as a political weapon to force the population into accepting the occupation. The army also profited by selling relief supplies at inflated prices. Such reports continually filtered out through Indonesian relief organizations, with rare reports and from refugees who made it to Portugal.

Even now, only a handful of independent relief workers are allowed to operate in East Timor. Any

Indonesian doing this work is automatically subject to
military coercion, thus the need for a foreign presence.   The supplies exist to alleviate East Timor's
suffering, but as of now, the Indonesian military is
still keeping out additional outside relief personnel
who are needed if things are to improve significantly.
More than 300,000 people are in need of relief at
present; only four foreigners are there to administer
the program--this, in a Connecticut-sized territory
with some of the most difficult terrain in Southeast
Asia.

Predictably, the State Department has supported
the Indonesian restrictions--restrictions that the U.S.
has been fighting in Cambodia. It is worth noting that
late last year, the International Red Cross said that
the East Timor situation was worse than that in Biafra
and potentially more serious than Cambodia.   With the
recent improvements in Cambodia, Timor has indeed fulfilled that dire prediction.   The situation is urgent;
Americans must work for the entry of large numbers of
foreign medical personnel, nutritionists and observers
if East Timor is to be saved.

THE BUDDHISTS OF TIBET

International Commission of Jurists

Introduction to the evidence on Chinese activities
in Tibet

The allegations against the People's Republic of
China can be fitted into three broad legal categories:

1) Systematic disregard for the obligations under
   the Seventeen-Point Agreement of 1951;

2) Systematic violation of the fundamental rights
   and freedoms of the people of Tibet;

3) Wanton killing of Tibetans and other acts
   capable of leading to the extinction of the
   Tibetans as a national and religious group, to
   the extent that it becomes necessaary to consider the question of Genocide.

There is some inevitable overlap between these
categories, for example, in the case of respect for
religious belief, where there is this obligation under
the Seventeen-Point Agreement [Article 7] and in the
Universal Declaration of Human Rights [Article 18].

The significance of these three legal categories
may be briefly explained. Violation of the 1951 Agreement by China can be regarded as a release of the Tibetan Government from its obligations, with the result
that Tibet regained the sovereignty which she surren-
dered under the Agreement. This question is discussed
in the part of this report entitled "The Position of
Tibet in International Law." For this reason the
violations of the Agreement by China amount to more
than a matter of domestic concern between Tibet and
China. What is at stake is the very existence of Tibet
as a member of the family of nations, and this matter
concerns the whole family of nations. Evidence showing
the systematic violation by China of the obligations
under the Agreement is therefore printed in extenso.

Any systematic violation of human rights in any
part of the world should, it is submitted, be a matter
for discussion by the United Nations. For this reason
the evidence which indicates violation on a systematic
scale of the rights of the Tibetan people as human

beings is printed in extenso. Most people will agree that in the sphere of human rights, some rights are fundamental. The rights of the Tibetans which appear to have been ruthlessly violated are of the most fundamental--even that of life itself. With violations of this gravity it is not a question of human rights being modified to meet the requirements of local conditions. It is a question of conduct which shocks the civilized world and does not even need to be fitted into a legal category. The evidence points to a systematic design to eradicate the separate national, cultural and religious life of Tibet.

Genocide is the gravest crime known to the law of nations. No allegation of Genocide should be made without the most careful consideration of evidence that killings, or other acts prohibited by the Genocide Convention, however extensive, are directed towards the destruction in whole or in part of a particular group which constitutes a race, a nation or a religion. The facts, as far as they are known are set out in extenso. It is submitted, with a full appreciation of the gravity of this accusation, that the evidence points at least to a prima facie case of Genocide against the People's Republic of China. This case merits full investigation by the United Nations.

The evidence submitted against China is printed verbatim in this report. Statements made by the official press and radio of the Chinese People's Republic are reproduced at perhaps inordinate length, and even so amount to no more than specimens of the Chinese account of the recent history of Tibet. Space does not permit a fuller inclusion, but it is considered that the selection is at least typical of the official Chinese accounts. The accounts given by Tibetan leaders in exile and refugees on the one hand, and Chinese spokesmen and Tibetan collaborators on the other are reproduced with a minimum of editing and running commentary. By and large the accounts given by Tibetans are self-evidently linked to the specific legal category under which they are cited; accounts from Chinese sources are by and large self-evidently inconsistent, though in this case there is a certain amount of running commentary.

At the beginning of each section of evidence presented is a summary of contents, an assessment of the effect of the evidence and, in some cases, a critical discussion of the Chinese accounts. Finally, a summary

of conclusions is offered. A note on the leading personalities involved precedes the general body of evidence, together with a list of abbreviations used in
the extracts and in the commentary.

From the whole tangled mass of propaganda, allegation and counter-allegations made by the principal
protagonists in the Tibetan situation, one statement
stands out. The Dalai Lama in his statement at
Mussoorie, India, on June 20th, 1959 said:

> I wish to make it clear that I have made
> these assertions against Chinese officials in
> Tibet in full knowledge of their gravity be-
> cause I know them to be true. Perhaps the
> Peiping Government are not fully aware of the
> facts of the situation but if they are not
> prepared to accept these statements let them
> agree to an investigation on the point by an
> international commission. On our part I and
> my Government will readily agree to abide by
> the verdict of such an impartial body.

The issue on the evidence submitted in this report
is to a large extent who is telling the truth. On this
issue this proposal by the Dalai Lama is of the utmost
importance. The International Commission of Jurists is
setting up its Legal Inquiry Committee, but it is not
known whether this Committee will be allowed to enter
Tibet. Nor is it certain that a United Nations Commission, if one is formed, will be able to make on the
spot inquiries in Tibet.   But if entry is refused it
will be by the Government of the People's Republic of
China.   That Government has not so far accepted the
Dalai Lama's proposal. On the question of credibility
the obvious inference is there to be drawn.

The Question of Genocide

Genocide is defined in the Convention for the
Prevention and Punishment of Genocide, 9th December
1948, which was agreed in pursuance of the resolution
by the General Assembly of the United Nations[1] that
Genocide is a crime against the law of nations. The
contracting parties undertook to prevent and punish
Genocide. There is therefore an obligation upon each
and every one of the States who were party to the
Convention to take action if a case of Genocide comes
to light.

The Convention defines both the _mens rea_[2] and the _actus reus_[3] of Genocide in specific terms. The _actus reus_ is committed in one or more of several ways as defined in Article 2:

a) killing;

b) causing serious bodily or mental harm;

c) subjection to living conditions leading to the total or partial destruction of the group;

d) measures intended to prevent the birth of children within the group;

e) forcible transfer of children of the group to another.

Conspiracy to commit Genocide, incitement to commit Genocide, attempted Genocide and aiding and abetting Genocide are all declared punishable by Article 3. The _mens rea_ of Genocide is defined as the intention to destroy in whole or in part a national, ethnic, racial or religious group as such.[4]

It cannot be overemphasized that one must deliberate carefully before making an allegation of Genocide. It is probably the gravest crime known to the law of nations. For this reason, the evidence must be very carefully considered, and all inferences from the evidence must be logically supportable.

Evidence of the Actus Reus of Genocide

(i) Religious groups: The evidence that there has been widespread killing of Buddhist monks and lamas in Tibet is clear and explicit. One need only refer to the evidence in this category under Section A (II). If this evidence is to be believed, there has been a destruction by killing of a part of a religious group. The International Commission of Jurists believes that this evidence raises at the very least a case which requires thorough and careful investigation.

(ii) National groups: The account of wanton killings in Tibet points to killings on a wider scale than that of religious groups. Particular attention should be paid to the evidence of indiscriminate air attacks, and of deliberate shooting of Tibetans who were in no way engaged in hostilities. Evidence of such killings is given in Section B. It should also be stressed that the alleged deportation of 20,000 Tibetan children is directly contrary to Article 2(e).[5] It is of the utmost importance that this report be fully investigated.

The Memorandum contains important evidence on the forcible removal of children to China:

> Above all they have made thousands of homes unhappy by forcing young boys and girls to go to China for de-nationalisation, thus getting them indoctrinated to revolt against our own culture, traditions and religion. To this end they have sent more than five thousand boys and girls up to now to China proper.

Here is clear prima facie evidence of a violation of Article 2(e) of the Genocide Convention.

Evidence of the Mens Rea of Genocide

It is very rarely in criminal trials that direct evidence of mens rea is available. The fact that there is no official Chinese policy statement directed towards the destruction of the Tibetans is no ground for withholding an accusation of Genocide if an inference of the requisite intention can properly be drawn. For this purpose it is permissible to take into account acts which point to the extinction of a national or religious group whether or not such acts are in themselves acts of Genocide. For if a systematic intention to destroy a nation or religion can be shown by acts which are not declared criminal by the Genocide Convention, the acts on which these inferences are based can properly be adduced as evidence of general intention. If in addition there are acts which are capable in law of amounting to Genocide, and such acts are part of a consistent pattern of destroying a nation or religion, the inference of intent in non-genocidal acts is equally valid in respect of acts which are within those prohibited by the Genocide Convention.

For this reason, the overall assessment of the evidence in Sections A and B is relevant and important. If such evidence points to an intention to destroy religion in Tibet, and to assimilate the Tibetan way of life to the Chinese, there is evidence of the required intent to destroy, in whole or in part, a national or religious group. It has been argued that the activities of the Chinese in Tibet point to the conclusion that this was the intention behind the Chinese acts in the fields described in Sections A and B. The ruthless efficiency is otherwise difficult to explain. The evidence in these two sections should be carefully studied.

This inference has been drawn from these and other facts by Tibetans from the Dalai Lama downwards. The Tibetan opinions on the Chinese intentions are as follows:

Statement of the Dalai Lama in Mussoorie, June 20, 1959

In the course of his press conference the Dalai Lama stated:

> The ultimate Chinese aim with regard to Tibet, as far as I can make out, seems to attempt the extermination of religion and culture and even the absorption of the Tibetan race...Besides the civilian and military personnel already in Tibet, five million Chinese settlers have arrived in eastern and north-eastern Tso, in addition to which four million Chinese settlers are planned to be sent to U and Sung provinces of Central Tibet. Many Tibetans have been deported, thereby resulting in the complete absorption of these Tibetans as a race, which is being undertaken by the Chinese.

Memorandum

The statement already quoted from the Memorandum on the actus reus of Genocide also contains the inference by the authors of the document that the aim was to get the children to "revolt against their own culture, traditions asnd religion."

Statement of Chaghoe Namgyal Dorje

> My experience of four years' work with the Chinese convinced me that their propaganda was false and that their real intention was

-249-

to exterminate us as a race and destroy our religion and culture.

Communists are enemies not only to Buddhism but to all religion. It has been told to me that more than 2,000 Lamas had been killed by the Chinese. I have personal knowledge of such attacks on 17 Lamas.

Even if no help is coming we shall fight to death. We fight not because we hope to win but that we cannot live under Communism. We prefer death.

We are fighting not for a class or sect. We are fighting for our religion, our country, our race. If these cannot be preserved we will die a thousand deaths than surrender these to the Chinese.

These inferences were drawn by people who know as no one outside Tibet can know the full extent of Chinese brutality in Tibet. They are in a better position than any outsider to assess the motives behind the Chinese oppression, including the slaughter, the deportations and the less crude methods, of all of which there is abundant evidence.

It is therefore the considered view of the International Commission of Jurists that the evidence points to:

(a) a prima facie case of acts contrary to Article 2(a) and (e) of the Genocide Convention of 1948.

(b) a prima facie case of a systematic intention by such acts and other acts to destroy in whole or in part the Tibetans as a separate nation and the Buddhist religion in Tibet.

Accordingly, the Commission will recommend to its Legal Inquiry Committee that existing evidence of Genocide be fully checked, that further evidence, if available, be investigated, that unconfirmed reports be investigated and checked. But the final reponsibility for this task rests with the formal organ of world authority and opinion. The Commission therefore earnestly hopes that this matter will be taken up by the United Nations. For what at the moment appears to be attempted Genocide may become the full act of Genocide unless prompt and adequate action is taken. The life of Tibet and the lives of Tibetans may be at stake, and somewhere there must be sufficient moral strength left in the world to seek the truth through the world's highest international organ.

Footnotes

1. Resolution 96(I) of December 11th, 1946.

2. *Mens* *rea*, a term from the criminal law, means the state of mind necesssary to make criminal the conduct which is prohibited.

3. *Actus* *reus* means the conduct which the law prohibits.

4. Article 2.

5. The report was contained in an article in the London "Daily Mail" on January 1st, 1959. Whilst a newspaper report cannot without more be regarded as an authentic primary source, the statement of a competent and reputable journalist (Mr. Noel Barber) raises at least a case for investigation.

THE SITUATION IN CAMBODIA

David Aikman

The enormity of the tragedy has been carefully reconstructed from the reports of many eyewitnesses. Some political theorists have defended it, as George Bernard Shaw and other Western intellectuals defended the brutal social engineering in the Soviet Union during the 1930s. Yet it remains perhaps the most dreadful infliction of suffering on a nation by its government in the past three decades. The nation is Cambodia.

On the morning of April 17, 1975, advance units of Cambodia's Communist insurgents, who had been actively fighting the defeated Western-backed government of Marshal Lon Nol for nearly five years, began entering the capital of Phnom Penh. The Khmer Rouge looted things, such as watches and cameras, but they did not go on a rampage, They seemed disciplined. And at first, there was general jubilation among the city's terrified, exhausted and bewildered inhabitants. After all, the civil war seemed finally over, the Americans had gone, and order, everyone seemed to assume, would soon be graciously restored.

Then came the shock. After a few hours, the black uniformed troops began firing into the air. It was a signal for Phnom Penh's entire population, swollen by refugees to some 3 million, to abandon the city. Young and old, the well and the sick, businessmen and beggars were all ordered at gunpoint onto the streets and highways leading into the countryside.

Among the first pitiful sights on the road, witnessed by several Westerners, were patients from Phnom Penh's grossly overcrowded hospitals, perhaps 20,000 people all told. Even the dying, the maimed and the pregnant were herded out stumbling onto the streets. Several pathetic cases were pushed along the road in their beds by relatives, the intravenous bottles still attached to the bedframes. In some hospitals, foreign doctors were ordered to abandon their patients in mid-operation. It took two days before the Bruegel-like multitude was fully under way, shuffling, limping and crawling to a designated appointment with revolution.

With almost no preparations for so enormous an exodus--how could there have been with a war

-252-

on?--thousands died along the route, the wounded from loss of blood, the weak from exhaustion, and others by execution, usually because they had not been quick enough to obey a Khmer Rouge order. Phnom Penh was not alone: the entire urban population of Cambodia, some 4 million people, set out on a similar grotesque pilgrimage. It was one of the greatest transfers of human beings in modern history.

The survivors were settled in villages and agricultural communes all around Cambodia and were put to work for frantic 16- or 17-hour days, planting rice and building an enormous new irrigation system. Many died from dysentery or malaria, others from malnutrition, having been forced to survive on a condensed-milk can of rice every two days. Still others were taken away at night by Khmer Rouge guards to be shot or bludgeoned to death. The lowest estimate of the bloodbath to date --by execution, starvation and disease--is in the hundreds of thousands. The highest exceeds 1 million, and that in a country that once numbered no more than 7 million. Moreover, the killing continues, according to the latest refugees.

The Roman Catholic cathedral in Phnom Penh has been razed, and even the native Buddhism is reviled as a "reactionary" religion. There are no private telephones, no forms of public transportation, no postal service, no universities. A Scandinavian diplomat who last year visited Phnom Penh--today a ghost city of shuttered shops, abandoned offices and painted-over street signs--said on his return: "It was like an absurd film; it was a nightmare. It is difficult to believe it is true."

Yet, why is it so difficult to believe? Have not the worst atrocities of the 20th century all been committed in the name of some perverse pseudo science, usually during efforts to create a new heaven on earth, or even a "new man?" The Nazi notion of racial purity led inexorably to Auschwitz and the Final Solution. Stalin and Mao Tse-tung sent millions to their deaths in the name of a supposedly moral cause--in their case, the desired triumph of socialism. Now the Cambodians have taken bloodbath sociology to its logical conclusion. Karl Marx declared that money was at the heart of man's original sin, the acquisition of capital. The men behind Cambodia's Angka Loeu (Organization on High) who absorbed such verities while students in the West, have decided to abolish money.

-253-

How to do that? Well, one simplistic way was to abolish cities, because cities cannot survive without money. The new Cambodian rulers did just that. What matter that hundreds of thousands died as the cities were depopulated? It apparently meant little, if anything, to Premier Pol Pot and his shadowy colleagues on the politburo of Democratic Kampuchea, as they now call Cambodia. When asked about the figure of 1 million deaths, President Khieu Samphan replied: "It's incredible how concerned you Westerners are about war criminals." Radio Phnom Penh even dared to boast of this atrocity in the name of collectivism: "More than 2,000 years of Cambodian history have virtually ended."

Somehow, the enormity of the Cambodian tragedy--even leaving aside the grim question of how many or how few actually died in Angka Loeu's experiment in genocide--has failed to evoke an appropriate response of outrage in the West. To be sure, President Carter has declared Cambodia to be the worst violator of human rights in the world today. And, true, members of the U.S. Congress have ringingly denounced the Cambodian holocaust. The U.N., ever quick to adopt a resolution condemning Israel or South Africa, acted with its customary tortoise-like caution when dealing with a Third World horror: it wrote a letter to Phnom Penh asking for an explanation of charges against the regime.

Perhaps the greatest shock has been in France, a country where many of Cambodia's new rulers learned their Marx and where worship of revolution has for years been something of a national obsession among the intelligentsia. Said New Philosopher Bernard-Henri Levy, a former leftist who has turned against Marxism: "We thought of revolution in its purest form as an angel. The Cambodian revolution was as pure as an angel, but it was barbarous. The question we ask ourselves now is, can revolution be anything but barbarous?"

Levy has clearly pointed out the abyss to which worship of revolution leads. Nonetheless, many Western European intellectuals are still reluctant to face the issue squarely. If the word "pure," when used by adherents of revolution, in effect means "barbarous," perhaps the best the world can hope for in its future political upheavals is a revolution that is as "corrupt" as possible. Such skewed values are, indeed, already rife in some quarters. During the 1960s, Mao's

Cultural Revolution in China was admired by many left-ist intellectuals in the West, because it was supposed-ly "pure,"--particularly by contrast with bureaucratic stodginess of the Soviet Union. Yet that revolution, as the Chinese are now beginning to admit, grimly impoverished the country's science, art, education and literature for a decade. Even the Chinese advocates of "purity" during that time, Chiang Ch'ing and her cron-ies in the Gang of Four, turned out to have been as corrupt as the people in power they sought to replace. With less justification, there are intellectuals in the West so committed to the twin Molochs of our day--"liberation" and "revolution"--that they can actually defend what has happened in Cambodia.

Where the insane reversal of values lies is in the belief that notions like "purity" or "corruption" can have any meaning outside an absolute system of values: one that is resistant to the tinkering at will by governments or revolutionary groups. The Cambodian revolution, in its own degraded "purity," has demon-strated what happens when the Marxian denial of moral absolutes is taken with total seriousness by its adher-ents. Pol Pot and his friends decide what good is, what bad is, and how many corpses must pile up before this rapacious demon of "purity" is appeased.

In the West today, there is a pervasive consent to the notion of moral relativism, a reluctance to admit that absolute evil can and does exist. This makes it especially difficult for some to accept the fact that the Cambodian experience is something far worse than a revolutionary aberration. Rather, it is the deadly logical consequence of an atheistic, man-centered syst-em of values, enforced by fallible human beings with total power, who believe, with Marx, that morality is whatever the powerful define it to be and, with Mao, that power grows from gun barrels. By no coincidence the most humane Marxist societies in Europe today are those that, like Poland or Hungary, permit the dilution of their doctrine by what Solzhenitsyn has called "the great reserves of mercy and sacrifice" from a Christian tradition. Yet if there is any doubt about what the focus of the purest of revolutionary values is, con-sider the first three lines of the national anthem of Democratic Kampuchea: "The red, red blood splatters the cities and plains of the Cambodian fatherland; the sublime blood of the workers and peasants; the blood of revolutionary combatants of both sexes."

THE BENGALIS OF EAST PAKISTAN

Rounaq Jahan

.....The birth of Bangladesh is in many ways a unique phenomenon and poses a number of interesting questions to students of political development. Pakistan is the first among the new states of Asia and Africa, with illogical boundaries and plural societies, to break down. Bangladesh is the first country to emerge out of a successful struggle against "internal colonialism" in the Third World countries. The emergence of Bangladesh, and especially the decisive Indian involvement in the last phase of the liberation movement, sent shock waves through the developing countries, many of whom are engaged in their own struggle to build nations out of disparate subnational groups. The question naturally arises: Was Bangladesh a special case or would it have a "domino" impact on other, similar movements? As this analysis has tried to show, the emergence of Bangladesh was indeed the result of a configuration of a number of forces which may not necessarily be repeated in other cases. Several factors may be cited to explain why the Bangladesh movement succeeded while similar movements in other countries have failed or are likely to fail.

First, the Bangladesh movement was truly a nationalist as well as a democratic struggle. The Bengalis formed the majority of Pakistan's population, but their efforts to participate in the decision-making process of the country through democratic electoral processes were thwarted repeatedly, in 1954, 1958, and 1971. The actual liberation movement started in Bangladesh in March 1971, when the Pakistani army tried to reverse with bullets the gains the Bengalis had achieved through the ballot box in the election of 1970. Unlike Biafra, where the liberation struggle was led by a military general, the Bangladesh movement was led by a political party, the Awami League, which had won an overwhelming election victory. The movement involved extensive mass participation and mass support, which was spontaneous. What the movement lost in organization from these spontaneous actions, it gained in numbers and popular support.

Second, the savage brutalities of the Pakistan army and the genocidal nature of their killings aroused a keen sense of unity among the Bengalis, broke down primordial sentiments, and stiffened their resistance. It was looked upon not only as a struggle for liberation but in fact as a struggle for the survival of a people. It is true that the Pakistan army had a number of select target groups, i.e., students, intellectuals, Hindus, Awami League supporters, slum dwellers, Bengali members of the army and police, etc.; but the burning of villages en masse and mass graves justified the Bengalis' apprehension over their survival as a group. Between one and three million people were reportedly killed during the nine-month struggle. The brutalities of the Pakistan army created world-wide sympathy for the Bengali cause, and the regime found it difficult to replenish its depleted defense budget from foreign sources. The brutalities of the army thus proved to be counterproductive,

Third, the separation of East and West Pakistan by a thousand miles of Indian territory created insurmountable logistic problems for Pakistan, which played a decisive role in the struggle. The cost of shipping men and arms across the Indian Ocean for nine months nearly bankrupted Pakistan. And when the actual war broke out at the end of November, Pakistan could not continue supplying its army in Bangladesh because of an effective Indian naval blockade.

Finally, the Indian sanctuary and Indian help played a key role. It would have taken Bangladesh several more years to emerge had India not joined with the Mukti Bahini in the third phase of the struggle. An India unfriendly to the cause of the liberation movement would, of course, have spelled disaster for the movement. Thus, the birth of Bangladesh was not only the culmination of a long struggle; it was the result of a combination of factors which might not be present elsewhere.

With the birth of Bangladesh, the major problem of Pakistan's integration is removed from the scene. The two successor states, Pakistan and Bangladesh, however, still face their own problems of national integration. For Pakistan it is the task of building a national community out of the four remaining subnational groups; for Bangladesh it is the task of building a national political system. One hopes that the policy-makers in both states have learned from the mistakes of the sixties; and that in the seventies, they will give priority to the task of nation-building through participation.

V.   THE IMPLICATIONS OF GENOCIDE

V.   THE IMPLICATIONS OF GENOCIDE

There are many complex issues raised by genocide. This section discusses some of them. Robert Jay Lifton, drawing on his work with Hiroshima survivors and Vietman War veterans, discusses the implications of future holocausts, especially nuclear war. He believes survivors will be subject to "psychic numbing," a diminished ability to think or feel. While he sometimes overgeneralizes, his essay is a poignant one. His work should be compared to Alan Rosenberg's essay at the beginning of this book.

Helen Fein, a New York sociologist, has made major contributions to our understanding of genocide with her sophisticated and hard-edged analyses.   Her essay should be read in conjunction with Section IV.   Her prognosis is pessimistic: the role of NGOs (nongovernmental organizations) has been belated and ineffectual and will continue to be so. She offers few solutions to this dilemma.

William Korey, long-time activist on behalf of Soviet Jewry and other human rights causes, delves into America's "shame" in not ratifying the Genocide Convention.   Perhaps he would agree with Helen Fein that little more would be done to curb genocide even if the U.S. did sign it.   Still the treaty is basically a moral document and the United States, despite everything, is a moral model to the world and should sign it.   Korey's history is a testament to ineffectual leadership in the United States on this matter.

The anthology concludes with an almost utopian ideal but one that should at least be attempted. Israel Charny, an American psychologist now teaching in Israel, has developed a simple, yet ingenious program-a genocide early-warning system based upon computer-fed files of political and economic data to pinpoint when and where genocide might occur. With such a tool it could be possible for governments and NGOs to alert possible victims and save them. Such a project would need constant maintenance, data, and feedback, but given enough support and money, it could work. We have early-warning military systems. Why not one to save human beings?

WITNESSING SURVIVAL

Robert Jay Lifton

Robert Jay Lifton, a professor of psychiatry at Yale University, has interviewed survivors of the atomic bombing of Hiroshima, veterans returning from the Vietnam war, and victims of the Buffalo Creek flood disaster, and has extensively studied the literature on the Nazi Holocaust. His message is clear: the study of holocausts is both vital and difficult. The study of past holocausts reveals how the meanings of life and death can become twisted in the hands of governments that have at their disposal increasingly effective means of killing. Lifton points out, moreover, that the survivors of holocausts suffer grievous trauma, both physically and mentally; in particular, survivors are susceptible to psychic numbing, in which the ability to feel and think is drastically diminished as a defense against meaninglessness and horror. Lifton's study of past holocausts underscores the importance of understanding and preventing future ones; a nuclear holocaust is likely to be unimaginably more pervasive and lethal, for both direct victims and survivors, than any holocaust in history.

One approaches the study of holocaust knowing that it is virtually impossible to convey the experience, to find words or concepts for the extremity of its horror. And we are faced with the paradox of making an effort to understand, in terms of human feeling, the most antihuman event in human history. The European Holocaust, after all, was invented by, and consumed, human beings. And its very extremity has something to teach us about our more ordinary confrontations with death and violence.

Investigators' Dilemmas

The word "holocaust," from Greek origins, means total consumption by fire. That definition applies, with literal grotesqueness, to Auschwitz and Buchenwald, and also to Nagasaki and Hiroshima. In Old

Testament usage there is the added meaning of the sacrificial, of a burnt offering. That meaning tends to be specifically retained for the deliberate, selective Nazi genocide of six million Jews--retained with both bitterness and irony (sacrifice to whom and for what?) I will thus speak of the Holocaust and of holocausts--the first to convey the uniqueness of the Nazi project of genocide, the second to suggest certain general principles around the totality of destruction as it affects survivors. From that perspective holocaust means total disaster: the physical, social, and spiritual obliteration of a human community. To observe common psychological responses of survivors, however, in no way suggests that the historical events themselves can be equated [to these responses].

Those of us who undertake this task face two additional problems. One is the inadequacy of ordinary psychological concepts, and yet the necessity to find connections between the extreme and the ordinary in our experience. Another is the nature of the investigator's own involvement--that combination which Buber called distance and relation.

On the part of psychological investigators there has been too much distance and not enough relation, a tendency to negate or minimize survivors' experiences, largely in response to our own psychic numbing. Yet there is also the danger of the kind of uneasiness before survivors that causes the investigator to romanticize or glorify their ordeal and thereby to divest it of its unsavory dimensions. Either stance--spurious neutrality or compensatory glorification--diminishes the survivor and interferes with our understanding both of what is particular to his ordeal, and what insight it may reveal about our own psychological and historical condition.

What follows draws upon my experience, direct and indirect, with survivors of four different holocausts: Hiroshima, where I lived and interviewed survivors over a period of six months in 1962; the Nazi death camps, mostly through others' studies and the writings of survivors; the Vietnam War, through intensive work with returning veterans from 1970 through 1973; and the Buffalo Creek flood disaster of 1972, through work with survivors in West Virginia from 1973 through 1975. Precisely because these four events differ so greatly-- the last in particular is of a separate order from the other three in terms of size and historical signifi-

cance--the fact that survivors share certain psychological responses takes on added importance.

Defining Survivors

Who is a survivor? A survivor is one who has
encountered, been exposed to, or witnessed death, and
has himself or herself remained alive. Albert Camus,
in his Nobel Prize acceptance speech of 1957, spoke of
"twenty years of absolutely insane history." Elsewhere
he asks a terrible rhetorical question: "Do you know
that over a period of twenty-five years, between 1922
and 1947, seventy million Europeans--men, women and
children--have been uprooted, deported, killed?" (The
"Do you know" means, do we let ourselves remember--do
we permit ourselves to feel!) One might well repeat
the question for the ensuing three decades, in relationship to Asians, Africans, and Latin Americans, who
have suffered similarly. Camus viewed such things, in
the words of one of his biographers, "as a scandal that
he himself finds impossible to evade." We can say that
he referred to our landscape of holocaust, from which
literature must emerge and life must be lived. On that
basis (and without in any way equating ordinary life to
the experience of holocaust) we can say that we all
have in us something of the survivor and witness.

Here, as in his other work, Camus expressed the
survivor's potential for confronting the death immersion and for seeking from it a measure of insight. But
a contrasting response is also possible--one of cessation of feeling or sustained psychic numbing. This is
the response of most ordinary people to the death
immersions of their time. And this numbed response can
be viewed as a second scandal of our time, the scandal
of our failure to be scandalized by manmade holocausts,
by mass murder.

A few more distinctions. An actual survivor of
holocaust undergoes a totality of psychological responses which cannot be duplicated in ordinary experience.
Yet separate elements of that death immersion do make
contact with general psychological principles. If
there is one thing Freud taught us, it is that no
single psychological tendency, however extreme or
disturbed, is totally alien from "normal" pyschic function. So we must study survivor experience both in its
uniqueness and in its connection with the rest of human
life. It follows that survivors vary enormously in

their capacities and inclinations--many extraordinary in their life-power, others capable of destructive behavior, each bringing a particular mixture of virtues and faults to a shared ordeal.

Psychological Themes

In previous writings I have described five psychological themes in survivors. The first of these is the death imprint with its related death anxiety. Involved here are indelible images not just of death but of grotesque and absurd (that is, totally unacceptable) forms of death. In Hiroshima the indelible image was likely to include grotesque shapes of the dead and the dying, as immediately encountered after the bomb fell-- scenes described to me seventeen years later and yet so immediate in tone that I felt myself virtually in the midst of them. With Nazi death camp survivors, the imagery can include many forms of cruel memory--the smoke or smell of the gas chambers, the brutal killing of a single individual, or simply separation from a family member never seen again. Vietnam veterans' images were of the bodies of close buddies blown apart and of the slaughter of Vietnamese civilians. In Buffalo Creek survivors described the terrifying advance of the "black water" and people disappearing in it. In all four cases imagery included something close to the end of the world, the "end of time," the destruction of everything. There can be a thralldom to this death imagery, the sense of being bound by it and of seeing all subsequent experience through its prism. The survivor may feel himself stuck in time, unable to move beyond that imagery, or he may find it a source of death-haunted knowledge--even creative energy--that has considerable value for his life.

The second category is that of death guilt--frequently termed survivor guilt, and much misunderstood. Death guilt is epitomized by the survivor's questions, "Why did I survive while he, she, or they died?" Even before he can ask this question, the beginnings of the process take shape around the indelible imagery mentioned earlier. Part of the survivor's sense of horror is his memory of his own inactivation--his helplessness --within the death imagery, of his inability to act in a way he would ordinarily have thought appropriate (save people, resist the victimizers, etc.) or even to feel the appropriate emotions (overwhelming rage toward victimizers, profound compassion for victims). Death guilt begins, then, in the gap between that physical and psychic inactivation and what one felt called upon (by that beginning image formation) to do and feel. That is one reason why the imagery keeps recurring, in dreams and in waking life. One could in fact define the survivor as one who is haunted by images of extremity that can neither be enacted (in the sense of a satisfactory original response) nor cast aside. Contained in this imagery is the survivor's sense of debt to the dead and responsibility toward them. One must be careful to distinguish these feelings of psychological guilt from moral and legal guilt, which involves ethical and social judgments concerning wrongdoing. Nowhere is the distinction more important than in the case of survivors of holocaust. Their paradoxical guilt is one of many undeserved residua of their experience, and perhaps the most ironic.

The third category is one I have emphasized in much of my work, that of psychic numbing or the diminished capacity to feel. In Hiroshima I was impressed by survivors' repeated statements to the effect that, after the bomb fell, they could see that people were dying, and understand that something dreadful had happened, but, very quickly, found themselves feeling almost nothing. They underwent what a Hiroshima writer described as "a paralysis of the mind," a dysfunction between perception and emotional response. I came to recognize psychic numbing as a necessary psychological defense against overwhelming images and stimuli. In such extreme situations one is simply unable to experience "ordinary" emotional responses and maintain either sanity or anything like adaptive physical and psychic function. I came to think of the process as something on the order of a temporary and partial deadening as a way of avoiding actual physical, or more or less permanent psychological, death. But psychic numbing could readily outlive its usefulness and give rise to later patterns of withdrawal, apathy, depression, and despair.

A fourth category has to do with survivors' sensitivity toward the counterfeit or suspicion of counterfeit nurturance. On one level the problem can be understood around questions of dependence and autonomy: the survivor feels the effects of his ordeal but frequently resents help offered because it is perceived as a sign of weakness. But perhaps more fundamentally, the issue has to do with the environment of moral inversion--the counterfeit universe--the survivor has

lived through. In Vietnam, for instance, the counterfeit universe consisted of what I called an "atrocity-
producing situation," which was so structured that the
slaughter of civilians became close to a psychological
norm. Living and dying are divested of moral structure
and lose all logic. Entrapped in such a world, one is
torn between the impulse to reject totally its counterfeit structure and the necessity to adapt to it, even
to internalize portions of it, in order to survive.

The fifth and final category is the survivor's
struggle for meaning, for a sense of inner form. Survivors of Nazi death camps have been called "collectors
of justice." They seek something beyond economic or
social restitution--something closer to acknowledgement
of crimes committed against them, and punishment of
those responsible, in order to reestablish at least the
semblance of a moral universe. The impulse to bear
witness, beginning with a sense of responsibility to
the dead, can readily extend into a "survivor mission"
--a lasting commitment to a project that extracts
significance from absurdity, vitality from massive
death. For many Jewish survivors of Nazi Holocaust,
the survivor mission took the form of involvement in
the creation of the State of Israel.

Survivor emotions can be very important in the
midst of war as well. It is not generally realized
that the night before the My Lai massacre, the "combat
briefing" was combined with a funeral ceremony for
membvers of the company who had died grotesquely in
mine explosions, and especially for a much admired,
fatherly, older sergeant. The men were exhorted to get
back at the enemy for the sake of (to bear witness to)
those dead buddies, and so great was their need for the
enemy that he had to be created from available Vietnamese civilians. For these reasons, and because the
whole process was manipulated from above partly around
competition for high "body counts," we can speak of
this process as "false witness."

Whether witness is false or true, it involves such
struggles around grief and mourning. Where death
occurs on the scale of Nazi genocide or atomic bomb-
ings, survivors are denied not only the physical
arrangements of mourning (the grave, the remains, place
of worship), but also the psychic capacity to absorb
and feel these deaths, to do the work of mourning.
Hence the extent to which the survivor's existence can
turn into a "life of grief." Impaired mourning becomes

equated with a more general inability to give inner form--again significance--to the death immersion, and therefore to the remainder of one's life. The survivor may then be especially vulnerable to various kinds of psychic and bodily disturbance, as well as to formulations of his experience around scapegoating and other kinds of false witness. Survivors require expressions of grief and mourning if they are to begin to derive from their experience its potential for some form of illumination.

Failure and Hope

Those of us who approach survivors and seek to understand holocaust have a part in this process as well. The professions have a dismal record in relationship to holocaust. More often than not they have lent themselves to a denial of its brutalizing effects. In psychiatry, organically minded practitioners have tried to ignore the effects of massive psychic trauma by insisting that psychiatric disturbance stems primarily from biological inheritance. And a few psychoanalysts have contributed to this charade by similarly limiting significant trauma to the first few years of life. Fortunately, sensitive and concerned psychiatric and psychoanalytic voices have strongly contested those assumptions. But the healing professions as a whole maintain a moral distance from these issues that keeps them in considerable ignorance.

My work in Hiroshima convinced me of the immorality of claiming professional neutrality in the face of ultimate forms of destruction. I was further troubled during my Vietnam work by the extent to which American professionals, notably psychiatrists and chaplains, could inadvertently employ their spiritual counseling in ways that reinforced the atrocity-producing process. In reexamining the history of the concept of the professions, I was struck by the extent to which its early religious connotations (the profession of faith or of membership in a particular religious order) were transformed almost totally into a matter of technique (or professional skill). Overall the shift was from advocacy based on faith to technique devoid of advocacy. What we require is not a return to a mere "profession of faith," but rather a fundamental critique of the technicism, the deification of technique, within the professions.

We need a new model of the professional that balances technique with advocacy, skill with ethical commitments. That kind of model would serve us well in approaching extreme forms of inhumanity. For psychiatric work in particular we require a shift in theoretical paradigm from Freud's model of instinct and defense to one of death and the continuity of life. The latter model can sensitize us to the kinds of struggles we witness in survivors around threats to physical and psychological existence and symbolization of vitality, and also around connections beyond the self--an area Tillich called "ultimate concern" and one I speak of as symbolic modes of immortality. We need such a model if we are to gain a better grasp of the psychological universe created by holocaust, including our own reactions to that universe.

We may be limited in our capacity to do so. But as professionals of any kind, as feeling human beings, we had better try. For only by understanding more of what happens to victims and survivors, and of what motivates victimizers, can we begin to imagine the future holocausts that threaten us, and thereby take steps to avoid them.

ON PREVENTING GENOCIDE

Helen Fein

Now is the time to consider how we will react to the next genocide. Although the hope that the judgments at Nuremberg would deter genocide and similar crimes against humanity in the postwar world, genocides have occurred without sanction since 1945. The best-documented cases I have studied include the attempted annihilation of Buddhism in Tibet by China (1950-59), the selective genocide of the Hutus in Burundi by the Government of Burundi (1972), the genocidal slaughter of Hindus in East Pakistan by the Government of Pakistan (1971), and the extermination of the Ache Indians of Paraguay from 1971 onward with the toleration or complicity of the Government of Paraguay.

Under the Pol Pot regime in Cambodia it has been estimated that about 2 million, or three out of ten Cambodians, were killed or died due to the regime's policies. Whether these murders, termed "autogenocide" by Anthony Paul, fit the definition of genocide under the Genocide Convention is open to question. Liquidating classes deemed potentially counterrevolutionary and labeling people enemies in order to kill them is not a new practice among Marxist-Leninist regimes. The Genocide Convention defines and proscribes acts leading to the direct or indirect physical destruction of the group when "such acts are committed with intent to destroy, in whole or in part, a national, ethnical, racial or religious group."

While the Soviet Union has imposed categorical punishments upon ethnic and national groups that may lead to their disappearance, including incarceration in the wasteland of the Gulag Archipelago and expulsion to new territory, most of its victims have been Russian and the manifest intent, it may be argued, was insuring political unity and obedience.[1] Robert Conquest estimates there were 20 to 30 million people killed in the USSR between 1917 and 1940, excluding those killed during the revolution or starved to death as a result of famines and plagues attributable to Soviet agricultural policies.[2] Although the People's Republic of China has stressed "thought-reform"--coercive reeducation--rather than liquidation, widespread executions were initiated in 1951 in response to threats voiced during the Korean War. Maurice Meisner concludes, on the basis of a speech by Zho Enlai in 1957 and by other government figures, that "the estimate...that there were 2,000,000 people executed during the first three years of the People's Republic is probably as accurate a guess as one could make."[3]

Nor are political murders limited to Communist regimes. In the name of self-defense against communism, Indondesia massacred about half a million people after the 1965 coup against Sukarno. Nazi Germany murdered at least half a million Germans in its misleadingly labeled "euthanasia" campaign that led to the genocide of "The Final Solution."

The preconditions of genocide and ideological massacres differ, although they are similar in form and organization, often drawing upon the same apparatus for execution. Genocides are always alike in one regard only: The victims are defined outside of the universe of obligation of the executioners. They are distinguished from the perpetrator by some stigma supposedly imposed on them by religious doctrine, racist dogma, or other in-group myth. The perpetrators of ideological massacres define their victims as enemies on the basis of class membership or suspected political sympathies. The definition of genocide by the Convention seems to imply that genocide is a function not of the nature of the crime alone but of a difference in race/religion/ ethnicity/nationality between the victim and the executioner. Thus, when China forced parents to send their children away so they could be stripped of their identity as Tibetan Buddhists, these acts were labeled genocide, but the same acts in China, separating children from parents, were not so labeled. Politically inspired categorical massacre of one's own people was deliberately excluded from the Convention upon Soviet insistence and this was one of the grounds upon which the American Bar Association justified its opposition (since reversed) to the Convention: "The proposed convention does not prohibit the only important genocide now going on, viz, in those countries where dissident groups and persons are regularly proceeded against on political grounds as enemies of the state."[4] Such slaughter is proscribed by the Convention on Civil and Political Rights, which embodies the norms first enunciated in the Universal Declaration of Human Rights as a universal goal. Because both genocide and ideological massacres are radical violations of human rights and we cannot discriminate whether a slaughter constitutes genocide until all the facts are in--which is too late--we will consider as one the problem of deterring or limiting genocide and mass slaughter.

Mass killings persist as a useful political weapon because they work, often serving to eliminate a class that is challenging its subordination. They work also because they are tolerated by other nations, allowing a ruling elite to profit from the destruction of potential opposition without incurring heavy costs. In none of the cases considered did the United Nations take any deterrent action or even condemn the perpetrator, except when it censured China--then a nonmember--in 1959. How the major powers defined these genocides depended on their relation to the perpetrator, their anticipation of future relations and opportunities, and their fear of establishing precedents that might justify what is misleadingly termed "interference in internal affairs." In every case, the perpetrator played a role in the international system as a client or ally of a major power. It is obvious that all powers can be rightly charged with opportunism and cynicism. France was in league with Burundi; the United States "tilted" toward Pakistan and continued to aid Paraguay; and the Soviet Union consistently sided with China in 1959.

The United Nations did not altogether ignore these massacres, but it defined them as disasters requiring humanitarian assistance, civil or tribal wars, and refused to recognize that a crime was being committed. International aid to the refugees was feeble compensation that did not redress their plight or protect their kin who were left behind. The perils of nonrecognition were illustrated in Burundi, where the U.N. became an unintentional accessory to the crime when its supply vehicles were appropriated by the government and used to transport and slaughter additional victims.

What role did the human rights nongovernmental organizations (NGOs) play in deterring or sanctioning these acts of genocide? The documentation compiled by some NGOs is invaluable in establishing the facts of such mass killings, but often long after the deed. The International Commission of Jurists (ICJ) cogently evaluated the evidence of genocide in Tibet and East Pakistan; the International League for Human Rights and the ICJ supported presentation of the evidence of genocide of the Ache in Paraguay to the United Nations and the Organization of American States. In these cases the presenting NGOs concluded categorically that these were genocides and held the perpetrators responsible for them. However, in the case of Burundi, the International League for Human Rights and the ICJ held no one to be responsible and recommended greater economic and social aid to the government that had authorized the massacres, observing: "When these international norms are violated openly by the new states, there is a certain leniency on the part of the international community."[5] The massacres were renewed in 1973.

In the case of Cambodia/Kampuchea, evidence of human rights violations was submitted in the summer of 1978 by Amnesty International and the ICJ to the U.N. Sub-Commission on Prevention of Discrimination and Protection of Minorities and to the U.N. Human Rights Commission (which had authorized a request for information to that government the previous spring). They did this only after several appeals by Amnesty to that government went unanswered.

Thus, NGOs recognize or label massacres of genocidal proportion in different ways and all have reacted belatedly, to say the least. There are several reasons for this. Some NGOs are so preoccupied with avoiding one type of error--arriving at a false judgment from unrepresentative or scattered evidence--that they slight their chance of committing another type of error --failing to infer a pattern that truly exists. They also use at times a double standard, as they did to exonerate the Government of Burundi, serving only to incite it to further killings. Where genocide is recognized, the conventional strategy of the NGOs devoted to human rights is persuasion; they appeal to publics, states, regional and international organizations. But their strategy, even were it not post facto, would be ineffectual in the case of genocide, and this for several reasons.

First, governments plotting genocide often play a zero-sum game: them or us. The more of them to survive, the fewer there will be of us. Such governments even firm up the sides and assure the continuance of the "game," for if the people they have staked out as victims are not actually enemies today, those who manage to evade death will surely be enemies tomorrow. Regimes relying on massacre and torture to inhibit opposition are the most unlikely candidates for self-reform; they know that under any democratic procedures they would be turned out. In these cases petitions to such regimes and to the U.N. are almost invariably a ritualistic exercise.

Second, the usual NGO strategy is to assist victims who are being processed legally through phases of transition--indictment, trial, judgment, incarceration, appeal, etc.   But if victims are mown down on the street or slaughtered at a clearing in the woods after a roundup only half an hour earlier, phases in which to intercede for the victims do not exist.   Victims of genocide often fail to reach the prisoner stage, and they are never "prisoners of conscience."   As human rights work goes, this is a disaster situation.

The disaster is not addressed by appealing to the U.N., which elevates evasion to a collective or organizational level, enabling all actors to evade responsibility.   The "disguised barter of one atrocity for another"[6] in the Human Rights Commission, its delay in investigation of, e.g., Uganda and Cambodia, and the silence of states outside the present majority coalition have long been noted.   Because of the mutual obligation to protect each other, only bloc isolates-Chile, South Africa, and Israel--have been subject to censure.

If we conclude that the NGOs' response has been both belated and ineffectual in these cases, two questions arise.   First, how can their response be explained?   Second, what strategies could they adapt that have been overlooked?

My answer to the first question must be tentative, since I did not study the NGOs as organizations and observe how widely they differ in membership, structure, and modes of functioning.   Ideologically, many leaders and staff members of NGOs are committed to belief in an expanding normative consensus that will-- someday, someway--inhibit nations from slaughter, torture, and repression.   Some members are committed to affirming the legitimacy of all governments that have arisen in decolonized states.   Others, for tactical reasons, act as if all states were legitimate.   Both may be inhibited in considering strategies that involve conflict, coercion, or which justify intervention. Another type of answer is that the human rights NGOs, like other organizations, may tend to repeat their modus operandi ritualistically; means become institutionalized regardless of how they accomplish ends.

To prevent future acts of genocide governments must be held politically responsible for perpetrating them and tolerating them in their sphere of influence and among their allies.   Prohibitions of unilateral

U.S. aid to nations violating basic human rights of their citizens could be extended to multilateral aid. Amending present legislation to give international observers the right to interview prisoners and inspect jails and all incarceration centers of aid recipients may be one way to implement this commitment. Guaranteeing visiting rights to relatives and counsel to prisoners is another way to keep them socially visible. Ratification of the Genocide Convention by the U.S. Senate is one step--and only a first step--to indicate our commitment to save people from extinction. The flaws in the Convention are presently irremediable: The victims cannot raise charges but must rely on their executioners to judge their acts; state signatories are responsible for enforcing the convention and thus for judging themselves, and there is no international authority to which signatories must submit. However, U.S. ratification would represent a significant acknowledgement of our international responsibility and help to articulate our generalized commitment to human rights.

An active citizens lobby is needed to press governments to go beyond rhetorical commitments. If our goal is to stop genocides, there are three stages to such a problem: First, genocide must be detected early and charges and countercharges evaluated; second, organizations must decide upon a strategy to press governments and other collective actors to, third, take steps to avert, deter, ameliorate, abort, or prevent the genocide.

The first step involves intelligence-gathering in the technical sense, i.e., securing information from actors who invoke secrecy. As detection on the site may be impossible due to entry barriers, investigators may have to rely on evaluating evidence supplied by refugees. Standing commissions, willing and able to fly to any site to gather such evidence, could be considered, adapting and revising models from the experience of, say, disaster-relief organizations. The advantage of a coalition of rights NGOs forming such a commission and pooling their sources of evidence is obvious. Tactics for gaining entry in situations where governments are uncooperative must be considered, including covert actions.

Strategies used by NGOs to achieve their objectives include persuasion, exchange, and coercion, the latter implying use of political or economic incentives and sanctions. Rights NGOs supported by a voting base may spur political insiders to press their government to use its influence and sanctions against perpetrators of genocide. They may themselves lobby for legislative sanctions and organize consumer boycotts, divestiture campaigns, and other strategies of economic coercion.

Strategies open to governments and organizations with military forces involve a choice of goals and tactics. One might stop genocides by persuading the perpetrator to cease and desist, by evacuating the victims, or by removing the perpetrators, fighting to oust them from the region inhabited by the victims (assuming the latter are geographically concentrated). Since the victims must flee or fight to save themselves, the range of choice may depend on their recognition of danger, their ability to defend themselves, and the readiness of access to outside aid. Many respected experts in international law maintain that the doctrine of "humanitarian intervention" justifies incursions across borders to remove or defend the victims of genocidal assault and is consistent with the U.N. Charter. Others disagree, asserting that such intervention is incompatible with the interdiction against aggression and interference in internal affairs in the Charter. Furthermore, they fear misuse of this doctrine to justify imperialistic adventures and Great Power self-aggrandizement.[7]

Such interventions imply responsibilities toward the perpetrator as well as toward the victims of genocide and toward other states. The prevalence of retributive genocide--annihilation of an opposing tribe viewed as challenging the order of domination--means that past oppressors may sometims correctly anticipate collective reprisals against their tribe or collectivity.

In the absence of internationally sanctioned interventions, the victims themselves must conclude that their defense rests on their own arms and/or the intervention of interested neighboring states. The latter may be considered a humanitarian intervention even after the fact. Although India justified its 1971 war against Pakistan as an act of self-defense, the International Commission of Jurists concluded that:

> India's armed intervention would have been
> justified if she had acted under the doctrine
> of humanitarian intervention, and further

that India would have been entitled to act unilaterally under this doctrine in view of the growing and intolerable burden which the refugees were casting upon India and in view of the inability of international organizations to take any effective action to bring to an end the massive violations in human rights in East Pakistan which were causing the flow of refugees.[8]

How genocide itself constitutes a threat to the peace, inviting foreign intervention, is again illustrated by the invasions of Cambodia and Uganda, the success of which is partly attributable to the nonresistance and cooperation of Cambodians and Ugandans. The international response to the former was characterized by evasion of the issue of the legitimacy of the former government of Cambodia while the military response threatened a new Indochinese war, diminishing interest in the justifications. One resolution to reconcile these values would have been to call upon all armies to withhold fire--including that of Pol Pot--and hold free elections guaranteed by an international peace force that excluded Chinese and Vietnamese troops. While such a resolution is unlikely to be offered in the United Nations by any major power, the human rights movement might do so.

Looking beyond the human rights NGOs to the broader human rights movement, it is clear the movement is divided by particular constituencies and ideological cleavages. Few are primarily concerned with the plight of what some have called "Fourth World" victims, such as the Ache in Paraguay. This invites inquiry into how the NGOs determine their priorities. How is the decimation of a small people--which may be great in terms of the percentage of its population annihilated-- weighed against the greater number of political deaths occurring in larger states? How are rights ranked in precedence? How much effort shall be devoted to protecting minorities and "deviant" groups (such as the Jehova's Witnesses) and protecting majorities? That organizations do not make such assessment explicit does not mean they do not make choices on these grounds. However, it does mean they make choices that cannot responsibly be debated.

Prospective scenarios for new genocides that will test the Western world abound. The crimes committed in Rhodesia have led the International Committee of the

Red Cross to denounce both sides publicly for "wanton and persistent cruelty," departing deliberately "from our habitual policy of diplomatic circumspection" (March 20, 1979). Other NGOs should heed the procedural and political implications of this decision. Human rights organizations--intergovernmental and nongovernmental--need to evaluate systematically the impact of corporate actors other than nation-states upon human rights, including terrorists, paramilitary and liberation groups, and multinational corporations. And all should heed the signals of what we may expect in the future. As Franz Schurmann puts it:

> Conflict becomes revolutionary when one class of people comes to believe that there is no solution to their oppressive misery except the destruction of the class which opposes them. In its most terrible form this conflict is genocide where the class differences are racial...In a world inflamed with nationalist passions, the spectre of genocide always haunts us.[9]

The use of collective massacre and reprisals in wars of liberation often evokes and may be intended to provoke counterterror and torture, as in Algeria, where the policy initiated by the FLN and the French response is estimated to have cost the lives of almost 300,000 Algerian natives--later Algeria claimed a million--and almost 100,000 French people and led to the expulsion of almost a million pieds noir and 100,000 Algerian Jews.[10] Genocide may be an intended or a latent consequence of such a strategy. If the human rights movement adapts a double standard or ignores this issue, it would increase the likelihood both sides will seek to annihilate each other, protected by the cynicism that charges of genocide may arouse. For charges would be magnified by partisans of both sides in order to discredit their adversaries, instigating sympathizers to deny or discredit reports of victimization by the party they oppose.

Rhodesia is viewed by many as merely a rehearsal for the impending conflict in the Union of South Africa. As threat increases, we know that racial solidarity and the potential for greater collective violence also increases. What can we anticipate? Will the white Afrikaners ruling South Africa, if confronted by internal rebellion, decide to go it alone within a constricted perimeter and carpet-bomb blacks in their midst in order either to exterminate them and/or terrorize them? Will the blacks of South Africa, after the last advocate of nonviolence has died at the hands of the South African police, remember Steven Biko and the others by retaliating collectively against whites with genocidal terror and massacres intended to expel them?

Other regions too are fertile arenas for genocides. May not Iran or Iraq attempt to resolve the Kurds' demands for autonomy by trying to eliminate them? Will the Soviet Union, seeking to squash both the Jewish and the dissident movements, amplify its hate-inciting campaign of anti-Semitism--masked as anti-Zionism--and begin to systematically deport Jews and dissidents (who might be labeled as Jews or sympathizers with the Zionist fifth column) to the Gulag Archipelago, where they can wither away unobserved under the polar sun?

If these scenarios are acted out, we will surely read about them at once in the New York Times. There will be the usual murmurings of governments in the West--perhaps some talk about the Helsinki pact--and the usual denials from the perpetrators, accusing others of human rights violations in their lands (as Kampuchea accused the United Kingdom in response to the U.N. Human Rights Commission inquiry). Constituencies sympathetic to Soviet Jewry and the South African blacks will organize ad hoc committees and mobilize public campaigns on their behalf; the Kurds and Afrikaners will fare less well. The NGOs will labor for anywhere from three years to a decade to produce volumes of documentation to submit to the U.N. Human Rights Commission.

Footnotes

1. However, the expulsion of nationalities and ethnic groups that has caused their decimation clearly fits under the convention. See Robert Conquest, The Nation-Killers; The Soviet Deportation of Nationalities (London, 1970).

2. The Human Cost of Soviet Communism (Washington, D.C., USGPO, 1971), p. 25.

3. Mao's China: A History of the People's Republic (New York, 1977), p. 107.

4. American Bar Association, Special Committee on Peace and Law Through the United Nations (Chicago, 1950), p. 11.

5. William J. Butler and George Obiozor, "The Burundi Affair 1972," IDOC Survey, no. 52 (April, 1973), p. 26.

6. Richard Arens, ed., Genocide in Paraguay (Philadelphia, 1976), p. 150.

7. Richard B. Lillich, ed., Humanitarian Intervention and the United Nations (Charlottesville, VA, 1973).

8. International Commission of Jurists, The Events in East Pakistan, 1971 (Geneva, 1972), p. 96.

9. Franz Schurmann, "On Revolutionary Conflict," in Conflict Resolution: Contributions of the Behavioral Sciences, ed. Clagget G. Smith (Notre Dame, Ind., 1971), p. 271.

10. Alistair Horne, A Savage War of Peace (New York, 1977, pp. 14, 538.

AMERICA'S SHAME: THE UNRATIFIED GENOCIDE TREATY

William Korey

Senator William Proxmire recently reminded his colleagues that no subject has been pending before the Senate as long as the Genocide Convention. The treaty has in fact been accumulating dust on the Senate shelf for 32 years--a dismal record that has brought the United States little but embarrassment in international forums.

What makes the neglect especially anomalous is the fact that it stands in striking contrast with the emphasis given human rights in American foreign policy. The genocide treaty was the very first United Nations human rights treaty, preceding even the Universal Declaration of Human Rights. That it remains unratified ineluctably raises questions about the commitment of the United States to the principles it espouses. Besides, if human rights is declared to be the keystone of U.S. statecraft and that which distinguishes America's government from most other regimes, failure to ratify the genocide treaty suggests a reluctance to translate such self-proclaimed features into international obligations that would flow from accession to binding agreements.

The point about international obligations draws attention to a second, equally distressing anomaly. The United States has relied heavily upon international law in making its case against Iran concerning our embassy hostages. The World Court's decision on this issue validated both the code of civilized nations and America's advocacy of international law. Were the United States to have been as dilatory in ratifying the Vienna Convention as it has in ratifying the genocide treaty, it would have been deprived of the centerpiece of its judicial appeal. Significantly, it was U.S. ratification of the Vienna Convention on Diplomatic Relations nearly 20 years ago that enabled the State Department to bring the hostage issue before the bar of international legal and moral opinion. Appealing to international standards and the assumption of obligations flowing from them were deeply rooted in America's post-World War II policy.

The concept of a treaty making genocide a crime had its roots in the struggle against Hitlerism and the overpowering public awareness of what unrestrained racism had wrought. The horrors of the Nazi crematoria and the unprecedented Holocaust stirred a profound sense of guilt and pricked mankind's uneasy conscience. The inextricable linkage between internal racism and external aggression had never been so terrifyingly demonstrated.

Three post-war sources were to shape the concept, provide it with an international forum, and finally, clothe it with binding international law. The first source was the Nuremburg Tribunal, of which the United States was a principal architect. Through the Tribunal the rule of law as applied to criminal violations of human rights was given a firm foundation. In November, 1946, President Harry Truman remarked that the "undisputed gain" of Nuremberg was precisely "the formal recognition that there are crimes against humanity." Recognized among the designated "crimes against humanity" were persecutions on political, racial, or religious grounds, whether or not sanctioned by domestic law.

The Tribunal, as one authority later noted, marked a "revolution in international criminal law" for it deeply eroded the earlier accepted principle of the exclusivity of domestic jurisdiction in the area of human rights. The second source was the United Nations General Assembly which, on December 11, 1946, legitimized the "revolution." Its famed Resolution 96(I) formally declared "that genocide is a crime under international law which the civilized world condemns and for the commission of which principals and accomplices are punishable." Again, the United States shepherded the resolution through the Assembly.

This Assembly decision and the far more important genocide treaty that emerged two years later would have been impossible without the intervention of the extraordinary "unofficial man", the self-defined description of Raphael Lemkin. Arriving at U.N. Headquarters in Lake Success during the fall of 1946, Lemkin became a one-man lobbyist who, with unflagging energy, zealous conviction, and persuasive logic expressed in a dozen different languages made genocide a household term in the international community and forced it to enact a treaty aimed at its prevention and punishment.

By the time Lemkin appeared in New York he had already coined the word "genocide." As he himself defined it, "Genocide comes from the Greek genos, meaning race, and the Latin cide, meaning killing. It is the mass murder of people for religious or racial reasons."

Lemkin understood from personal experience what it meant. The large Polish Jewish Lemkin family, some 70 persons, were almost wiped out in the Nazi carnage: only Raphael and a brother survived. A brilliant legal scholar who also served as a public prosecutor in Warsaw long before his personal trauma, he began to outline at international legal meetings the conception that would lead to the Genocide Convention. The trauma simply gave the conception a sense of urgency, indeed, of necessity.

Representing no government and no organization, Lemkin was one of those rare individuals who by the force of his person dared to move and, indeed, succeeded in moving history. At the time, the intense, gaunt figure, with graying hair and thick spectacles, wearing shabby clothes, seemed just another Don Quixote tilting at political windmills. But he literally buttonholed every Assembly delegate, pressing his case with patience and determination. When U.S. Ambassador Warren R. Austin succumbed to his impeccably logical blandishments, the outcome was virtually predetermined: Austin led the Assembly to adopt Resolution 96(I).

For Lemkin, it was only the beginning. Tirelessly, for the next two years, he prodded, pleaded, and pressed for a genocide treaty, often volunteering to write, in appropriate languages, speeches for the delegates. When the Assembly finally adopted the convention, Lemkin desperately wanted the United States to be among the first contracting parties to the treaty. At his death in August 1959, he was still waiting.

On December 9, 1948, things looked much more hopeful. The historic significance of the General Assembly action could not be doubted. It was the first human rights treaty of the United Nations, adopted one day before the Universal Declaration of Human Rights. The President of the General Assembly, Herbert V. Evatt, Foreign Minister of Australia, commented on the meaning of the event: "In this field, relating to the sacred right of existence of human groups, we are proclaiming today the supremacy of international law once and for all."

If the dream of an international treaty barring genocide was Lemkin's, the structure and form was largely the U.S.'s. Today, it is all but forgotten that the United States delegation to the U.N. played the key role in the actual drafting of the text. The irony is all the greater in that past and current opposition to ratification draws upon an assumption that the drafting of the treaty was done by foreigners or by U.N. officials. The assumption is without foundation. The text itself reflected the reality of American draftsmanship. Its sources were terms familiar in Anglo-American legal theory. And, indeed, the formulations were couched in the language of traditional common-law concepts, including the very precise wording of common-law crimes long accepted in American jurisprudence. Of critical importance, in this connection, was U.S. insistence that proof of <u>intent</u> to commit genocide must be clearly demonstrated <u>before</u> an offender can be punished.

Nor was American involvement limited to mere legal counselling and draftsmanship. It was the U.S. delegation at the General Assembly session in Paris that led the fight from the floor for its adoption. American lobbyists were everywhere promoting a positive vote at the Palais de Chaillot. Th head of the delegation, Assistant Secretary of State Ernest A. Gross (a prominent attorney and churchman in private life) took a personal hand in the campaign: he demanded that "positive action...be taken now."

The U.S. efforts were impressively successful. Unanimous endorsement was won for the Genocide Convention; to testify to its commitment, the U.S. delegation rushed to affix the U.S. signature to the treaty. The signing of a treaty, in the context of international law, is a solemn and formal act by a government. It signifies both a commitment to fulfill the purpose of the treaty and an intent to ratify it. Nearly 32 years later, that intent is yet to be fulfilled.

For Raphael Lemkin, the Convention on the Prevention and Punishment of the Crime of Genocide was merely the formalization of an idea whose time had come. Neither he nor his supporters in the various U.N. delegations ever expected serious opposition, certainly not from the democratic world that had engaged in a massive effort to destroy Hitlerism.

The treaty contained 19 articles, the last 10 of which were procedural. The first nine articles were substantive, with Article I confirming that genocide is a crime under international law. The second article was the core of the convention. It outlawed "acts committed with an intent to destroy, in whole or in part, a national, ethnical, racial, or religious group as such." Delineated among the "acts" were killing, the causing of serious "mental harm," the inflicting of "conditions of life calculated" to lead to physical destruction, and the imposition of measures intended to prevent reproduction of a group.

The treaty specified actions that would be subjected to punishment: genocide; conspiracy or attempt to commit genocide; direct and public incitement to commit genocide; and complicity in the act of genocide. The convention made clear that no one was immune from punishment--rulers, public officials, or private individuals. Persons charged with the crime of genocide were to be tried by a competent tribunal of the state in the territory in which the act was committed. This would require extradition; the convention stresses that genocide is not, under any circumstances, to be considered a political crime.

If the language of the text was drawn from traditional American jurisprudence, opposing arguments offered in various legal circles, also had a uniquely American ring. One argument, taking its inspiration from Charles Evans Hughes's guideline that the treaty-making power must be used only "with regard to matters of international concern," contended that genocide, along with human rights generally, is essentially a domestic concern. To the extent that it was alleged to be a domestic matter, genocide, it was said, did not meet the relevant test of the Supreme Court as to whether the treaty is "properly the subject of negotiations with a foreign country."

In fact, human rights have been dealt with and protected by international treaties since the 16th century. During the 19th century, the United States itself was a party to dozens of treaties regulating the slave trade. Moreover, the U.S. has ratified treaties relating to the activities of its own citizens when those activities have a transnational character--narcotics, public health, natural conservation. Certainly the critical lesson of World War II, as the Nuremburg Tribunal demonstrated, was that genocide was quintessentially an international concern, far more so that even slavery during the 19th century.

A second objection sprang from the Federal character of the U.S. It was argued that ratification would create a Constitutional issue by tilting the balance of authority on criminal matters between the Federal government and the states to the former. (Murder, it was emphasized, is a state crime.) The argument failed, however, to take account of the specific constitutional provision that Congress has the power "to define and punish offenses against the law of Nations," and genocide has been firmly declared to be an offense against international law. Besides, as indicated in various civil rights statutes which were adopted later on, Federal authority was recognized as having priority in various human rights fields.

Arguments were also advanced over certain ambiguities in the convention. What did "in whole or in part" mean in the crucial Article II of the convention? Fears were apparent in various segregationist circles that the reference to "in part" might be applied to a limited form of race violence, such as lynchings. The phrase "mental harm" also raised concern. Some who pointed to the centrality of civil liberties expressed doubts about reference to direct incitement even though Supreme Court decisions made clear that such activity was not protected by the First Amendment.

The ambiguities did not constitute insoluble problems, providing there was good will on the part of the critics. They could be handled by clarifications, called "understandings" or, more accurately, "reservations". And, indeed, this is the way the matter would ultimately be handled. The Constitutional controversy, on the other hand, was a more serious obstacle.

The kind of resistance involving legitimate questions and concern was reinforced--and complicated--by extremist movements in the political Far Right. A dozen such organizations are capable of generating a substantial flow of mail and telegrams to the Senate. Among the groups that have led vehement campaigns against the Genocide Convention are the Liberty Lobby, which denounced the treaty as a "Communist hoax," the Christian Crusade, which dubbed the treaty "fraudulent," and the John Birch Society, which called it "pernicious" and a "surrender of the Constitutional rights of American citizens."

At the time, however, no serious difficulties were anticipated. After a short, appropriate interval of six months, President Truman transmitted the treaty to the Senate for its advice and consent. The Senate Foreign Relations Committee assigned a subcommittee the task of holding hearings. Promptly held in January and February, 1950, the hearings elicited a favorable response from representatives of most public, non-governmental organizations. And the spokesman for the government, Deputy Under-Secretary of State Dean Rusk, was unusually effective. He made two principal points: ratification was essential to "demonstrate to the rest of the world that the United States is determined to maintain its moral leadership in international affairs;" also, it would show that the U.S. intends "to participate in the development of international law on the basis of human justice."

The two themes--moral leadership and international law--echoed, of course, a distinctive strand in U.S. foreign policy, especially since the era of Woodrow Wilson's administration. The genocide convention reflected the twin features of the Wilson heritage: morality and the law. The International Court of Justice appeared to make this point when it held that the convention "was manifestly adopted for a purely humanitarian purpose. It is indeed difficult to imagine a convention that might have this dual character to a greater degree, since its object on the one hand is to safeguard the very existence of certain human groups and on the other to confirm and endorse the most elementary principles of morality."

In May, 1950, the Senate subcommittee, only a few months after the hearings, reported favorably. Yet to meet the objections of the legal profession, the subcommittee recommended that four "understandings" and one "declaration" be embodied in the resolution consenting to ratification. One "understanding" (later termed "reservation") dealt with the phrase "in whole or in part." "In part" was interpreted to mean "a substantial portion of the group concerned." A second "understanding" defined "mental harm" as "permanent physical injury to mental faculties." A third understanding clarified "complicity in genocide" as meaning "participation before and after the facts and aiding and abetting in the commission of the crime of genocide." The last understanding was minor. The declaration dealt with the key federal-state balance issue by citing explicitly from the Constitution's Article I the right of Congress to punish "offenses against the law of Nations."

Significantly, the same clarifying statements would appear as "reservations" when the Senate Foreign Relations Committee approved the genocide treaty 21 years later. But in 1950, the entire Committee never got the opportunity to vote on the issue. A month after the subcommittee's recommendation, North Korea launched the invasion of South Korea; a new era was ushered in profoundly affecting the fabric of American society. The war unleashed powerful xenophobic forces that significantly bolstered the earlier anti-Communist witch hunt. The genocide convention was perceived in these quarters as undermining American sovereignty and serving the interests of Communism.

Paralysis set in among supporters of the genocide treaty. They were simply overwhelmed, less by the arguments of conservative spokesmen or ABA officials than by the resurgent home grown rightist forces. Formally, the treaty came into effect on January 12, 1951, but no action by the United States was even contemplated. Indeed, with the ascendancy of a kind of neo-isolationism, there would appear a movement both in and out of the Senate, under John Bricker's leadership, aimed at limiting the treaty-making authority of the Executive. Senator Bricker of Ohio, a pronounced enemy of international authority and of imagined forces threatening American sovereignty, was certain a new danger was beginning to emanate from the United Nations, where the drafting of international covenants on human rights had just started (not until December, 1966, would they be completed). Bricker proposed an amendment to the Constitution designed to preclude forever the possibility of the U.S. being "subverted" through the action of an administration representative at the U.N. Presidential authority to sign treaties dealing with human rights would simply be forbidden. That such an amendment challenged the intrinsic and traditional power of the President in foreign affairs was a matter of indifference to the powerful Ohio Senator.

The newly-elected Eisenhower administration, it-self an expression, at least in part, of resurgent rightist tendencies, put an end to all further discussion of the genocide treaty and, indeed of any human rights treaty. The official pronouncement came early in the administration--April 6, 1953--and was articulated by John Foster Dulles, Secretary of State. The occasion was a hearing of the Senate Judiciary Committee, and Dulles, acutely conscious of the challenge to Presidential authority posed by the Bricker movement forces, was anxious to use the opportunity to deprive the movement of its raison d'etre. If firm commitments were given to the Senate that the administration would never contemplate signing a human rights treaty let alone transmitting it to the Senate for action, then the Bricker phenomenon might disintegrate for want of a rationale.

But the Secretary of State went even further. He gave formal expression to the very isolationist and xenophobic impulses that impinged on the administration from Right-wing sources. At the same time, the formulation was dressed up in the legal terminology advanced in principal arguments of the ABA. The administration, Dulles promised, would never "become a party to any (human rights) covenant or present it as a treaty for consideration by the Senate." If human rights were to be promoted by the United States, this would be accomplished by "methods of persuasion, education and example," and not by "formal undertakings" such as treaties. Indeed, the treaty-making power, Dulles assured the Senate, cannot and must not be used "as a way of effectuating reforms, particularly in relation to social matters." In his view, echoing the ABA and, at the same time, satisfying Bricker, there were "traditional limits" of the exercise of treaty-making and those "limits" would be trespassed by striving to effect "internal social changes" through treaties.

If the Secretary's assurances caused the Bricker movement to disintegrate, they also erected a virtually impregnable obstacle for Senate action on any human rights treaty. His was, after all, a solemn commitment from the administration. Once formally articulated and accepted, the assurance took on a life of its own and, by force of inertia, prevented new legislative initiatives in the human rights field. Such efforts would inevitably take on a Sisyphean character. Ironically, Dulles himself, as a member of the U.S. delegation to the U.N. General Assembly in 1948, had urged the drafting of a covenant that would translate human rights into law. In a rather pointed and effective address, he drew an analogy, on the one hand, between the Declaration of Independence and the Constitution, and on the other, the Universal Declaration of Human Rights and the International Covenants on Human Rights. Dulles had observed in 1948 that legally binding instruments followed and gave force to inspirational moral declarations. In 1953 this was conveniently forgotten.

The genocide treaty, to the extent that it, too, was a human rights treaty, was clearly living on borrowed time. Dulles was hesitant about declaring null and void a treaty in which the U.S. had invested so much and to which it had made the strongest commitments, including the formal signature. To avoid the embarrassment of previously-extended solemn obligations, Dulles noted that the USSR had not yet ratified the genocide convention and, therefore, it "could better be reconsidered at a later date." But when the USSR did ratify the treaty in 1954, no notice was taken of the action by the Eisenhower administration. The issue was dead, buried by the Dulles doctrine, which had also wrought the internment of those foreign policy goals, given emphasis during and after World War II, that underscored the necessity of extending the rule of law, including human rights law, to the world arena.

A glacial silence now settled upon international human rights undertakings generally and the genocide treaty specifically. If there were momemts of awkwardness, that was the price that had to be paid for the new policy. How, for example, should a U.S. representative conduct himself in U.N. debates about individual articles of the draft covenants on human rights? No clear guidelines were possible, since the U.S. had already pre-judged the outcome so far as our own rejection of ratification was certain. Perhaps the better part of valor was non-participation--hardly a posture that could help shape effectively the character and language of the covenants or, for that matter, a favorable image of the United States.

Not until a decade later did cracks appear in the monolith of Washington indifference. President Kennedy sounded a renewed hope and vigor with respect to traditional obligations in the human rights field by his historic speech at American University on June 10, 1963. The powerful rhetoric of the address made human rights, a little more than 10 years after Dulles's commitment in the Senate, a critical feature of America's foreign policy thinking. Peace itself was declared to be "in the last analysis a matter of human rights."

Nor was it an uncertain trumpet that had sounded. A month after the American University speech, Kennedy, in a breakthrough move, sent to the Senate three international human rights treaties that had lain dormant for some time. One dealt with practices akin to slavery, a second with forced labor, and the last with the political rights of women. In his message asking for the Senate's consent to ratification, the President wrote: "The United States cannot afford to renounce responsibility for support of the very fundamentals which distinguish our concept of government from all forms of tyranny."

Yet the action scarcely exemplified unusual cour- age. Kennedy chose the least controversial of the international treaties. About the Genocide Convention, he did not urge action, although a White House spokes- man publicly noted that "we share the views that promp- ted President Truman to urge consent of the Senate." The far more significant development, sparked by the new administration posture, was the creation in 1964, of a clearing house for public action by over 50 non- governmental organizations. Called the Ad Hoc Committeee on the Human Rights and Genocide Treaties, the coalition, drawn from religious, ethnic, and labor groups, initiated a major lobbying effort with the Senate.

The thrust of the Johnson administration parallel- ed its predecessor, particularly as the embarrassment of non-ratification became increasingly difficult to bear. The changed atmosphere was even beginning to erode support for the Dulles doctrine in the legal profession. Virtually every section and committee of the ABA with specialized competence in the area of human rights or the rule of law adopted resolutions calling for ratification of the genocide treaty. In 1968, a blue ribbon committee of lawyers, chaired by retired Supreme Court Justice Tom Clark, publicly denounced as "anachronistic" the standard argument of the ABA and its Senate supporters that the treaty- making power of the Executive should not be used for human rights purposes.

The year 1968 marked the 20th anniversary of the Universal Declaration of Human Rights (as well as the Genocide Convention). Commemoration activities brought to the fore a sense of shame and embarrassment surroun- ding the genocide treaty. Chief Justice Earl Warren captured the altered mood in an anniversary address in December: "We, as a nation should have been the first to ratify the genocide convention...Instead, we may well be near the last."

Catharsis, through oratorical breast-beating, was undoubtedly helpful, but no meaningful change appeared

to register in the Senate. What some diagnosed as a
"lingering Brickeritis" continued to pervade the upper
legislative chamber. In 1967 Senator Proxmire had initiated an educational campaign among his colleagues by
delivering a daily appeal for ratification of human
rights treaties. His appeal largely fell on deaf ears.
The genocide treaty was tightly wrapped in Senate moth-
balls; hope for its removal appeared remote. Neither
the Kennedy not the Johnson administration dared to
challenge Senate indifference to genocide.

It was left to a Republican administration, and a
conservative one at that, to demand a reversal of the
Dulles doctrine. On February 17, 1970, President
Nixon, for the first time since Truman had called for
legislative action 21 years earlier, formally asked the
Senate "to consider anew this important convention." In
his message, Nixon emphasized that ratification was
necessary to "demonstrate unequivocally our country's
desire to participate in the building of an international order based on law and justice." The language, strikingly, was almost an exact replica of that
used by the spokesman of the Truman administration.

What prompted Nixon to break with the outlook of
the Eisenhower administration is probably similar to
what brought about the change with respect to recognition of Communist China. Alert and sensitive to emergent public attitudes, and not burdened by fears of
possible charges from the Right of national "betrayal,"
the administration was keenly aware that the altered
atmosphere made legitimate a complete break with an
anachronistic past posture. Encouragement in this
direction was provided by a young Republican lawyer
from New York, Rita Hauser, whose service as a key
member of the U.S. delegation to the U.N. convinced her
that non-ratification only generated an attitude of
disdain and contempt and evoked unnecessary criticism
from friendly and neutral countries. Besides, a Republican championing ratification could not go unnoticed
and unrewarded in liberal and intellectual circles.
Her recommendation was politically useful and at the
same time cloaked the administration in a statesmanlike
garb.

The administration did make important inroads with
the Senate Foreign Relations Committee. In 1971 that
powerful body, which had failed to act upon the basis
of recommendations of its sub-committee in 1950, moved
to hold hearings and, in May of that year, to render a

landmark rejection of the ABA decision. By a vote of 10-4, it announced that "we find no substantial merit in the arguments against the convention" and urged the Senate to "give its advice and consent to ratification of the genocide convention by an overwhelming vote."

The decisive Committee vote should have resolved the problem and ended a national embarrassment. Prior to the Committee action, Justice Arthur Goldberg, speaking on behalf of the Ad Hoc Committee on the Human Rights and Genocide Treaties, told the Senate body: "It is inconceivable that we should hesitate any longer in making an international commitment against mass murder." The statement failed to take account of technical or procedural considerations which, when buttressed by the usual legal opposition, by fierce resistance from extremist forces, and by the unanticipated and immeasurable force of inertia, became insuperable obstacles.

In December, 1971, Proxmire, joined by another intrepid advocate of ratification, Senator Jacob Javits, asked the Majority Leader, Senator Mike Mansfield, to put the treaty on the legislative calendar for action. Mansfield demurred on grounds that "a propitious time ...has not arisen." He wanted evidence of "sufficient numbers" before he would place it before the Senate. There was some logic to this position, since a failure to win a two-thirds vote in the Senate--a form of overt rejection--could prove even more disastrous for America's image than the stigma of non-ratification.

What constituted "sufficient numbers?" It was known that various Senators were reluctant to tip their hands in advance lest they open themselves up to an endless mail barrage from extremists. The Senate leadership initially decided upon assurances by 50 Senators--a "Constitutional majority." To obtain a definitive list, Proxmire and Javits, along with Frank Church and Hugh Scott (the Chairman and the Minority Leader of the Foreign Relations Committee), on February 24, 1972, sent around a petition asking their colleagues to demonstrate a clear commitment to support ratification. The timing of the petition was deliberate. A week earlier, the Attorney-General had transmitted to Congress a formal legislative proposal designed to implement the Genocide Convention. Such implementing legislation is required by the act of ratification.

Despite the fact that the petition contained 53 signatures and several other Senators orally indicated

a willingness to support it--by August, there were 60
definite votes available--a new bottleneck presented
itself. A filibuster was threatened by a pillar of the
Senate, Sam Ervin of North Carolina. With a determined
adherence to the strict construction of the Constitution, Ervin found the arguments of the ABA valid,
indeed, unassailable. A filibuster would tie up the
Senate calendar and a cloture vote required the same
two-thirds (later to be changed to three-fifths or 60).
But a two-thirds vote on cloture was far more difficult
to obtain as Senatorial courtesy was at stake. In the
intimate Senate club, the shutting off of debate evoked
the deepest kind of reluctance.

A kind of "Catch 22" now prevailed. The Senate
leadership would not move without assurances on ratification that in turn required assurances on cloture.
But the leadership was profoundly reluctant to support
cloture. The paralysis of the vicious circle had set
in. Once again, in 1973, the Senate Foreign Relations
Committee called for ratification. In 1974, two
attempts at invoking cloture for ending the filibuster
failed. To resolve the dilemma, the Senate leadership
reached a decision that would reject all further debate, let alone action, on the Genocide Convention
without absolute assurances of a two-thirds favorable
vote on the treaty as well as a reasonable expectation
for cloture. Since such preconditions, in the absence
of strong leadership either in the Congress or the
White House, were politically almost inconceivable, the
question of ratification was back to square one.

Still, despite the dismal Congressional reality
the year 1976 ushered in a new era of hope for the
Genocide Convention. The House of Delegates of the
ABA, meeting in Philadelphia, finally voted on February
17 to support ratification. The reversal, after more
than a quarter of a century of willful intransigence
and resistance, eliminated at long last the aura of
respectability in which the opposition to ratification
had been enveloped. Javits, in a joyous mood, rose in
the Senate on March 4 to greet "the new propitious
conditions" created by the ABA decision which would
result in the Genocide Convention being "ratified as a
treaty of the United States as well as of all those
other countries in the world." At long last, he said,
positive action was certain for "this terribly delayed,
almost unbelievably delayed, simple statement of human
truth and human decency." If the sharp indictment of
the past had to be made--and it was done eloquently-it

was deliberately subordinated to the glow of hope and optimism. Even The New York Times editorially was convinced that there could be no "doubt about the affirmative outcome of the next Senate vote."

The problem, however, was getting the Senate to vote. The filibuster obstacle remained, even if a significant procedural breakthrough now required only 60 votes for cloture, instead of the earlier two thirds. More significantly, the residue of the long-time powerful ABA opposition constituted a serious hurdle. Its arguments would continue to be marshalled in various hostile quarters, particularly among fringe rightist elements who had a way of mobilizing intense vocal and letter opposition. Javit's hope for action in 1976 dwindled.

By the following year, two additional developments augured encouragement. Sam Ervin retired from the Senate race, removing the single most commanding presence of opposition. To that extent, the challenge of an effective filibuster diminished. And, into the White House moved Jimmy Carter whose verbal commitment to human rights was far greater than any previous President. It was to be the "soul" of his foreign policy which, in the Inaugural Address, was given powerful articulation. No President addresssed himself to the genocide treaty ratification as often and as vigorously as Carter. Four times in the course of a three year period he called for Senate action, the first time in a major U.N. speech just two months after his inauguration and most recently in connection with a special and unusually impressive observance of the Holocaust. His Commission on the Holocaust, chaired by Elie Wiesel, on September 27, 1979 formally joined "in urging the Senate to ratify the Genocide Convention" on the grounds that "the knowledge that perpetrators will be held responsible for the crime of genocide can play some role in preventing such acts in the future."

But the President's commitment did not translate itself into strong and effective leadership.

Informal polls of the Senate taken by human rights activists and by State Department specialists reveal that approximately 60 Senators were prepared to vote for the genocide treaty. This figure was but a few votes shy of the necessary two-thirds--67 votes--required for ratification. Few doubt that the balance could be obtained once the issue is directly confronted on the Senate floor, and the Senate leadership as well as the administration pull their respective weight.

The Senate leadership, however, may still be hesitant, and that hesitancy may constitute an obstacle. Confronted by a hesitant Senate leadership, and a zealous, if limited, opposition, most will opt for inertia, a do-nothing philosophy. For the average Senator, the genocide treaty offers little to attract voter support. Earlier voter constituencies on behalf of ratification have all but evaporated in the face of repeated failure, of apathy and frustration. On the other hand, open support for the genocide treaty in states with strong conservative tendencies can evoke powerful opposition.

Without a strong administration initiative and a willingness to invest political capital in lobbying and in making the necessary trade-offs, no progress will be made. Soundings by the Ad Hoc Committee in 1979 repeatedly elicited from White House sources that the SALT ratification issue, of necessity, must receive priority. SALT, of course, is no longer on the Senate agenda, having been removed by the administration as a response to the Soviet invasion of Afghanistan. Nonetheless, no indication had been signaled by the Carter White House that was now prepared to make the all-out fight. Not has the Reagan administration made its position clear.

"Lingering Brickeritis" has been a costly malaise. The United States has found it difficult, if not impossible, to promote any meaningful human rights project in international forums. Non-ratification of the genocide treaty assures the U.S. of an extraordinary status, a kind of splendid isolation. All the other democratic countries have ratified it as have all the other Great Powers, all our allies, and virtually all of Europe and Latin America. Only in Africa, and among the new countries of Asia and the Caribbean, has there been a delay. In all, 83 countries have formally acceded to the treaty. Delegates at international forums find the U.S. posture inexplicable and indefensible. Even among our allies and friendly neutrals, there is a unanimity of dismay. Acute embarrassment is the U.S. delegate's lot when the issue is raised, as it often is, both in public and in private meetings. Arthur Goldberg, several years after he served as U.S. Ambassador to the U.N., recalled: "When I was United States Ambassador to the United Nations, I was often asked to explain our failure to ratify the genocide convention. Frankly, I never found a convincing answer. I doubt that anyone can."

The task of ratification remains unfulfilled. Nothing is more urgent. For genocide goes to the very heart of elemental human rights--the right to survive. It is time to end the shame and the embarrassment, and to consummate the dream of Raphael Lemkin. A conservative Reagan administration could conceivably complete the Nixon initiative by pursuing this goal.

A GENOCIDE EARLY WARNING SYSTEM[1]

Israel W. Charny

The following is a proposal of a new way of treating, so to speak, the Holocaust and its survivors. Athough I am a practicing psychotherapist, I am not referring to treatment of Holocaust survivors in the sense to which Holland and Israel are committed. There are, of course, times when I also "treat" survivors, but these are essentially incidental to the larger flow of my practice, and not a focus of my work or an area to which I have dedicated myself as many of you have done so devotedly and meaningfully over the years.

Let me sketch for you briefly the trail which has led me to this Netherlands-Israel Conference on the Impact of Persecution. In my "over-privileged" position as an American Jew, I suddenly realized that there was one question I cared about more deeply than all others: namely, how could it be that normal human beings were capable of executing the Holocaust--and so many other genocides throughout history? From there the trail led through a series of explorations, studies and projects.

We organized a study group which met over a period of years. It included, among others, a Quaker psychiatrist who was deeply concerned with the absence of aggression in typical Quaker patients on the one hand, and also with the images and archetypes of war and apocalypse; a theatre director who saw the drama as a vehicle for _affective_ education of children, teaching them how to confront the violences within them and about them; a famous philosopher and novelist; and others. In time, the trail moved on to the forum of the American Orthopsychiatric Association, where for several years, I served as Chairman of the Study Group on Mental Health Aspects of Aggression, Violence and War.[2]

Odyssey to Israel

On behalf of the American Orthopsychiatric Association, I also participated in the Inaugural Meeting of the Consortium on Peace Research, Education and Development at the University of Colorado and subsequently served on its Advisory Council. And finally my per-

sonal professional trail led me to Israel in 1973 and
my affiliation with the Henrietta Szold National Insti-
tute for Research in the Behavioral Sciences here in
Jerusalem, directed by my dear colleague, Dr. Chanan
Rapaport, who is co-director for the project we call a
Genocide Early Warning System.[3]

The plan of operation for a genocide early warning
system project is remarkably simple.

No Archives of Past Genocides

It may surprise you, as it surprised us, to learn
that nowhere in the world today is there a systematic
archive of information about past genocides. Nor is
there to our knowledge any systematic compilation of
information about current genocidal events. At any
given moment there are many actually taking place or
about to occur in different parts of our world.

As if this were not enough, it turns out that
although there is a great deal more information available about the human rights status of peoples around
the world, there is no systematic compilation of information about major violations of human rights in
different countries around the world. There are
admittedly partial assemblies; for example, Amnesty
International's increasingly effective compilation of
information; but these focus mostly on specific cases
of prisoners of conscience rather than on the total
picture of groups of people summarily executed, interned in concentration camps, inprisoned, or tortured.
Patterns of human rights violations directed against
identifiable cultural or racial or religious or political entities are not included.

The immediate goal of our early warning system is
to assemble the information of genocide and other major
human rights violations--defined as assaults upon and
insults to the human body and the right to a physically
healthy life, as these are reported all around the
world.

Genocides Differ in Different Eras

The early warning system will be built around a
computer bank of information both about ongoing events
and about past events. In the pilot study which we

have projected at this time, our goal is to enter the computer base with the information of one current year, as well as to trace back the data of the three preceding years.

The categories of the data system which we have created are, first of all, descriptively or phenomenologically simple. They refer to the sources of information, the specific events described, the stages of the events described, (according to a classification we have prepared for the sequences in which human rights violations build toward their possible culmination in the ultimate crime of mass murder), and the causes reported for the human rights violation, if any.

On another level, we propose also to enter these same events into the data bank according to a more analytical set of social indicators which are relevant to our longer range plans for researches of the sequences of social, cultural and political processes in any given society, which may point to the emerging likelihood of more and more serious injustices and violences to human beings. For it is our conviction that although the story of genocide is different in different eras--in one case it is against a given religion, in another case against a political group, in a third case against people of a different color or race; and although the ostensible central figures in genocide vary with different historical circumstances--in one era, there is an evil strong man, other times genocide is in direct fulfillment of a national policy of conquest and territorial expansion, still other times genocide springs from relatively spontaneous mass movements and uprisings--there are common characteristics in the unfolding genocidal momentum, and the choice points they pass through, which we can learn to read. However, it is premature for me to develop this aspect of our work at this time; and we have, in any case, more than enough to interest us in the first goal of the pilot project, which is the assembly and simple categorization of informations of human rights violations and genocide.

The Sources of Information

What is also extraordinarily simple in this project is that we are using everyday sources of information. For we have made the decision not to be drawn into any kind of investigative role. The news sources

-299-

to which we will turn are, first of all, a series of established news-gathering agencies around the world. Specifically, we have chosen a group of newspapers around the globe which are acknowledged, by prevailing Western standards of objectivity, to attempt a reasonably fair and objective recording of events, and which are acknowledged, by and large, to be free of specific ideological biases or attempts at controlled news. We also plan to use the "raw" data which go on the wires of major news-gathering services, such as AP and Reuters. These presumably will also include some of the "unconfirmed reports" or some of the early-stage reports that many editors will not allow themselves to print. In addition, we also propose to rely on the seasoned journalism of certain major news magazines as well as on established archival sources such as Facts on File or Kiesings Archives. Finally, we propose also to tap the reports of several agencies which are specifically dedicated to investigate reports of torture and murder, such as Amnesty International, the International League for the Rights of Man, The International Commission of Jurists, and so on.

It is true that, even without a Genocide Early Warning System, we have information available to us. After all, the information we intend to work with is right there in our newspapers and magazines. But what now happens to a great extent is that we read reports of genocide in our newspaper, and we don't know what to make of them. For one thing, these reports are often rendered with reservations that they are, as yet, unconfirmed--which often means that it takes incontrovertible evidence of dead bodies before the information will be accepted as credible. Furthermore, we get a feeling that we are being treated to information more in the interest of news, to entertain us with the exciting dramas of our times, the best and the worst that human actors can produce, than out of any intent to mobilize caring and action by us or by relevant governmental or religious, welfare or other humanitarian services. Our experience also tells us that we are not necessarily going to be treated to follow-up information in the days ahead, often because the news of this kind of genocide will no longer be that "interesting" as to warrant repetition when it is "no longer news," or because there will be nothing new to report.

Limitations of Current Sources

For example, how much have we read these last years about the fate of the million people who were marched out of Phom Phen? Even if the Cambodians have sealed off new information, does this mean that the spotlight of our news wires should not remain focused on the terrible questions of what happened and what is now happening? In short, current news reports of genocide tend more than anything else to remind us of our terrible aloneness and vulnerability, and our overwhelming impotence in the face of bitter human injustices.

Role of the Early Warning System

In contrast, the charge of a duly constituted Genocide Early Warning System, as a responsible social agency, is to issue repeated, sequential reports and follow-up reports, systematically bringing up to date the human rights problems of people everywhere. No less important, these reports will convey not only the information that is collated from the best news gathering sources in our world, but also a message that there is an agency delegated by our society to express serious concern and caring about the fate of peoples. This in itself will already be an antidote to some of the overwhelming feelings of isolation and hopelessness that we usually experience when we discover random, uncorrelated reports of genocide and human rights violations in the "voyeuristic," uncaring press.

Altogether, the purpose of assembling these data is to provide a powerful information feedback system to our contemporary world. As you know, the concept of feedback is increasingly important in our psychological and behavioral sciences. Years ago we learned that people develop far greater control over behavior when they are given information about what they are doing and what is happening to them. For example, typists improve their skill remarkably when they are able to see their errors as they make them rather than long after on a corrected page, and in recent years we have learned that there are exciting possibilities for control of unconscious, autonomic nervous system processes through biofeedback information. The concept of social feedback is similar, namely, giving human beings more current and authoritative information in a context which encourages them to care and act on this information for their best interests.

Inviting Talent From a Variety of Disciplines

People are likely to improve their situations considerably, whether through citizen's groups, bringing pressure on their governments, via programs of social and welfare agencies or religious institutions, or through the powerful interventions of international business interests, and so on. How exciting it would be if many more such agencies chose to take action whenever they became aware of human beings facing violation of their rights to physically safe lives.

Moreover, it is our intention to invite outstanding talents in fields of communication to help us design as effective a program for communicating the information of the computer bank to the world's news media, national and international political leaders, religious leaders, health and welfare caretakers, and world public opinion at large. We intend to ask the help of social psychologists, public opinion pollsters, media executives, and professionals in advertising. For it is our hope to build the Genocide Early Warning System's information program around a recognizable message or slogan which inspires people to dare to care about human life everywhere. If a slogan "We try harder" can help sell automobile rentals, and "All the news that's fit to print" can sell newspapers as well as help build an enviable image and tradition, perhaps we can find a simple motto which will accompany all information about genocide and human rights violations that will "sell" people around the world on the dignity and value of human life!

Helping Prospective Victims to Help Themselves

Now it is not only foolhardy but fundamentally wrong to be drawn into any kind of fantasy that the early warning system we are describing, at its very best, will solve the problem of genocide or of other violations of the human being in our time or even into the foreseeable future. This is a messianic fantasy, or, as psychotherapists know, an exaggeration of the wish to heal or an expression of omnipotence which only gets in the way of possible real help. In the treatment of suicide, for example, no therapist should ever take on himself reponsibility for his patient's life; but a therapist certainly should take responsibility for giving his patient the best help there is that might help the patient himself to be able to choose the way of life. Paradoxically, taking over too much responsibility for patients often ends in the worst treatment because the clinician then is so concerned about himself, and the outcome of his own wishes for perfection, or his own fears of imperfection, that he fails to help his patient. We propose the Genocide Early Warning System not as a cure or solution, but as a new tool which we believe will provide a new basis for researches and, we trust, the development of still other tools as we get more and more information as to how genocides build.

In the final analysis, even if the early warning system leads only to a few instances of constructive pressure against genocide, it will have proved worthwhile.

Even if the early warning system alerts only a few prospective victims to escape their fates, it will be worthwhile.

Footnotes

1. Presented at the Netherlands/Israel Conference on the Impact of Persecution, Jerusalem, October, 1977.

2. Strategies Against Violence, a volume resulting from a series of conferences of the association was released by Westview Press in Boulder, Colorado.

3. In this special context of a conference in Israel on the treatment of Holocaust survivors, I will allow myself to call to your attention what I do not always openly note, namely, that if you sound the first letters of our project title with a soft g, you have GEWS! This is my private way of remembering the very special, but not exclusive, role of our Jewish people in history as recurrent bellwethers for the emergence of genocidal destruction.

APPENDIX

APPENDIX

This appendix contains two documents, a bibliography, and a reference section. The first document, the U.N. Genocide Convention, sets the stage for the definition of genocide, the means to prevent and punish the perpetrators of genocide, the parties to the Convention, and other matters. It is a valuable document to examine closely despite (or perhaps because of) its historical and political impotence. The second document is Raphael Lemkin's classic description of genocide, written some 40 years ago during World War II by the man who first coined the term. See also the articles in this anthology by Alan Rosenberg, James Tashjian, Helen Fein, William Korey, and the editor's introduction for further analyses of these documents. (The U.N. statement on human rights should also be examined.)

The bibliography contains articles and books on various aspects of genocide as well as sections on particular genocides described in this anthology, plus those that could be called "questionable genocides" (e.g., homosexuals under the Third Reich, Afro-Americans, American Indians, the Biafra-Nigeria struggle, among others.) The appendix concludes with a reference section of major research centers and journals, again divided according to victims. Several of these centers and journals are, of course, the repositories of all types of genocide materials despite their title.

THE UNITED NATIONS GENOCIDE CONVENTION

Aimed at Preventing Destruction of Groups and at Punishing Those Responsible

Genocide is a modern word for an old crime. It means the deliberate destruction of national, racial, religious or ethnic groups.

History had long been a grim witness to such acts, but it remained for the twentieth century to see those acts carried out on the largest and most inhuman scale known when the Nazi Government of Germany systematic- ally annihilated millions of people because of their religion or ethnic origin. A shocked world then rejected any contention that such crimes were the exclusive concern of the State perpetrating them, and punishment of the guilty became one of the principal war aims of the Allied nations. The charter of the International Military Tribunal at Nuremberg, approved by the Allies in 1945, recognized that war criminals were not only those who had committed crimes against peace, and violations of the laws or customs of war, but those who had carried out "crimes against humanity" whether or not such crimes violated the domestic law of the country in which they took place.

During its first session in 1946, the United Nations General Assembly approved two resolutions. In the first, the Assembly affirmed the principles of the charter of the Nuremberg Tribunal. In the second--the basic resolution on genocide--the Assembly affirmed that genocide was a crime under international law and that those guilty of it, whoever they were and for whatever reason they committed it, were punishable. It asked for international cooperation in preventing and punishing genocide and it invited Member States to enact the necessary national legislation. In a final provision, The Assembly called for studies aimed at creating an international legal instrument to deal with the crime. That was the origin of the Convention on the Prevention and Punishment of the Crime of Genocide unanimously adopted by the Assembly on 9 December 1948.

The term convention in international law means an agreement among sovereign nations. It is a legal com- pact which pledges every Contracting Party to accept certain obligations.

How the Convention Was Prepared

In 1946 the General Assembly requested the Economic and Social Council to undertake the necessary studies for drawing up a draft Convention on the crime of genocide. In 1947 the Secretary-General, at the request of the Economic and Social Council, prepared a first draft of the Convention and circulated it to Member States for comments. At that stage, the Secretary-General was assisted by a group of international law experts, among them the late Dr. Raphael Lemkin, who in 1944 had coined the term "genocide." In 1948 the Economic and Social Council appointed an ad hoc Committee of seven members to submit to it a revised draft. That the Committee did, and after a general debate, the Council decided on 26 August to transmit the draft to the General Assembly. At the Paris session of the General Assembly the draft was debated by the Legal Committee and adopted by the Assembly on 9 December 1948.

The Definition of Genocide in the Convention

Genocide, the Convention declares, is the committing of certain acts with intent to destroy--wholly or in part-- a national, ethnic, racial or religious group as such.

What are the acts? First, actual killing. But it is possible to destroy a group of human beings without direct physical extermination. So the Convention includes in the definition of genocide the acts of causing serious bodily or mental harm; deliberate infliction of conditions of life "calculated to bring about" physical destruction; imposing measures to prevent birth, and, finally, forcibly transferring children of one group to another group. Those acts, the Convention states, constitute "genocide." In accordance with the Convention, related acts are also punishable: conspiracy to commit genocide, direct and public incitement to commit genocide, an attempt to commit the crime and complicity in its commission.

To Prevent and To Punish

The Convention first declares that genocide "whether committed in time of peace or in time of war" is a crime under international law which the contracting States "undertake to prevent and to punish."

Main principles established by the Convention are:

(1) Contracting States are bound to enact the laws needed to give effect to the provisions of the Convention, in particular to provide effective penalties.

(2) States undertake to try persons charged with those offences in their competent national courts.

(3) Parties to the Convention agree that the acts listed shall not be considered as political crimes. Therefore, they pledge to grant extradition in accordance with their laws and treaties.

All those pledges are for national action. The Convention also envisages trial by an international penal tribunal should one be set up and should the Contracting Parties accept its jurisdiction. Furthermore, it provides that any of the contracting States may bring a charge of genocide, or of any of the related acts, before the competent organs of the United Nations and ask for appropriate action under the Charter.

If there is any dispute between one country and another on the interpretation, application or fulfillment of the Convention, the dispute must be submitted to the International Court of Justice at the request of any of the Parties.

Who May Be Punished?

Article IV of the Convention declares that those guilty of genocide and the other acts listed shall be punished "whether they are constitutionally responsible rulers, public officials or private individuals." That clause makes it impossible for a person to plead immunity because he was the head of a State or a public official.....

Other Activities of the United Nations Related to the Genocide Convention

Various subjects debated by United Nations bodies, such as the preparation of a draft Code of Offences against the Peace and Security of Mankind; the punishment of war criminals and of persons guilty of crimes against humanity; _apartheid_ and measures to be taken against nazism and other totalitarian ideologies, and practices based on incitement to hatred and racial intolerance, have also raised questions connected with the Genocide Convention.

In 1969, the Economic and Social Council approved the decision of the Sub-Commission on Prevention of Discrimination and Protection of Minorities of the Commission on Human Rights to undertake a study on the prevention and punishment of the crime of genocide. That study is in progress.

Prospects for the Genocide Convention

Throughout the world people aware of the importance and vital necessity of the Genocide Convention are working for its general acceptance and for its observance. The basis of their support transcends religious beliefs and crosses political lines.

Perhaps the best expression of the Convention's appeal was made by the late Gabriela Mistral, the famous Chilean poet who won the Nobel Prize for Literature in 1945.

"With amazing regularity genocide has repeated itself throughout history," she wrote. "Despite all advances in our civilization the twentieth century must unfortunately be considered as one of those most guilty of the crime of genocide. Losses in life and culture have been staggering. But deep in his heart man cherishes a fervent yearning for justice and love; among small nations and minorities the craving for security is particularly alive. The success of the Genocide Convention today and its greater success tomorrow can be traced to the fact that it responds to necessities and desires of a universal nature. The word genocide carries in itself a moral judgement over an evil in which every feeling man and woman concurs."

Text of the Convention

THE CONTRACTING PARTIES,

HAVING CONSIDERED the declaration made by the General Assembly of the United Nations in its resolution 96(I) dated 11 December 1946 that genocide is a crime under international law, contrary to the spirit and aims of the United Nations and condemned by the civilized world;

RECOGNIZING that at all periods of history genocide has inflicted great losses on humanity; and

BEING CONVINCED that, in order to liberate mankind from such an odious scourge, international co-operation is required:

HEREBY AGREE AS HEREINAFTER PROVIDED:

Article I

The Contracting Parties confirm that genocide, whether committed in time of peace or in time of war, is a crime under international law which they undertake to prevent and to punish.

Article II

In the present Convention, genocide means any of the following acts committed with intent to destroy, in whole or in part, a national, ethnical, racial or religious groups, as such:

(a) Killing members of the group;

(b) Causing serious bodily or mental harm to members of the group;

(c) Deliberately inflicting on the group conditions of life calculated to bring about its physical destruction in whole or in part;

(d) Imposing measures intended to prevent births within the group;

(e) Forcibly transferring children of the group to another group.

Article III

The following acts shall be punishable:

(a) Genocide;

(b) Conspiracy to commit genocide;

(c) Direct and public incitement to commit genocide;

(d) Attempt to commit genocide;

(e) Complicity in genocide.

Article IV

Persons committing genocide or any of the other acts enumerated in Article III shall be punished, whether they are constitutionally responsible rulers, public officials or private individuals.

Article V

The Contracting Parties undertake to enact, in accordance with their respective Constitutions, the necessary legislation to give effect to the provisions of the present Convention and, in particular, to provide effective penalties for persons guilty of genocide or of any of the other acts enumerated in Article III.

Article VI

Persons charged with genocide or any of the other acts enumerated in Article III shall be tried by a competent tribunal of the State in the territory of which the act was committed, or by such international penal tribunal as may have jurisdiction with respect to those Contracting Parties which shall have accepted its jurisdiction.

Article VII

Genocide and the other acts enumerated in Article III shall not be considered as political crimes for the purpose of extradition.

The Contracting Parties pledge themselves in such cases to grant extradition in accordance with their laws and treaties in force.

Article VIII

Any Contracting Party may call upon the competent organs of the United Nations to take such action under the Charter of the United Nations as they consider appropriate for the prevention and suppression of acts of genocide or any of the other acts enumerated in Article III.

Article IX

Disputes between the Contracting Parties relating to the interpretation, application or fulfilment of the present Convention, including those relating to the responsibility of a State for genocide or for any of the other acts enumerated in Article III, shall be submitted to the International Court of Justice at the request of any of the parties to the dispute.

Article X

The present Convention, of which the Chinese, English, French, Russian and Spanish texts are equally authentic, shall bear the date of 9 December 1948.

Article XI

The present Convention shall be open until 31 December 1949 for signature on behalf of any Member of the United Nations and of any non-member State to which an invitation to sign has been addressed by the General Assembly.

The present Convention shall be ratified, and the instruments of ratification shall be deposited with the Secretary-General of the United Nations.

After 1 January 1950 the present Convention may be acceded to on behalf of any Member of the United Nations and of any non-member State which has received an invitation as aforesaid.

Instruments of accession shall be deposited with the Secretary-General of the United Nations.

Article XII

Any Contracting Party may at any time, by notification addressed to the Secretary-General of the United Nations, extend the application of the present Convention to all or any of the territories for the conduct of whose foreign relations that Contracting Party is responsible.

Article XIII

On the day when the first twenty instruments of ratification or accession have been deposited, the Secretary-General shall draw up a proces-verbal and transmit a copy thereof to each Member of the United Nations and to each of the non-member States contemplated in Article XI.

The present Convention shall come into force on the ninetieth day following the date of deposit of the twentieth instrument of ratification or accession.

Any ratification or accession effected subsequent to the latter date shall become effective on the ninetieth day following the deposit of the instrument of ratification or accession.

Article XIV

The present Convention shall remain in effect for a period of ten years as from the date of its coming into force.

It shall thereafter remain in force for successive periods of five years for such Contracting Parties as have not denounced it at least six months before the expiration of the current period.

Denunciation shall be effected by a written notification addressed to the Secretary-General of the United Nations.

Article XV

If, as a result of denunciations, the number of Parties to the present Convention should become less than sixteen the Convention shall cease to be in force

as from the date on which the last of these denunciations shall become effective.

Article XVI

A request for the revision of the present Convention may be made at any time by any Contracting Party
by means of a notification in writing addressed to the
Secretary-General.

The General Assembly shall decide upon the steps,
if any, to be taken in respect of such request.

Article XVII

The Secretary-General of the United Nations shall
notify all Members of the United Nations and the non-
member States contemplatd in Article XI of the
following:

(a) Signatures, ratifications and accessions
received in accordance with Article XI;

(b) Notifications received in accordance with
Article XII;

(c) The date upon which the present Convention
comes into force in accordance with Article
XIII;

(d) Denunciations received in accordance with
Article XIV;

(e) The abrogation of the Convention in accordance
with Article XV;

(f) Notifications received in accordance with
Article XVI.

Article XVIII

The original of the present Convention shall be
deposited in the archives of the United Nations.

A certified copy of the Convention shall be transmitted to each Member of the United Nations and to each
of the non-member States contemplated in Article XI.

Article XIX

The present Convention shall be registered by the Secretary-General of the date of its coming into force.

I. Genocide - A New Term and New Conception
For Destruction of Nations

New conceptions require new terms. By "genocide" we mean the destruction of a nation or of an ethnic group. This new word, coined by the author to denote an old practice in its modern development, is made from the ancient Greek word genos (race, tribe) and the Latin cide (killing), thus corresponding in its formation to such words as tyrannicide, homocide, infanticide, etc.[1] Generally speaking, genocide does not necessarily mean the immediate destruction of a nation, except when accomplished by mass killings of all members of a nation. It is intended rather to signify a coordinated plan of different actions aiming at the destruction of essential foundations of the life of national groups, with the aim of annihilating the groups themselves. The objectives of such a plan would be disintegration of the political and social institutions, of culture, language, national feelings, religion, and the economic existence of national groups, and the destruction of the personal security, liberty, health, dignity, and even the lives of the individuals belonging to such groups. Genocide is directed against the national group as an entity, and the actions involved are directed against individuals, not in their individual capacity, but as members of the national group.

The following illustration will suffice. The confiscation of property of nationals of an occupied area on the ground that they have left the country may be considered simply as a deprivation of their individual property rights. However, if the confiscations are ordered against individuals solely because they are Poles, Jews, or Czechs, then the same confiscations tend in effect to weaken the national entities of which those persons are members.

Genocide has two phases: one, destruction of the national pattern of the oppressed group; the other, the imposition of the national pattern of the oppressor. This imposition, in turn, may be made upon the oppressed population which is allowed to remain, or upon the territory alone, after removal of the population and the colonization of the area by the oppressor's own nationals. Denationalization was the word used in the past to describe the destruction of a national pattern. The author believes, however, that this word is inadequate, because: (1) it does not connote the destruction of the biological structure; (2) in connoting the destruction of one national pattern, it does not connote the imposition of the national pattern of the oppressor; and (3) denationalization is used by some authors to mean only deprivation of citizenship.

Many authors, instead of using a generic term, use currently terms connoting only some functional aspect of the main generic notion of genocide. Thus, the terms "Germanization," "Magyarization", "Italianization," for example are used to connote the imposition by one stronger nation (Germany, Hungary, Italy) of its national pattern upon a national group controlled by it. The author believes that these terms are also inadequate because they do not convey the common elements of one generic notion and they treat mainly the cultural, economic, and social aspects of genocide, leaving out the biological aspect, such as causing the physical decline and even destruction of the population involved. If one uses the term "Germanization" of the Poles, for example, in this connotation, it means that the Poles, as human beings, are preserved and that only the national pattern of the Germans is imposed upon them. Such a term is much too restricted to apply to a process in which the population is attacked, in a physical sense, and is removed and supplanted by populations of the oppressor nations.

Genocide is the antithesis of the Rousseau Portalis Doctrine, which may be regarded as implicit in the Hague Regulations. This doctrine holds that war is directed against sovereigns and armies, not against subjects and civilians. In its modern application in civilized society, the doctrine means that war is conducted against states and armed forces and not against populations. It required a long period of evolution in civilized society to mark the way from wars of extermination, which occurred in ancient times and in the Middle Ages, to the conception of wars as being essentially limited to activities against armies and states. In the present war, however, genocide is widely practiced by the German occupant. Germany could not accept the Rousseau-Portalis Doctrine: first, because Germany is waging a total war; and secondly, because, according to the doctrine of National Socialism, the nation, not the state, is the predominant factor. In this German conception the nation provides the biological element for the state. Consequently, in enforcing the New Order, the Germans prepared, waged, and continued a war not merely against states and their armies but against peoples. For the German occupying authorities war thus appears to offer the most appropriate occasion for carrying out their policy of genocide. Their reasoning seems to be the following:

The enemy nation within the control of Germany must be destroyed, disintegrated, or weakened in different degrees for decades to come. Thus the German people in the post-war period will be in a position to deal with other European peoples from the vantage point of biological superiority. Because the imposition of this policy of genocide is more destructive for a people than injuries suffered in actual fighting, the German people will be stronger than the subjugated peoples after the war even if the German army is defeated. In this respect genocide is a new technique of occupation aimed at winning the peace even though the war itself is lost.

For this purpose, the occupant has elaborated a system designed to destroy nations according to a previously prepared plan. Even before the war Hitler envisaged genocide as a means of changing the biological interrelations in Europe in favor of Germany. Hitler's conception of genocide is based not upon cultural but upon biological patterns. He believes that "Germanization can only be carried out with the soil and never with men."

When Germany occupied the various European countries, Hitler considered their administration so important that he ordered the Reich Commissioners and governors to be responsible directly to him. The plan of genocide had to be adapted to political considerations in different countries. It could not be implemented in full force in all the conquered states, and hence the plan varies as to subject, modalities, and degree of intensity in each occupied country. Some groups--such as the Jews--are to be destroyed completely. A distinction is made between peoples considered to be related by blood to the German people (such as Dutchmen, Norwegians, Flemings, Luxemburgers), and peoples not thus related by blood (such as the Poles, Slovenes, Serbs). The populations of the first group are deemed worthy of being Germanized. With respect to

-319-

the Poles particularly, Hitler expressed the view that it is their soil alone which <u>can</u> <u>and</u> <u>should</u> <u>be</u> <u>profitably</u> <u>Germanized</u>.

II. <u>Techniques</u> <u>of</u> <u>Genocide</u> <u>in</u> <u>Various</u> <u>Fields</u>

The techniques of genocide, which the German occupant has developed in the various occupied countries, represent a concentrated and coordinated attack upon all elements of nationhood. Accordingly, genocide is being carried out in the following fields:

Political

In the incorporated areas, such as western Poland, Eupen, Malmedy and Moresnet, Luxemburg, and Alsace-Lorraine, local institutions of self-government were destroyed and a German pattern of administration imposed. Every reminder of former national character was obliterated. Even commercial signs and inscriptions on buildings, roads, and streets, as well as names of communities and of localities, were changed to a German form. Nationals of Luxemburg having foreign or non-German first names are required to assume in lieu thereof the corresponding German first names; or, if that is impossible, they must select German first names. As to their family names, if they were of German origin and their names have been changed to a non-German form, they must be changed again to the original German. Persons who have not complied with these requirements within the prescribed period are liable to a penalty, and in addition German names may be imposed on them. Analogous provisions as to changing of names were made for Lorraine.

Special Commissioners for the Strengthening of Germanism are attached to the administration, and their task consists in coordinating all actions promoting Germanism in a given area. An especially active role in this respect is played by inhabitants of German origin who were living in the occupied countries before the occupation. After having accomplished their task as members of the so-called fifth column, they formed the nucleus of Germanism. A register of Germans (<u>Volksliste</u>) was established and special cards entitled them to special privileges and favors, particularly in the fields of rationing, employment, supervising enterprises of local inhabitants, and so on. In order to disrupt the national unity of the local population, it was declared that non-Germans, married to Germans, may upon their application be put on the Volksliste.

In order further to disrupt national unity, Nazi party organizations were established, such as the Nasjonal Samling Party in Norway and the Mussert Party in the Netherlands, and their members from the local population were given political privileges. Other political parties were dissolved. These Nazi parties in occupied countries were also given special protection by courts.

In line with this policy of imposing the German national pattern, particularly in the incorporated territories, the occupant has organized a system of colonization of these areas. In western Poland, especially, this has been done on a large scale. The Polish population have been removed from their homes in order to make place for German settlers who were brought in from the Baltic States, the central and eastern districts of Poland, Bessarabia, and from the Reich itself. The properties and homes of the Poles are being allocated to German settlers; and to induce them to reside in these areas the settlers receive many privileges, especially in the way of tax exemptions.

Social

The destruction of the national pattern in the social field has been accomplished in part by the abolition of local law and local courts and the imposition of German law and courts, and also by Germanization of the judicial language and of the bar. The social structure of a nation being vital to its national development, the occupant also endeavors to bring about such changes as may weaken the national spiritual resources. The focal point of this attack has been the intelligentsia, because this group largely provides national leadership and organizes resistance against Nazification. This is especially true in Poland and Slovenia (Slovene part of Yugoslavia), where the intelligentsia and the clergy were in great part removed from the rest of the population and deported for forced labor in Germany. The tendency of the occupant is to retain in Poland only laboring and peasant class, while in the western occupied countries the industrialist class is also allowed to remain, since it can aid in integrating the local industries with the German war economy.

Cultural

In the incorporated areas the local population is forbidden to use its own language in schools and in printing. According to the decree of August 6, 1940, the language of instruction in all Luxemburg schools was made exclusively German. The French language was not permitted to be taught in primary schools; only in secondary schools could courses in that language continue to be given. German teachers were introduced into the schools and they were compelled to teach according to the principles of National Socialism.

In Lorraine general compulsory education to assure the upbringing of youth in the spirit of National Socialism begins at the age of six. It continues for eight years, or to the completion of the grammar school (Volksschule), and then for three more years, or to the completion of a vocational school. Moreover, in the Polish areas Polish youths were excluded from the benefit of liberal arts studies and were channeled predominantly into the trade schools. The occupant apparently believes that the study of the liberal arts may develop independent national Polish thinking, and therefore he tends to prepare Polish youths for the role of skilled labor, to be employed in German industries.

In order to prevent the expression of the national spirit through artistic media, a rigid control of all cultural activities has been introduced. All persons engaged in painting, drawing, sculpture, music, literature, and the theater are required to obtain a license for the continuation of their activities. Control in these fields is exercised through German authorities. In Luxemburg this control is exercised through the Public Relations Section of the Reich Propaganda Office and embraces music, painting, theater, architecture, literature, press, radio, and cinema. Every one of these activities is controlled through a special chamber and all these chambers are controlled by one chamber, which is called the Reich Chamber of Culture (Reichskulturkammer). The local chambers of culture are presided over by the propaganda chief of the National Socialist Party in the given area. Not only have national creative activities in the cultural and artistic field been rendered impossible by regimentation, but the population has also been deprived of inspiration from the existing cultural and artistic values. Thus, especially in Poland, were national monuments destroyed and libraries, archives, museums, and galleries of art carried away. In 1939 the Germans burned the great library of the Jewish Theological Seminary at Lublin, Poland. This was reported by the Germans as follows:

> For us it was a matter of special pride to destroy the Talmudic Academy which was known as the greatest in Poland... We threw out of the building the great Talmudic library, and carted it to market. There we set fire to the books. The fire lasted for twenty hours. The Jews of Lublin were assembled around and cried bitterly. Their cries almost silenced us. Then we summoned the military band and the joyful shouts of the soldiers silenced the sound of the Jewish cries.

Economic

The destruction of the foundations of the economic existence of a national group necessarily brings about a crippling of its development, even a retrogression. The lowering of the standard of living creates difficulties in fulfilling cultural-spiritual requirements. Furthermore, a daily fight literally for bread and for physical survival may handicap thinking in both general and national terms.

It was the purpose of the occupant to create such conditions as these among the peoples of the occupied countries, especially those peoples embraced in the first plans of genocide elaborated by him--the Poles, the Slovenes, and the Jews.

The Jews were immediately deprived of the elemental means of existence. As to the Poles in incorporated Poland, the purpose of the occupant was to shift the economic resources from the Polish national group to the German national group. Thus the Polish national group had to be impoverished and the German enriched. This was achieved primarily by confiscation of Polish property under the authority of the Reich Commissioner for the Strengthening of Germanism. But the process was likewise furthered by the policy of regimenting trade and handicrafts, since licenses for such activities were issued to Germans, and only exceptionally to Poles. In this way, the Poles were expelled from trade, and the Germans entered that field.

As the occupant took over the banks a special policy for handling bank deposits was established in order to strengthen the German element. One of the most widely patronized Polish banks, called the Post Office Savings Bank (P.K.O.), possessed, on the day of the occupation, deposits of millions of Polish citizens. The deposits, however, were repaid by the occupant only to the German depositors upon production by them of a certificate of their German origin. Thus the German element in Poland was immediately made financially stronger than the Polish. In Slovenia the Germans have liquidated the financial cooperatives and agricultural associations, which had for decades proved to be a most efficient instrumentality in raising the standard of living and in promoting national and social progress.

In other countries, especially in Alsace-Lorraine and Luxemburg, genocide in the economic field was carried out in a different manner. As the Luxemburgers are considered to be of related blood, opportunity is given them to recognize the Germanic elements in themselves, and to work for the strengthening of Germanism. If they do not take advantage of this "opportunity," their properties are taken from them and given to others who are eager to promote Germanism.

Participation in economic life is thus made dependent upon one's being German or being devoted to the cause of Germanism. Consequently, promoting a national ideology other than German is made difficult and dangerous.

Biological

In the occupied countries of "people of non-related blood," a policy of depopulation is pursued. Foremost among the methods employed for this purpose is the adoption of measures calculated to decrease the birthrate of the national groups of non-related blood, while at the same time steps are taken to encourage the birthrate of the Volksdeutsche living in these countries. Thus in incorporated Poland marriages between Poles are forbidden without the special permission of the Governor (Reichsstatthalter) of the district; and the latter, as a matter of principle, does not permit marriages between Poles.

The birthrate of the undesired group is being further decreased as a result of the separation of males from females by deporting them for forced labor elsewhere. Moreover, the undernourishment of the parents, because of discrimination in rationing, brings about not only a lowering of the birthrate, but a lowering of the survival capacity of children born of underfed parents.

As mentioned above, the occupant is endeavoring to encourage the birthrate of the Germans. Different methods are adopted to that end. Special subsidies are provided in Poland for German families having at least three minor children. Because the Dutch and Norwegians are considered of related blood, the bearing, by Dutch and Norwegian women, of illegitimate children begotten by German military men is encouraged by subsidy.

Other measures adopted are along the same lines. Thus the Reich Commissioner has vested in himself the right to act as a guardian or parent to a minor Dutch girl if she intends to marry a German. The special care for legitimation of children in Luxemburg, as revealed in the order concerning changes in family law of March 22, 1941, is dictated by the desire to encourage extramarital procreation with Germans.

Physical

The physical debilitation and even annihilation of national groups in occupied countries is carried out mainly in the following ways:

1. Racial Discrimination in Feeding. Rationing of food is organized according to racial principles throughout the occupied countries. "The German people come before all other peoples for food," declared Reich Minister Goring on October 4, 1942. In accordance with this program, the German population is getting 93 per cent of its pre-war diet, while those in the occupied territories recive much less: In Warsaw, for example, the Poles receive 66 per cent of the pre-war rations and the Jews only 20 per cent. The following shows the difference in the percentage of meat rations received by the Germans and the population of the occupied countries: Germans, 100 per cent; Czechs, 86 per cent; Dutch, 71 per cent; Poles (Incorporated Poland), 71 per cent; Lithuanians, 57 per cent; French, 51 per cent; Belgians, 40 per cent; Serbs, 36 per cent; Poles (General Government), 36 per cent; Slovenes, 29 per cent; Jews, 0 per cent.

The percentage of pre-war food received under present rations (in calories per consumer unit) is the following: Germans, 93 per cent; Czechs, 83 per cent; Poles (Incorporated Poland), 78 per cent; Belgians, 66 per cent; Poles (General Government), 66 per cent; Norwegians, 54 per cent; Jews, 20 per cent.

As to the composition of food, the percentages of required basic nutrients received under present rations (per consumer unit) are as follows:

Consumer Unit	Carbohydrates	Proteins	Fats
	%	%	%
Germans..................	100	97	77
Czechs...................	90	92	65
Dutch....................	84	95	65
Belgians.................	79	73	29
Poles(Incorporated Poland)	76	85	49
Poles(General Government)	77	62	18
Norwegians...............	69	65	32
French...................	58	71	40
Greeks...................	38	38	1.14
Jews.....................	27	20	0.32

The result of racial feeding is a decline in health of the nations involved and an increase in the deathrate. In Warsaw, anemia rose 113 per cent among Poles and 435 among Jews. The deathrate per thousand in 1941 amounted in the Netherlands to 10 per cent; in Belgium to 14.5 per cent; in Bohemia and Moravia to 13.4. The Polish mortality in Warsaw in 1941 amounted in July to 1,316; in August to 1,729; and in September to 2,160.

2. Endangering of Health. The undesired national groups, particularly in Poland, are deprived of elemental necessities for preserving health and life. This latter method consists, for example, of requisitioning warm clothing and blankets in the winter and withholding firewood and medicine. During the winter of 1940-41, only a single room in a house could be heated in the Warsaw ghetto, and children had to take turns in warming themselves there. No fuel at all has been received since then by the Jews in the ghetto.

Moreover, the Jews in the ghetto are crowded together under conditions of housing inimical to health, and in being denied the use of public parks they are even deprived of the right to fresh air. Such measures, especially pernicious to the health of children, have caused the development of various diseases. The transfer, in unheated cattle trucks and freight cars, of hundreds of thousands of Poles from Incorporated Poland to the Government General, which took place in the midst of a severe winter, resulted in a decimation of the expelled Poles.

3. <u>Mass Killings</u>. The technique of mass killings is employed mainly against the Poles, Russians, and Jews, as well as against leading personalities from among the non-collaborationist groups in all the occupied countries. In Poland, Bohemia-Moravia, and Slovenia, the intellectuals are being "liquidated" because they have always been considered as the main bearers of national ideals and at the time of occupation they were especially suspected of being the organizers of resistance. The Jews for the most part are liquidated within the ghettos, or in special trains in which they are transported to a so-called "unknown" destination. The number of Jews who have been killed by organized murder in all the occupied countries, according to the Institute of Jewish Affairs of the American Congress in New York, amounts to 1,702,500.

Religious

In Luxemburg, where the population is predominantly Catholic and religion plays an important role in national life, especially in the field of education, the occupant has tried to disrupt these national and religious influences. Children over fourteen years of age were permitted by legislation to renounce their religious affiliations, for the occupant was eager to enroll such children exclusively in pro-Nazi youth organizations. Moreover, in order to protect such children from public criticism, another law was issued at the same time imposing penalties ranging up to 15,000 Reichsmarks for any publication of names or any general announcement as to resignations from religious congregations. Likewise in Poland, through the systematic pillage and destruction of church property and persecution of the clergy, the German occupying authorities have sought to destroy the religious leadership of the Polish nation.

Moral

In order to weaken the spiritual resistance of the national group, the occupant attempts to create an atmosphere of moral debasement within this group. According to this plan, the mental energy of the group shoud be concentrated upon base instincts and should be diverted from moral and national thinking. It is important for the realization of such a plan that the desire for cheap individual pleasure be substituted for the desire for collective feelings and ideals based upon a higher morality. Therefore, the occupant made an effort in Poland to impose upon the Poles pornographic publications and movies. The consumption of alcohol was encouraged, for while food prices have soared, the Germans have kept down the price of alcohol, and the peasants are compelled by the authorities to take spirits in payment for agricultural produce. The curfew law, enforced very strictly against Poles, is relaxed if they can show the authorities a ticket to one of the gambling houses which the Germans have allowed to come into existence.

III. Recommendations for the Future

Prohibition of Genocide in War and Peace

The above-described techniques of genocide represent an elaborate, almost scientific, system developed to an extent never before achieved by any nation. Hence the significance of genocide and the need to review international law in the light of the German practices of the present war. These practices have surpassed in their unscrupulous character any procedures or methods imagined a few decades ago by the framers of the Hague Regulations. Nobody at that time could conceive that an occupant would resort to the destruction of nations by barbarous practices reminiscent of the darkest pages of history. Hence, among other items covered by the Hague Regulations, there are only technical rules dealing with some (but by no means all) of the essential rights of individuals; and these rules do not take into consideration the interrelationship of such rights with the whole problem of nations subjected to virtual imprisonment. The Hague Regulations deal also with the sovereignty of a state, but they are silent regarding the preservation of the integrity of a people. However, the evolution of international law, particularly since the date of the Hague Regulations, has brought about a considerable interest in national groups as distinguished from states and individuals. National and religious groups were put under a special protection by the Treaty of Versailles and by specific minority treaties, when it became obvious the minorities were compelled to live within the boundaries of states ruled by governments representing a majority of the population. The constitutions which were framed after 1918 also contain special provisions for the protection of the rights of national groups. Moreover, penal codes which were promulgated at that time provide for the protection of such groups, especially of their honor and reputation.

This trend is quite natural, when we conceive that nations are essential elements of the world community. The world represents only so much culture and intellectual vigor as are created by its component national groups. Essentially the idea of a nation signifies constructive cooperation and original contributions, based upon genuine traditions, genuine culture and a well-developed national psychology. The destruction of a nation, therefore, results in the loss of its future contributions to the world. Moreover, such destruction offends our feelings of morality and justice in much the same way as does the criminal killing of a human being: the crime in the one case as in the other is murder, though on a vastly greater scale. Among the basic features which have marked progress in civilization are the respect for and appreciation of the national characteristics and qualities contributed to world culture by the different nations--characteristics and qualities which, as illustrated in the contributions made by nations weak in defense and poor in economic resources, are not to be measured in terms of national power and wealth.

As far back as 1933, the author of the present work submitted to the Fifth International Conference for the Unification of Penal Law, held in Madrid in October of that year in cooperation with the Fifth Committee of the League of Nations, a report accompanied by draft articles to the effect that actions aiming at the destruction and oppression of populations (what would amount to the actual conception of genocide) should be penalized. The author formulated two new international law crimes to be introduced into the penal legislation of the thirty-seven participating countries, namely, the crime of barbarity, conceived as oppressive and destructive actions directed against individuals as members of a national, religious, or racial group, and the crime of <u>vandalism</u>, conceived as malicious destruction of works of art and culture because they represent the specific creations of the genius of such groups. Moreover, according to this draft these new crimes were to be internationalized to the extent that the offender should be punished when apprehended, either in his own country, if that was the situs of the crime, or in any other signatory country, if apprehended there.

This principle of universal repression for genocide practices advocated by the author at the above-mentioned conference, had it been accepted by the conference and embodied in the form of an international convention duly signed and ratified by the countries there represented in 1933, would have made it possible, as early as that date, to indict persons who had been found guilty of such criminal acts whenever they appeared on the territory of one of the signatory countries. Moreover, such a project, had it been adopted at that time by the participating countries, would prove useful now by providing an effective instrument for the punishment of war criminals of the present world conflict. It must be emphasized again that the proposals of the author at the Madrid Conference embraced criminal actions which, according to the view of the author, would cover in great part the fields in which crimes have been committed in this war by the members of the Axis Powers. Furthermore, the adoption of the principle of universal repression as adapted to genocide by countries which belong now to the group of non-belligerents or neutrals, respectively, would likewise bind these latter countries to punish the war criminals engaged in genocide or to extradite them to the countries in which these crimes were committed. If the punishment of genocide practices had formed a part of international law in such countries since 1933, there would be no necessity now to issue admonitions to neutral countries not to give refuge to war criminals.

It will be advisable in the light of these observations to consider the place of genocide in the present and future international law. Genocide is, as we have noted, a composite of different acts of persecution or destruction. Many of those acts, when they constitute an infringement upon honor and rights, when they are a transgression against life, private property

-330-

and religion, or science and art, or even when they encroach unduly in the fields of taxation and personal services, are prohibited by Articles 46, 48, 52, and 56 of the Hague Regulations. But other acts falling within the purview of genocide, such as, for example, subsidizing children begotten by members of the armed forces of the occupant and born of women nationals of the occupied area, as well as various ingenious measures for weakening or destroying political, social, and cultural elements in national groups, are not expressly prohibited by the Hague Regulations. The entire problem of genocide needs to be dealt with as a whole; it is too important to be left for piecemeal discussion and solution in the future. Many hope that there will be no more wars, but we dare not rely on mere hopes for protection against genocidal practices by ruthless conquerors. Therefore, without ceasing in our endeavors to make this the last war, we must see to it that the Hague Regulations are so amended as expressly to prohibit genocide in any war which may occur in the future. De lege ferenda, the definition of genocide in the Hague Regulations thus amended should consist of two essential parts: in the first should be included every action infringing upon the life, liberty, health, corporal integrity, economic existence, and the honor of the inhabitants when committed because they belong to a national, religious, or racial group; and in the second, every policy aiming at the destruction or the aggrandizement of one of such groups to the prejudice or detriment of another.

Moreover, we should not overlook the fact that genocide is a problem not only of war but also of peace. It is an especially important problem for Europe, where differentiation in nationhood is so marked that despite the principle of political and territorial self-determination, certain national groups may be obliged to live as minorities within the boundaries of other states. If these groups should not be adequately protected, such lack of protection would result in international disturbances, especially in the form of disorganized emigration of the persecuted, who would look for refuge elsewhere. That being the case, all countries must be concerned about such a problem, not only because of humanitarian, but also because of practical, reasons affecting the interest of every country. The system of legal protection of minorities adopted in the past, which was based maninly on international treaties and the constitutions of the respective countries, proved to be inadequate because not every European country had a sufficient judicial machinery for the enforcement of its constitution. It may be said, in fact, that the European countries had a more efficient machinery for enforcing civil and criminal law than for enforcing constitutional law. Genocide being of such great importance, its repression must be based not only on international and constitutional law but also on the criminal law of the various countries. The procedure to be adopted in the future with respect to this matter should be as follows:

An international multilateral treaty should provide for the introduction, not only in the constitution but also in the criminal code of each country, of provisions protecting minority groups from oppression because of their nationhood, religion, or race. Each criminal code should have provisions inflicting penalties for genocide practices. In order to prevent the invocation of the plea of superior orders, the liability of persons who <u>order</u> genocide practices, as well as of persons who <u>execute</u> such orders, should be provided expressly by the criminal codes of the respective countries. Because of the special implications of genocide in international relations, the principle of universal repression should be adopted for the crime of genocide. According to this principle, the culprit should be liable to trial not only in the country in which he committed the crime, but also, in the event of his escape therefrom, in any other country in which he might have taken refuge. In this respect, genocide offenders should be subject to the principle of universal repression in the same way as other offenders guilty of the so-called <u>delicta juris gentium</u> (such as, for example, white slavery and trade in children, piracy, trade in narcotics and in obscene publications, and counterfeiting money). Indeed, genocide should be added to the list of <u>delicta juris gentium.</u>

International Control of Occupation Practices

Genocide as described above presents one of the most complete and glaring illustrations of the violation of international law and the laws of humanity. In its several manifestations genocide also represents a violation of specific regulations of the Hague Convention such as those regarding the protection of property, life, and honor. It is therefore essential that genocide procedures be not only prohibited by law but prevented in practice during military occupation.

In another important field, that of the treatment of prisoners of war, international controls have been established in order to ascertain whether prisoners are treated in accordance with the rules of international law (see Articles 86 to 88 of the Convention concerning the Treatment of Prisoners of War, of July 27, 1929). But the fate of nations in prison, of helpless women and children, has apparently not seemed to be so important as to call for supervision of the occupational authorities. Whereas concerning prisoners of war the public is able to obtain exact information, the lack of direct-witness reports on the situation of groups of population under occupation gravely hampers measures for their assistance and rescue from what may be inhumane and intolerable conditions. Information and reports which slip out from behind the frontiers of occupied countries are very often labeled as untrustworthy atrocity stories because they are so gruesome that people simply refuse to believe them. Therefore, the Regulations of the Hague Convention should be modified to include an international controlling agency vested with specific powers, such as visiting the occupied countries and making inquiries as to the manner in which the occupant treats nations in prison. In the situation as it exists at present there is no means of providing for alleviation of the treatment of populations under occupation until the actual moment of liberation. It is then too late for remedies, for after liberation such populations can at best obtain only reparation of damages but never restoration of those values which have been destroyed and which cannot be restored, such as human life, treasures of art, and historical archives.

Footnote

1. Another term could be used for the same idea, namely, ethnocide, consisting of the Greek word "ethnos"--nation--and the Latin word "cide."

SELECTED BIBLIOGRAPHY ON GENOCIDE

SELECTED BIBLIOGRAPHY ON GENOCIDE

These series of bibliographies are not meant to be complete or exhaustive. The literature is simply too vast. I request of the reader to check the reference sections of the various articles in this anthology for more information. I have also included some sources on genocidal victims that are either not covered in this book or do not strictly fit the definition of genocide according to some scholars and according to international law (homosexuals in Nazi Europe, for example).

I have also listed periodicals and resource centers (divided by victim group) that should also be useful. I would like to thank Prof. Byron Sherwin for compiling, along with Susan G. Ament, an extensive list of Holocaust and genocide resource centers in their book Encountering the Holocaust (Impact Press, 1979; distributed by Hebrew Publishing Company, New York City). I refer readers to their excellent anthology.

General, Theoretical, and Comparative Works

Barkun, Michael, "Survivors: Social Movements and the Sense of Victimization," paper presented at the annual meeting of the Society for the Scientific Study of Religion, Milwaukee, Wisconsin, October 24-26, 1975.

Bishop, William W. (ed.), International Law Cases and Materials, Boston: Little, Brown, 1962.

Carter, Jimmy, "Speech on Anniversary of Human Rights Declaration" (excerpts), New York Times, Thursday, December 7, 1978, p. A10.

Charny, Israel W. (ed.), Strategies Against Violence: Design for Nonviolent Change, Boulder, CO: Westview Press, 1978.

Dadrian, Vahakn N., "Cultural and Social Psychological Factors in the Study of Survivors of Genocide," Anali, Proceedings of 3rd Intern. Congress of Social Psychiatry, Zagreb, September 21-27, 1970.

_____, "Factors of Anger and Aggression in Genocide," Journal of Human Relations, Vol. 19, No. 3, 1971.

_____, "The Structural-Functional Components of Genocide," in Israel Drapkin and Emilio Viano (eds.), Victimology, Lexington, MA: D.C. Heath, 1974.

_____, "A Typology of Genocide," International Review of Sociology, 5,2, Autumn, 1975, pp. 201-212.

_____, "A Theoretical Model of Genocide," The Armenian Review, Vol. 31, 1979, pp. 115-136; also appeared in Sociology Internationalis, January 1980.

Elliot, Gil, The Twentieth Century Book of the Dead, New York: Ballantine, 1972.

Fein, Helen, "Genocide in the Post-Holocaust Era: What Has/Can Be Done?" paper presented at the 73rd meeting of the American Sociological Association, September 4-8, 1978, San Francisco, CA.

_____, "A Formula for Genocide: Comparison of Turkish Genocide (1915) and German Holocaust (1939-1945), Comparative Studies in Sociology, Vol. 1, 1978, pp. 271-293.

Friedmann, Wolfgang G., The Changing Structure of International Law, New York: Columbia University Press, 1964.

Horowitz, Irving Louis, Taking Lives: Genocide and State Power, third edition, New Brunswick, NJ: Transaction Books, 1980.

Kelman, Herbert C., "Violence Without Moral Restraint," Journal of Social Issues, Vol. 29, No. 4, 1973, pp. 25-61.

Knoll, Erwin and Judith Nies McFadden, War Crimes and the American Conscience, New York: Holt, Rinehart and Winston, 1970.

Lemkin, Raphael, Axis Rule in Occupied Europe, New York: Fertig, 1973 (originally published in 1944).

McDougal, Myres S. and Richard Ahrens, "The Genocide Convention and the Constitution," Vanderbilt Law Review, Vol. 3, No. 4, June 1950.

Mendelsohn, Beniamin, "Victimology and the Needs of Contemporary Society," The Israel Annals of Psychiatry and Related Disciplines, 11, 3, 1973, pp. 189-198.

Mosse, George L., Toward the Final Solution: A History of European Racism, New York: Harper and Row, 1978.

Nanda, Ved P., James Scarritt, and George Shepard, Jr. (ed.), Global Human Rights, Boulder, CO: Westview Press, 1981.

Porter, Jack Nusan, Conflict and Conflict Resolution: A Sociological Introduction with Historical Bibliography, New York: Garland Press, (forthcoming).

Robinson, Nehemiah, "The Genocide Convention," Jewish Frontier, Vol. 18, 1, (189), January 1951, pp. 7-14.

Sanford, Nevitt and Craig Comstock and Associates, *Sanctions for Evil*, San Francisco: Jossey-Bass, 1971.

Simpson, George Eaton and J. Milton Yinger, *Racial and Cultural Minorities*, Fourth Edition, New York: Harper and Row, 1972.

Snyder, Louis L., *Encyclopedia of the Third Reich*, New York: McGraw-Hill, 1976.

Stone, Julius, *Legal Controls of International Conflict*, New York: Holt, Rinehart, and Winston, 1959, rev. ed.

U.S. Senate, Subcommittee on Genocide Convention of the Committee on Foreign Relations, Statements of Senator Sam Ervin and the Honorable Arthur J. Goldberg, March 10, 1971. See also the Congressional Record, Senate, March 13, 1973, S4479-4482, S6177-S6181.

U.S. House of Representatives, Hearings, Committee on International Relations, *Investigation into Certain Past Instances of Genocide and Exploration of Policy Options for the Future*, Ninety-Fourth Congress, second session, May 11; August 30, 1976.

Viano, Emilio (ed.), various issues of *Victimology: An International Journal*, especially Vol. 1, No. 1, Spring 1976 and Vol. 1, No. 2, Summer 1976.

Weisbord, Robert G., *Genocide, Birth Control and the Black American*, Westport, Conn.: Greenwood Press, 1975.

Plus, the *Encyclopedia of the Social Sciences*, listings under "International Crimes," "Human Rights," and "Criminal Law."

The Jews

Ainstein, Reuben, Jewish Resistance in Nazi-Occupied Europe, New York: Barnes and Noble, 1974.

Bauer, Yehuda, The Holocaust in Historical Perspective, Seattle, WA: University of Washington Press, 1978.

Dawidowicz, Lucy, The War Against the Jews, 1933-1945, The War Against the Jews, 1933-1945, New York: Holt, Rinehart, and Winston, 1975. Excellent bibliography.

Eckman, Lester and Chaim Lazar, The Jewish Resistance, New York: Shengold Publishers, 1977.

Epstein, Helen, Children of the Holocaust, New York: G. P. Putnam, 1979.

Fein, Helen, Accounting for Genocide, New York: The Free Press, 1979.

Fogelman, Eva and Bella Savran, "Therapeutic Groups for Children of Holocaust Survivors," Int. J. of Group Psych., Vol. 29, No. 2, April 1979.

Hilberg, Raul, The Destruction of the European Jews, Chicago: Quadrangle, 1967.

Levin, Nora, The Holocaust: The Destruction of European Jewry, 1933-1945, New York: Schocken Books, 1973.

Porter, Jack Nusan (ed.), Jewish Partisans: A Documentary of Jewish Resistance in the Soviet Union During WW II, Washington, DC: University Press of America, 1981.

Rabinowitz, Dorothy, New Lives: Survivors of the Holocaust, New York: Avon Books, 1977.

Reitlinger, Gerald, The Final Solution, New York: A. S. Barnes, 1961.

Robinson, Jacob and Philip Friedman, Guide to Jewish History Under Nazi Impact, New York: KTAV Publishing House, 1973.

Sherwin, Byron L. and Susan G. Ament (eds.), Encountering the Holocaust, Chicago: Impact Press, distri-

buted by Sanhedrin Press, Division of Hebrew
Publishing Company, New York City, 1979.

Suhl, Yuri (ed.), They Fought Back: The Story of Jewish
Resistance in Nazi Europe, New York: Schocken
Books, 1975.

Armenians

Arlen, Michael J., Passage to Ararat, New York: Farrar,
Straus & Giroux, 1975.

Bedoukian, Kerop, Some of Us Survived: The Story of an
Armenian Boy, New York: Farrar, Straus, and
Giroux, 1978.

Boyajian, Dickran H., Armenia: The Case for a Forgotten
Genocide, Westwood, N.J.: Educational Book Craft-
ers, 1972.

Bryce, Viscount James, The Treatment of Armenians in
the Ottoman Empire, 1915-1916, London: HMSO, 1916,
Edited by Arnold J. Toynbee.

Dadrian, Vahakn N., "The Common Features of the Armen
ian and Jewish Cases of Genocide," in Israel
Drapkin and Emilio Viano (eds.), Victimology: A
New Focus: Violence and Its Victims, Boston: D.C.
Heath, 1975, pp. 99-120.

Fein, Helen, Accounting for Genocide, New York: The
Free Press, 1979, especially pages 3-18.   Good
bibliography.

Hovannisian, Richard G., Tne Armenian Holocaust,
Cambridge, MA: Armenian Heritage Press, 1978.
Excellent bibliography and research tool.

Morgenthau, Henry, Sr., Ambassador Morgenthau's Story,
Garden City, N.Y.: Doubleday, Page, 1918.

Sarkisian, E.K. and R.G. Sahakian, Vital Issues in
Modern Armenian History, Watertown, Mass.: Library
of Armenian Studies, 1965.

Tashjian, James H., Turkey: Author of Genocide: The
Centenary Record of Turkey, 1822-1922, Boston:
Commemorative Committee of the 50th Anniversary of
the Turkish Massacres of the Armenians, 1965.

The Turkish Armenocide, Documentary Series, (Vol. 2), Newtown Square, Pennsylvania: Armenian Historical Research Association, 1965. Contains two accounts: "The Beginnings of Genocide" by Joseph Guttman and "The Memoirs of Naim Bey" by Aram Andonian.

Gypsies

Acton, Thomas, Gypsy Politics and Social Change, London and Boston: Routledge and Kegan Paul, 1974.

Cohn, Werner, The Gypsies, Reading, Mass.: Addison Wesley, 1973.

Doring, Hans-Joachim, Die Ziguener im Nationalsozialis tischen Staat, Hamburg: Kriminalistik Verlag, 1964.

Friedman, Philip, "How the Gypsies Were Persecuted," Weiner Library Bulletin, Nos. 3-4, 1950.

Kenrick, Donald and Grattan Puxon, The Destiny of Europe's Gypsies, New York: Basic Books, Inc., 1972. Excellent bibliography.

Max, Frederic, "Le Sort des Tsiganes dans les Prisons et les Camps de Concentration de L'Allemagne Hitlerienne," Journal of Gypsy Lore Society, Vol. 25, No. 1/2, January-April 1946, pp. 24-32.

Novitch, Myriam, Le Genocide des Tziganes sous le Regime Nazi, Paris, 1968 (pamphlet).

Puxon, Grattan, Rom: Europe's Gypsies, London: Minority Rights Group, Report No. 14, March 1973.

Schechtman, Joseph, "The Gypsy Problem," Midstream, November, 1966, 52-60.

Tyrnauer, Gabrielle, "The Hidden Americans," Yankee Magazine, May 1981, pp. 74-79, 130-143.

Yates, Dora E., "Hitler and the Gypsies,", Commentary, Vol. 8, No. 5, November 1949, pp. 455-459.

Yoors, Jan, The Gypsies, New York: Simon and Shuster, 1967.

_____, _Crossing_, New York: Simon and Shuster, 1971.

South American Indians

Arens, Richard (ed.), _Genocide in Paraguay_, Philadelphia: Temple University Press, 1976.

_____, _The Forest Indians in Stroessner's Paraguay: Survival or Extinction?_ London: Survival International.

Davis, Shelton H., _Victims of the Miracle: Development and the Indians of Brazil_, Cambridge: Cambridge University Press, 1977.

Savon, H., _Du Cannibalisme au Genocide_, Paris, Hachette, 1972.

North American Indians

Brown, Dee, _Bury My Heart at Wounded Knee_, New York: Holt, Rinehart, and Winston, 1971.

Costo, Rupert (ed.), _Textbooks and the American Indian_, Indian History Press, 1969.

Dadrian, Vahakn N., "The Victimization of the American Indian," _Victimology: An International Journal_, Vol. 1, No. 4, Winter 1976, pp. 517-537.

Deloria, Vine, _Custer Died For Your Sins_, New York: Macmillan, 1969.

_____, _We Talk, You Listen_, New York: Macmillan, 1970.

Josephy, Alvin, _Indian Resistance: The Patriot Chiefs_, New York: Viking Press, 1971.,

Lafarge, Oliver, _A Pictorial History of the American Indian_, New York: Crown, 1974, rev. ed.

Momaday, N. Scott, _House Made of Dawn_, New York: Harper and Row, 1968.

Ortiz, Roxanne Dunbar, "Wounded Knee 1890 to Wounded Knee 1973: A Study in United States Colonialism," The Journal of Ethnic Studies, Vol. 8, No. 2, Summer 1980, pp. 1-15.

Peithmann, Irving, M., Broken Peace Pipes: A Four-Hundred Year Old History of the American Indian, Springfield, Ill.: Charles C. Thomas, 1964.

Sandoz, Mari, Cheyenne Autumn, New York: Hastings House, 1975.

Burundi

Lemarchand, Rene, Rwanda and Burundi, New York: Praeger, 1970.

Lemarchand, Rene and David Martin, Selective Genocide in Burundi, London: Minority Rights Group, Report No. 20, July 1974.

Melady, Thomas P., Burundi: The Tragic Years, New York, Orbis Books, 1974.

Morris, Roger, et al., Passing By: The United States and Genocide in Burundi, 1972, Special Report, New York/Washington, D.C.: Carnegie Endowment for International Peace, 1973.

Weinstein, Warren and Robert Schrire, Political Conflict and Ethnic Strategies: A Case Study of Burundi, Syracuse, N.Y.: Maxwell School of Citizenship and Public Affairs, 1976, Report No. XXIII, Comparative Studies--Eastern Africa.

Williams, Roger M., "Slaughter in Burundi," World, 21, November 1972, 20-24.

East Pakistan

Deutschman, Paul, "Pakistan: What Never Gets Said," The Nation, November 8, 1971, pp. 457-460.

International Commission of Jurists, The Events in East Pakistan, 1971, Geneva, 1972.

Jahan, Rounaq, Pakistan: Failure in National Integration, New York: Columbia University Press, 1972. Excellent bibliography.

Menon, B.P., "The Ashes of Bangla Desh," The New Leader, September 20, 1971.

White Paper on the Crisis in East Pakistan, Islamabad, Pakistan: Ministry of Information, Government of Pakistan, August 5, 1971. Series of Documents and apologetic statements.

Buddhists in Tibet

International Commission of Jurists, Tibet and the Chinese People's Republic, Geneva, 1960.

Patterson, George N., Tibet in Revolt, London: Faber and Faber, 1960.

Peissel, Michael, The Secret War in Tibet, Boston: Little, Brown, 1972. Small and select bibliography.

Cambodia and Other Asian Genocides

Barron, John and Anthony Paul, Murder of a Gentle Land, New York: Thomas Y. Crowell, 1977.

Chomsky, Noam and Edward S. Herman, "Distortions at Fourth Hand" (Review Essay), The Nation, June 25, 1977, pp. 789-794.

Groueff, Stephane, "The Nation as Concentration Camp," National Review, September 2, 1977, pp. 988-990.

Hildebrand, George C. and Gareth Porter, Cambodia: Starvation and Revolution, New York: Monthly Review Press, 1976.

Kamm, Henry, "The Silent Suffering of East Timor," The New York Times Magazine, February 15, 1981, pp. 34-35 cf.

Levey, Robert, "Indonesia's Grab for Power," Boston Sunday Globe, U.S. and World section, January 20, 1980, p. 39.

Ponchaud, Francois, Cambodge Annee Zero, Paris: Juilliard Press, 1977.

Wallace, James N., "The Death of a Million Cambodians,"
U. S. News and World Report, August 8, 1977, p.
33.

Homosexuals

Bleuel, Hans Peter, Sex and Society in Nazi Germany,
New York: Lippincott, 1973, especially pages
23-24, 95-101, 118-119, 217-225.

Bullough, Vern L., Homosexuality: A History, New York:
New American Library, 1979.

Garde, Noel I., Jonathan to Gide: The Homosexual in
History, New York: Nosbooks, 1969, (1964 copy-
right, Vantage Press); see especially pp. 674-677,
679-683, and 722-727, the sections on Magnus
Hirschfeld, Prince Euelenberg-Hertefeld, and Ernst
Rohm.

Heger, Heinz, The Men with the Pink Triangle, Boston:
Alyson Publications, Inc., 1980. Trans. by David
Fernbach.

Lauritsen, John and David Thorstad, The Early Homo
sexual Rights Movement (1864-1935), New York:
Times Change Press, 1974.

Lautman, Rudiger and Erhard Vismar, Pink Triangle: The
Social History of Anti-Homosexual Persecution in
Nazi Germany, 1979, unpublished manuscript. Based
on original German documents.

Steakley, Jim, Body Politic, Nos. 9, 10, 11, Toronto,
Canada, series on homosexual movement in Germany.

Young, Allen, "Magnus Hirschfeld: Gay Liberation's
Zeyde (Grandfather)", in Chutzpah: A Jewish
Liberation Anthology, San Francisco: New Glide
Publications, 1977, pp. 158-160. (Short, secon-
dary source based on the primary research of Jim
Steakley and John Lauritsen/David Thorstad, op.
cit.)

Questionable Genocide

The following are just a sampling of articles dealing with genocide that has been seriously questioned by many. If the victim is not obvious in the title, then it will be noted in brackets.

Bedau, Hugo Adam, "Genocide in Vietnam?" in Virginia Held, Sidney Morgenbesser, and Thomas Nagel (eds.), Philosophy, Morality, and International Affairs, New York: Oxford University Press, 1974, pp. 5-46. Another version can be found in the Boston University Law Review, Vol. 53, No. 3, May 1973, 574-622.

Fields, Rona M., "Psychological Genocide," paper presented at the American Sociological Association Convention, New York City, 1976. [Catholics in Northern Ireland.]

Morel, E.D., The Black Man's Burden, New York: Monthly Review Press, 1969. Originally published in Great Britain in 1920.

Patterson, William L. (ed.), We Charge Genocide: The Historical Petition to the United Nations for Relief from a Crime of the US Against the Negro People, New York: International Publishers, 1961.

Perham, Margery, "Nigeria's Civil War," Contemporary Africa Record, 1967-1968, pp. 1-12. [Biafra.]

St. Joree, John de, The Brother's War: Biafra and Nigeria, Boston: Houghton-Mifflin, 1972, esp. pp. 284-287.

PERIODICALS

The following periodicals contain information on genocide and human rights and are open to articles on these subjects.

General Publications

Matchbox; Amnesty International Reports; Universal Human Rights; Bulletin of the International Commission of Jurists; Minority Rights Group Report (London); United Nations human rights reports; United Nations governmental hearings on foreign policy and international relations; Victimology: An International Journal.

Jewish Periodicals

Leo Baeck Yearbook (New York and London); Martyrdom and Resistance (N.Y.); News of Yivo, YIVO Annual of Jewish Social Science (N.Y.); Shoah: A Review of Holocaust Studies and Commemorations (N.Y.); Wiener Library Bulletin (London); Yad Vashem Studies (Jerusalem); and other Jewish journals such as Midstream, Commentary, Jewish Social Studies and the American Jewish Yearbook.

Armenians

The Armenian Review (Boston); Ararat (New York); Armenian Action ("Hye Sharzhoom").

Gypsies (Rom)

Etudes Tziganes (Paris); Journal of Gypsy Lore Society (England).

Homosexuals

Journal of Homosexuality; Mattachine Review; One.

Africa

Africa Report; World; Journal of Modern African Studies: West Africa; Africa Quarterly; Atlas: World Press Review; and European newspapers.

RESEARCH CENTERS

The following institute, university, and research centers contain material on genocide and human rights.

General Centers

Library of Congress; United Nations; Amnesty International; Minority Rights Group (London); International Commission of Jurists (Geneva); National Center for Genocide Studies (Boston).

Jewish Centers

American Jewish Archives (Cincinnati, Ohio); American Jewish Committee; American Jewish Congress; American Jewish Historical Society (Boston); American Jewish Joint Distribution Committee; Archives of Kibbutz Arzi-Hashomer Hazair Movement (Merchavia, Israel); Berlin Document Center (BDC); Bund Archives for the Jewish Labor Movement; Canadian Jewish Congress (Montreal); Center for Holocaust Studies (Brooklyn, N.Y.); Central Zionist Archives (Jerusalem); Kibbutz Lohamei Hageta'ot (Haifa, Israel); Jabotinsky Institute in Israel (Tel Aviv); Leo Baeck Institute; Wiener Library and Research Institute (London); Yad Vashem (Jerusalem); YIVO Institute for Jewish Research; Brookline Holocaust Center (Brookline, Mass.); National Institute on the Holocaust (Philadelphia); National Jewish Conference Center; St. Louis Holocaust Center; Simon Weisenthal Center for Holocaust Studies (Los Angeles); Anti-Defamation League of Bnai Brith; and Institute of Contemporary Jewry (Jerusalem). Where site of center is not mentioned, it means New York City.

Armenian Centers

Armenian Historical Research Association; Armenian Information Center (Boston); The Armenian Assembly (various resource centers in the USA); The National Association for Armenian Studies and Research (Cambridge, Mass.); Armenian Student Association; Armenian General Benevolent Union; Armenian National Museum and Cultural Center (Fresno, CA).

Gypsy Centers

World Romani Congress; Gypsy Council (England); Comite International Rom (Geneva); Weiner Library and Research Institute (London); Minority Rights Group (London).

Homosexuals

Institute for Sex Research (University of Indiana, Bloomington, Indiana); Weiner Library and Research Institute (London, on the Nazi era).

Indians

Institute for the Development of Indian Law (USA); Minority Rights Group (London); Bureau of Indian Affairs (Washington, D.C.), Indian Law Resource Center (Washington, D.C.).

CONTRIBUTORS

Yehuda Bauer is Jonah M. Machover Professor of Holocaust Studies and Head of the Institute of Contemporary Jewry at Hebrew University, Jerusalem, Israel.

Alan Rosenberg teaches in the department of philosophy at Queens College, CUNY, in Flushing, New York.

Henry L. Feingold teaches in the history department of Baruch College, CUNY, in New York City.

Jack Nusan Porter is a Boston sociologist, editor, writer, and political activist.

Marjorie Housepian is Associate Dean of Studies at Barnard College, Columbia University, New York City.

Leon Chorbajian teaches in the sociology department of the University of Lowell in Massachusetts.

James Tashjian is editor of The Armenian Review in Boston, Massachusetts.

The late Philip Friedman was one of the most important scholars in the fields of Holocaust studies and European Jewish life.

The late Dora E. Yates was secretary of the Gypsy Lore Society in London.

Jerzy Ficowski is a Polish scholar and writer.

Gabrielle Tyrnauer is a Research Associate at Harvard's Center for European Studies, has published works on Gypsies in New England and in the Northwest United States. An anthropologist (Cornell Ph.D.) and journalist, she has recently spent several months in Germany studying the European Rom.

Rene Lemarchand is professor of political science and former director of the African Studies Center, University of Florida, Gainesville, Florida.

Richard Arens is professor of law at the University of Bridgeport (CT).

Mike Chamberlain works for Clergy and Laity Concerned and the Asian Center at Oberlin College.

David Aikman was the last *Time* magazine staffcorrespondent to leave Cambodia, a few days before Phnom Penh fell to the Khmer Rouge.

Rounaq Jahan is a professor of political science at Dacca University, Bangladesh. He received his Ph.D. from Harvard University and was research associate at the Southern Asia Institute of Columbia University.

Robert Jay Lifton is a professor of psychiatry at Yale University.

Helen Fein is Director of Indochinese Refugee Sponsorship Development of the Dutchess County (NY) Interfaith Council.

William Korey is director of international policy research for the B'nai Brith, New York City.

Israel W. Charny is a professor at Tel Aviv University and director of several projects in the field of Holocaust studies in Jerusalem, Israel.

ABOUT THE AUTHOR

JACK NUSAN PORTER is a sociologist, author, editor and political activist. Born in the Ukraine and raised in Milwaukee, he graduated cum laude from the University of Wisconsin-Milwaukee and received his Ph.D in sociology from Northwestern University in 1971.

He has published fifteen books and anthologies and nearly 150 articles, including Student Protest and the Technocratic Society, The Study of Society (contributing editor), Jewish Radicalism (with Peter Dreier), The Sociology of American Jews, The Jew as Outsider: Collected Essays, Kids in Cults (with Irvin Doress), Conflict and Conflict Resolution, Jewish Partisans (two volumes), and Genocide and Human Rights. He has made many contributions to reference books and journals including the Encyclopedia Judaica, Encyclopedia of Sociology, Society, Midstream, and Writer's Digest.

He is the founder of the Journal of the History of Sociology and the Sociology of Business Newsletter and the winner of the John Atherton fellowship from the Breadloaf Writers Conference as well as fellowships from the Memorial Foundation for Jewish Culture and the World Jewish Congress. He is listed in Who's Who in the East, American Men and Women of Science, Who's Who in Israel, and Contemporary Authors.

Dr. Porter has lectured widely on American social problems and political/religious movements. He has testified before several government commissions including the White House Conference on Families and the National Peace Academy hearings. Long active in Israel and Jewish communal activities, he is considered one of the founders of the Jewish student movement in the USA and Canada in the late 1960s.

He lives in Boston with his wife Miriam and their son Gabriel, and is at present the Massachusetts representative of the American-Israel Securities Corporation.